COMPLETE GUIDE TO FILM SCORING

3rd Ed.

The Art and Business of Writing Music for Movies & TV

RICHARD DAVIS and **ALISON PLANTE**

Berklee Press

Editor in Chief: Jonathan Feist

Senior Vice President of Pre-College, Online, and Professional Programs/
CEO and Cofounder of Berklee Online: Debbie Cavalier

Earlier Editions:

Contributing Editor: David Franz

Original Cover Design: Moore Moscowitz

ISBN: 978-0-87639-231-7

1140 Boylston Street
Boston, MA 02215-3693 USA
(617) 747-2146

Visit Berklee Press Online at
www.berkleepress.com

Distributed By

Visit Hal Leonard Online
www.halleonard.com

Berklee Press, a publishing activity of Berklee College of Music, is a not-for-profit educational publisher.
Available proceeds from the sales of our products are contributed to the scholarship funds of the college.

CONTENTS

ACKNOWLEDGMENTS

With a now twenty-five year span between the first and third editions of this text, countless people deserve our gratitude for their time, insight, and support of this work. In addition to all of the interviewees and helpers from the first and second editions, we would like to extend a special thanks in this third edition to our gracious interview subjects: Keith C. Anderson, Jane Applegate, Ben Bromfield, Miriam Cutler, Mason Daring, Germaine Franco, Lena Glikson, Evyen Klean, Haim Mazar, Woody Pak, Ro Rowan, Shie Rozow, Òscar Senén, Kara Talve, Thanh Tran, and Ayako Tsuchiya. We are honored to include their voices along with ours, especially in sharing their special areas of expertise.

We'd also like to thank Eli Slavkin for his work getting the second edition text into shape for what turned out to be a "down to the studs" renovation project, and Erin Collins for providing some invaluable cross-checking of our understanding for some of the business topics. And of course, we'd like to thank the staff at Berklee Press, particularly Editor in Chief Jonathan Feist who has devoted countless hours to meticulously editing and assembling this manuscript, through all three editions.

We also want to acknowledge the role of Berklee College of Music, and especially the Screen Scoring Department, in the formation of this book. Much of the thinking behind its content developed from courses in the Film Scoring major, going back to the early days of the department under the leadership of Founding Chair Don Wilkins and Assistant Chair Michael Rendish.

From Richard Davis:

As we will mention several times in the book, the world of film scoring has changed dramatically since the first edition was published. One of the newer paradigms in the industry is that more and more projects have become collaborations between two or more composers. So in a very appropriate manner, the third edition of this book has been, in every way, a collaboration with Alison Plante. We took the original text down to its bare bones and built it back up, chapter by chapter. I have the most appreciation and highest level of gratitude for the new interviews Alison conducted, for her thorough organization and focused work ethic, for her clarity in writing, and for the spirit of collaboration that allowed us to create a new edition where the whole is greater than the sum of the parts.

From Alison Plante:

When Richard Davis was about to retire from teaching at Berklee College of Music, I asked him if this life change might provide time to pen the much-needed third edition of this book. When he demurred, I offered to take it on in his place, and he gave his blessing to do so. At that point, I thought I would be doing most of the work alone, in my solitary writing cave. However, once we got started, we found that we worked together seamlessly. I feel incredibly fortunate to have been able to build on Richard's already comprehensive and invitingly written book, and to have had a writing partner who was knowledgeable, rigorous, collaborative, and open-minded. I'd also like to thank current Berklee Screen Scoring Department Chair Sean McMahon for supporting my sabbatical semester, which gave me time to focus exclusively on this work.

PREFACE TO THE THIRD EDITION

Just as in going from the first to the second editions of this book, in writing this third edition, the scoring world has both changed drastically in some ways and at the same time remained the same in many of the fundamentals. It is the same in that there is still the opportunity to write and record great music that will be heard by millions of people. Composers and directors still must meet eye-to-eye (though often that now means over video chat) and achieve the director's vision of a film. There are still improbably tight deadlines to meet, tight budgets, and a rocky political landscape to negotiate between director, producer, studio, and composer. And the exciting challenge of finding just the right music to tell the story, sell the world of the film, and express the inner life of its characters remains the same.

Technology, not surprisingly, has come a long way and continues to change and influence composers' workflows. Unlike in the second edition, where we could still relegate technology to its own chapter, digital tools are now so infused into everything we do that discussion of these advances are now integrated into most of the chapters and topics rather than standing alone. As of this writing, developments in generative AI promise to further disrupt scoring, as with many other fields, though it is too early yet to know exactly how. When possible, rather than focusing on specific tools, we have emphasized their underlying principles that are more evergreen.

The business of scoring has also continued to change, with an increasing share of projects set up as "package deals," which require composers to also function as savvy business people, hiring ever-larger teams and changing the entry-level jobs in the industry and the routes to success. Performance royalties, on which so many media composers have depended to make a decent living, are under constant threat that so far has been fended off by grassroots action, although composers are still without a union or guild.

As new forms of media emerge, there are also differences in aesthetics and business strategy in various scoring genres, from production music libraries to trailer music to documentary and nonfiction scoring. We have added new chapters in this edition to dive deeper into some of these areas and illuminate avenues that can be explored beyond the scoring of scripted feature films.

One particularly welcome development is that the face of film scoring is changing—literally. Historically underrepresented groups have organized to advance their causes and increase their visibility. Some studios have launched initiatives devoted to creating opportunities for fresh compositional voices, and the advent of streaming and other forms of media has opened new doors. To choose one example, the percentage of women scoring the top 250 highest grossing Hollywood films grew from 2 percent in 2013 to 8 percent in 2022[1]—a four-fold increase, though still quite low even by Hollywood standards. The global marketplace in the age of streaming has also found increasing interest in non-Hollywood films, with international followings for films from countries such as South Korea. In this third edition, we have embraced these broader perspectives by adopting inclusive language and including a wider variety of examples from a broader range of composers and others working in related fields, both in the U.S. (still our primary point of reference) and around the world.

One additional and significant change in the scoring field since the second edition was published that we have consciously chosen not to address in this book is the rise of video games and other interactive media. Though there is much in common between scoring linear (film and television, e.g.) and interactive media, and many composers these days work on both forms, there is enough that is specific to the field of video game and interactive scoring as to merit its own major course of study at Berklee. We encourage all students of scoring to at least acquaint themselves with interactive scoring as well.

Finally, just as we decided to keep our focus on linear media, we have also kept the original title, rather than broadening it to "The Complete Guide to Screen Scoring" as our department at Berklee has done. Though much has changed, as noted, the field of scoring owes its origins to film, and films are still a disproportionately influential space even for other forms of media. Moreover, "film scoring" is still understood by most to include the scoring of other linear forms of media. That said, one especially notable development since the second edition is the world of streaming, which has created an enormously expanded need for music and a corresponding growth in the number of opportunities for composers.

—Richard Davis and Alison Plante, May 2024

INTRODUCTION

This book is for anyone interested in writing music for film or television (with "television" here used as a shorthand for episodic media, including, for example, those on the various streaming services). It covers the art of scoring step-by-step, from the history of the field, through the process of writing the score, and finally to an explanation of the music business as it pertains to film and television composers. Being composers ourselves, we have worked in genres spanning fiction and nonfiction, film and episodic media, and short and long form works. In preparing this book, we interviewed dozens of practitioners—composers, music editors, orchestrators, music supervisors, agents, and others—and included their observations and anecdotes.

Successful scoring is not a matter of just writing good music; it is writing good music that supports a dramatic situation. After teaching scoring at Berklee College of Music for over forty years, collectively, we both agree that the most important thing for the aspiring media scorer to learn is how to think like a filmmaker while practicing their art as a composer. This means finding the heart of the film—or perhaps its soul—and expressing that in music. No one can get inside a composer's head and tell them which notes to write. Every musician brings their own personal experience and musical point of view to a composition. But they can be guided and pointed in a certain direction, either by a teacher, a director, or simply a gut reaction to a particular scene. We have found that the best creative guidance we can give is to help someone find that heart of the picture in order to know what they want to express about it. That expression can then combine with other skills—compositional, technical, creative, business, and communication skills—to make a successful score and a successful composer.

This is our approach in the Screen Scoring Department at Berklee, and there are several dimensions to our program that are reflected in the structure of this book.

First, it is invaluable to have an appreciation of the context of film scores past and present. The chapters on the history of film scoring give an overview, and hopefully will inspire you to further study.

Second, every composer hoping to work in film scoring must understand certain things about the process of film making and the evolution of a score. The chapters in part II will help you understand this process that many established composers had to learn on the job.

Third, and the most difficult to impart in a book, are the chapters on creating the score. With the help of our composer colleagues, we focus on the important concepts in writing a film score. Again, our aim is to point you in the right direction, though not to teach you composition principles. Hopefully, as an interested student of scoring, you will take the advice of several of the composers in this book and pursue your own studies diligently in this area.

The final chapters discuss an issue that is necessary to the livelihood of every professional musician: the music business. Royalties, agents, attorneys, copyrights, and other topics of the film music business are addressed at length, and with specific case studies of particular genres and types of media. This provides the grounding required for anyone entering the field.

How does music end up on the screen? What does it take to be able to compose it? Who chooses the composer? Who chooses what the music should sound like? How long does it take? How do the finances work? This book answers these questions and many others about the art and business of scoring for film and television.

PART I

History

CHAPTER 1

Early Films and Music: The Silent Era

Music and drama. Drama and music. Either way, these two branches of the performing arts have been linked together for thousands of years in many cultures around the world. There is Japanese Noh and Kabuki, Indian Bharatanatyam, and the Balinese Monkey Dance. The early Greeks and Romans used choruses and orchestras to accompany their dramatic plays. In Europe, during medieval times, there were pagan festivals that used music to accompany stories of gods and heroes, as well as liturgical dramas that portrayed various biblical stories through singing and dramatic action. During the Renaissance, music was used in various scenes in the plays of Shakespeare and others. In the Baroque period of classical music, we find early opera and ballet—forms of musical drama that continue today. And finally, in this century, we have the huge popularity of Broadway plays and film music.

In all these examples, the music and drama can be separated into independent entities, but their combination as a whole is greater than the sum of their individual parts. Overtures and arias from Mozart's or Verdi's operas are often performed independently and are musically satisfying. Some of these same operas exist as plays or books. But hear the aria as part of the staged opera and the effect is profound in a way that the play or music by itself cannot approach. Music for film is similar. Certainly, a film composer can write good music that stands on its own without the film, and there are many acclaimed live performances of music that originated in film and other media. However, when heard in conjunction with the visuals of the film, both the music and the film have the potential to take on another dimension.

THE DAWN OF CINEMA

It is often difficult for modern audiences to appreciate the experience of moviegoers at the turn of the twentieth century, when the technology of moving pictures was new. But try, for a moment, to put yourself in the shoes of a filmgoer in 1895. The common forms of long-distance communication were letters and the telegraph. The cutting edge of communication technology was the telephone, and only a tiny percentage of city dwellers had one in their homes or had ever used one. Horses and trains were still the primary modes of travel; automobiles were about as common as telephones, and the flight of the first airplane was still ten years away. Electric lights were only fifteen years old, and gas lamps were still the prevailing method of artificial light. Einstein had yet to propose his theory of general relativity. Stravinsky was only thirteen years old, and Schoenberg's twelve-tone system of music was more than two decades in the future. Music lovers were most familiar with Brahms, Wagner, Mozart, Verdi, Beethoven, and other eighteenth- and nineteenth-century composers.

Imagine, now, that you enter a small theater, or even a café with curtains closed against the light. A very noisy machine in the middle of the room starts up, and across a screen in the front, you see the images of people, animals, and buildings. To you, the almost turn-of-the-century filmgoer, this is like a miracle. And yet at the same time, the images seem disembodied, for there is no accompanying sound. The mouths might move, the horse might gallop, the car spews its fumes, but there are no words, there is no clippety-clop, and there is no chugging and banging of the engine. All is left to your imagination, for the only sounds you hear are the loud and noisy rotations of the projector's motor.

However, imagine you are in the same room, and there is a pianist or small group of musicians playing while the picture moves on the screen. This adds another dimension to your experience, and even if the music is just background music with no dramatic importance, your previous impression of empty, disembodied images is transformed into a more complete experience. There are still no words, no hooves, no automobile engine noises. But the addition of music somehow makes the images on the screen more complete and less like two-dimensional shadows.

From the very beginning, there were probably musical accompaniments to films, though the first documented incidents were in 1895 and 1896 when the Lumière family screened some of its early films in Paris and London with musical accompaniment. These were a great success, and soon, orchestras were accompanying films in the theaters.

The music that went with these films was taken from anywhere: classical favorites, popular songs, folk songs, or café music. At first, there was little or no attempt to give the music a dramatic importance; it was there to enliven the audience's experience. But as the industry and audience grew, the musicians providing accompaniment to the films realized that, as in opera, they could make a direct dramatic commentary on what was being viewed.

As the film industry grew and became more sophisticated, music in the theaters grew as well. Depending on the size and location of the theater, there could be anywhere from one piano or organ to a small orchestra. The player or music director would choose various pieces from the already existing literature and prepare them for performances.

In 1908, again in France, Camille Saint-Saëns was commissioned to write what is believed to be the first film score tailored for a specific film, *L'Assassinat du Duc de Guise*. This score was successful, but because of the added expenses of commissioning a composer, preparing the music, and hiring the ensemble, the concept of scores specifically composed for a film did not yet take hold. However, many people in the industry were becoming aware that there was a need for having music accompany films, whether or not it was specifically composed for them.

MUSIC FAKE BOOKS

What did take hold at this point was a method of standardizing the musical experience of the audience, and a way of codifying what the musicians played. This happened with the publication of several books that provided many different pieces of music with different moods that could cover almost any dramatic situation. These books, of which the most well-known are the *Kinobibliothek* (or *Kinothek*) by Giuseppe Becce, *the Sam Fox Moving Picture Music volumes* by J. S. Zamecnik, and *Motion Picture Moods* by Erno Rapée, organized the musical selection to be played by dramatic category. The music director could simply determine the mood or general feeling of a particular scene, look up that idea in the book, and choose one of several possibilities. If, for example, the film needed music for a very dramatic scene set in an evil castle, the music director might have seen these possibilities, among others, in *Motion Picture Moods* by Rapée:

- Grotesque: "Misterioso #1" by Otto Langley
- Horror: "Abduction of the Bride" by Grieg
- Misterioso: "March of the Dwarfs" by Grieg or "The Erl-King" by Schubert
- Sinister: "Carolina Overture" by Beethoven

In addition, there were many other moods and also other main categories: Love, Lyrical Expression, Nature, Nation & Society, and Church & State.

The use of these books could be a cumbersome process, especially if there was more than one musician playing. The music director in each theater would view the film several times with a stopwatch and time each scene, and then choose the individual pieces to be played, noting how many seconds each piece should run. Much was dependent on the ability of the conductor or player to anticipate a scene change and to be able to extend or compress a piece. One of the most problematic areas became the transitions between scenes that had different pieces of music. A change in key center, tempo, instrumentation, or overall mood could be very awkward without a written-out transition. Therefore, many musical directors created such transitions themselves.

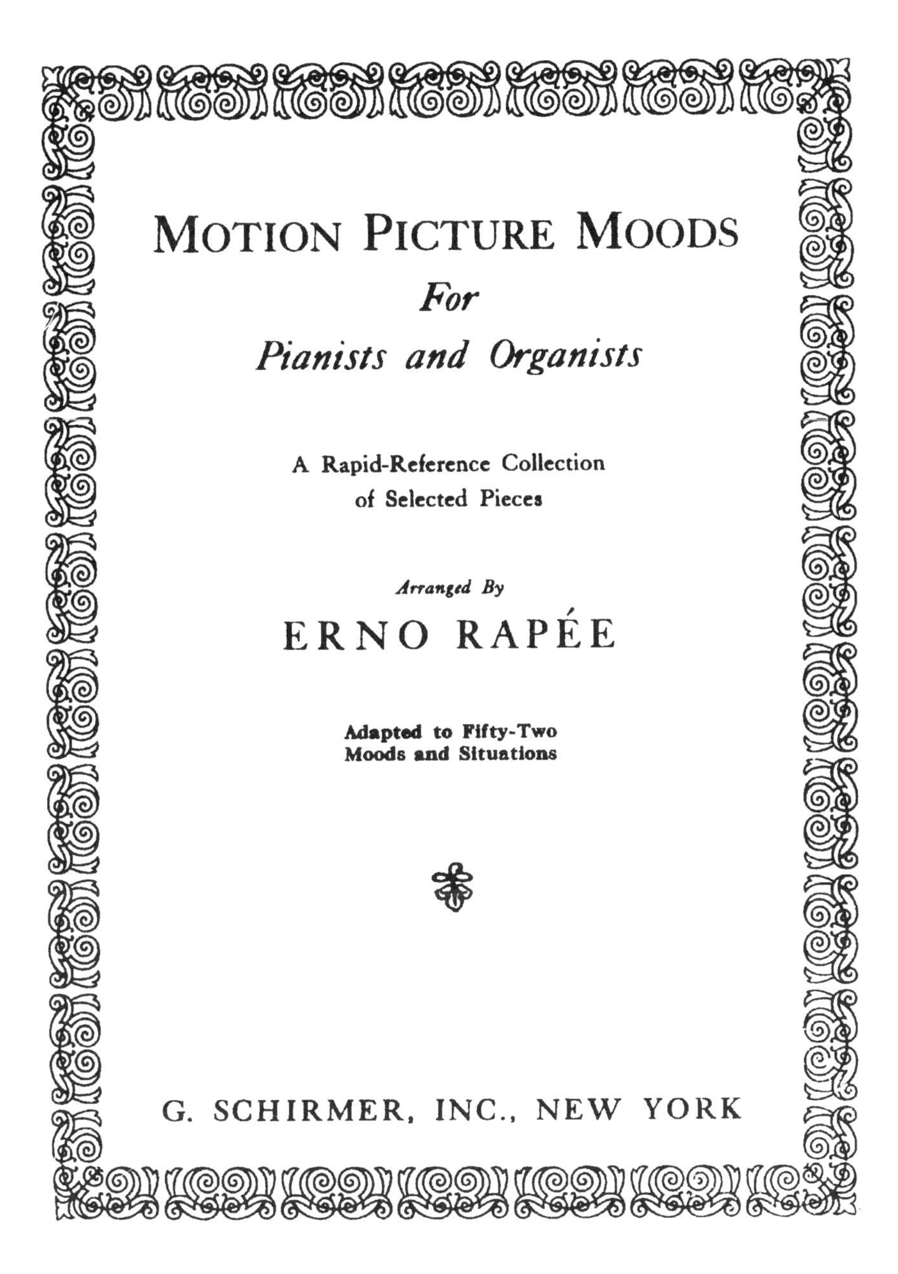
MOTION PICTURE MOODS

For

Pianists and Organists

A Rapid-Reference Collection
of Selected Pieces

Arranged By

ERNO RAPÉE

**Adapted to Fifty-Two
Moods and Situations**

G. SCHIRMER, INC., NEW YORK

FIG. 1.1. Rapée's *Motion Picture Music* Title Page, 1916. Used by Permission of Hal Leonard LLC.

Table of Contents

[vi]

FIG. 1.2. *Motion Picture Music* Table of Contents Excerpt (Rapée). Used by Permission of Hal Leonard LLC.

FIG. 1.3. "Agitato No. 3" by Otto Langey. Included in *Motion Picture Music* (Rapée) in the "Battle" category. Used by Permission of Hal Leonard LLC.

The fake books were successful, since they created a set musical script that any musician could follow. However, their dramatic effectiveness was limited by the ability of each theater's musical director.

A concurrent system whose inception actually predates the use of fake books was developed by Max Winkler, a clerk at Carl Fischer Music Store and Publishing Company in New York. Winkler realized that if he could see the films before they were released, he could then make up what he called "cue sheets" for each film (not to be confused with modern-day cue sheets). These cue sheets would lay out the choice of music and give timings for how long to play each piece, as well as present guidelines for interpretation, in order to stay synchronized. The publisher would preview the film, create a cue sheet, then organize and sell a book for each film that was provided to the music director of each theater. This benefited the film maker, for it provided a set musical script with rough timings. It also benefited the publishers of the music, for they could make a profit selling or renting the music itself to theaters.

In actuality, both the Kinothek and Max Winkler methods were destined for short lives. They were published between 1912 and 1919, and by the late 1920s, the revolution of "talkies," the first movies with their characters actually speaking and even singing in synchronized sound, were being distributed. It was this technological advancement that began the modern use of music in movies.

CHAPTER 2

The First Talkies: The Beginning of Synchronized Music

The use of sound in films revolutionized the way movies were made. Not only was there an amazing new dimension to the audience's experience, but the way a story was communicated had to be completely rethought. Previously, when the actors were silent, the film maker often had to convey or amplify an emotion, or make a certain point by use of lighting or camera angles. Because the actors were now talking on-screen, directors felt that they had to highlight them with clear, bright light. In addition, the camera angles stayed more static in order to focus on the speakers and the reactions of those listening. (This was also a technological requirement, because the cameras were still very noisy and had to be enclosed in bulky, soundproof cubicles that were cumbersome to move around the set.) The effect of all of this was that the dialogue became the focal point of the film. The imagination of the audience was curtailed as the actors explained everything happening.

This meant several things for the musicians. First, a composer could continue to provide needed insight into the emotional and psychological drama through the music. Second, the music composed would accompany the film wherever it was shown. Third, the shift towards sound pictures meant that thousands of theater musicians would be put out of work.

One of the interesting side-stories to the development of the film industry is that in the late 1920s there were quite a few studio owners who believed that the talkies were a passing fad.

However, there were others who saw the commercial possibilities of movies with synchronized dialogue. During the mid 1920s, different technologies were being experimented with to synchronize picture and dialogue. In 1925 and 1926, several shorts were screened to the public by the Warner Bros. Studio to gauge the audience reaction. These were not dramatic films; they simply showed opera singers, trains, or other mundane events that included synchronized sound. Although the reaction was mixed, the studio decided to move forward with the new technology.

In 1927, nervous Warner Bros. executives premiered *The Jazz Singer* in New York. Starring vaudeville singer Al Jolson, this film had several musical numbers featuring synchronized sound. With almost a century of hindsight, it is easy for us to think, "What was the big deal? Of course, everyone would love this new technology." But the reality of the time is that no one knew how audiences would react after thirty years of silent pictures. Although much of the spoken dialogue was still silent and the story told by narration "cards," when Jolson sang "Blue Skies" and "My Mammy," and the sound appeared to come from his mouth, the audience was thrilled. *The Jazz Singer* did terrific box-office business and became the film that showed the industry the way to go. It opened up a whole new era.

For several reasons, both commercial and technical, many of the first successful talkies were musicals. For about three years, until about 1931, a steady stream of musicals was produced. This was probably because of their entertainment value; not only did the actors speak, they also sang and danced. In fact, "All Singing, All Dancing" began as a slogan to advertise one of these new films, before entering the English language as an idiom to mean any shiny new technology. In addition, there was the logistical advantage of having the musicians on the set and often on camera. However, after several years of a steady diet of musicals, the public's interest in them waned. When this happened, many studio executives thought there was no longer a need for musicians, and many of the studio orchestras were laid off. A yearlong period of adjustment ensued until the same executives found out how much they really did need music for dramatic films.

Adding music to films at this time was an expensive, cumbersome, and problematic process. In the very early days of talkies, there was no way to record the music separately from the rest of the production. All the musicians had to be present on the set, positioned in such a way as to be heard but not cover up the actors' lines. They could not make a mistake lest a whole take be ruined. This was a nightmare for all involved: musicians, actors, director, and sound recordists. Sometimes, a short song could take two or three days to record. In addition, there could be no edits afterward or the music would be ruined; the soundtrack would have jumps and blips.

The technology that was to free the music from the confines of the shooting set was the ability to add the music at a separate time. Developed about 1931, this technique allowed the music to be recorded on its own *scoring stage*, so-called to distinguish the music recording building from the *sound stage* or film set building. It allowed the film maker to be able to place the music anywhere in the film, and it originated the process we now call "dubbing" or "re-recording" when the music, dialogue, and sound effects are mixed together. Dubbing was a major technological advance, as it gave the director or producer control not only over where the music and sound effects would go, but also over how loud they would be in relation to the dialogue.

This new technology made the process of including music in films much more flexible and less expensive, and by the early 1930s, directors and producers began to accept that the film's underscore was a critical component. However, many still believed that the source of any music needed to be accounted for visually. For example, if two lovers were shown having a picnic in the woods, the filmmakers may have introduced a random, wandering violinist to justify having the full orchestra playing a love theme in the underscore. This is one example of the cautious steps taken by many film makers in the early days of sound films. Audiences had been accepting music with no need for a visual justification from the beginning of films. However, it was a period when the industry was finding its way and discovering what worked and what did not work in these new sound movies.

To address the perceived necessity that all music be justified visually, two distinct and diametrically opposed solutions for music use came into vogue. One was the use of constant music—a score that started at the opening credits and did not stop until the picture ended. The other was no music at all. Neither of these solutions was ideal, and it took some trial and error on the part of film makers to find out what worked. Ultimately, a system of bringing the music in and out of the picture as the drama required became the standard practice, and still is adhered to today.

It is interesting to note that between these early days of talkies and the contemporary films of today, there have been very few successful movies that had absolutely no music. A revealing anecdote is that of *The Lost Weekend*, a 1945 film starring Ray Milland. This intense film about an alcoholic on a weekend bender was originally released without any music at all. When first shown in the theaters, at the most dramatic scenes of Milland's descent into an alcoholic blur, the audience snickered and giggled—exactly the opposite of the film maker's intent. It was quickly pulled from circulation, and almost permanently shelved. However, composer Miklós Rózsa was brought in to compose a score, and the movie was rereleased to great acclaim. It went on to win best actor, best picture, and best director, but the score was not acknowledged at the time, even though it was the only thing added to the original, failed version.

During the period of film music's infancy between 1927 and 1931, a clear progression can be seen. At first, the most common and obvious use of music in the talkies was as part of a musical with song and dance numbers. Upon the arrival of re-recording, producers went to the extremes and thought they didn't need music at all or had to have it all the time. Experiments were made with various kinds of source music (music that comes from a "source" on-screen), as in the Marlene Dietrich film, *The Blue Angel* (1930). Theme songs were used, just as they are today, in order to promote the film and sell records and sheet music. And finally, directors began to play with the idea that music could come in and out of the soundtrack to support various types of scenes. Watching old films, you will notice that the concept of constant music was slow to die and was used in many films. However, the notion that music was a necessary part of film took hold, and the underscore as we know it today began to take shape.

CHAPTER 3

The Hollywood Studio System

Much has been written about the Hollywood studio system, in effect from the silent film era until the 1960s. Although we are primarily concerned with how this worked in relation to composers and musicians in general, it is worthwhile to briefly describe the overall studio system.

In the early days of Hollywood, there were several large movie studios that produced the majority of films. These studios grew up during the days of the silent films, and the system of production they established then carried over to the talkies. Warner Bros. Studios, Metro-Goldwyn-Mayer (MGM), Universal Studios, Paramount Studios, RKO, Twentieth Century-Fox, and United Artists were the most productive and longest lasting. As still happens today, many of these entities were constantly shifting in ownership and had varying degrees of profitability. They were also each known for having certain kinds of films. For example, Warner Bros. was known for swashbuckling adventure stories, Universal for steady production of B horror and comedy movies, and MGM for grand dramas.

This was the most productive time in the history of the film business in terms of the sheer numbers of films produced. Back then, people would frequently spend the afternoon seeing a double feature. In the 1930s, approximately 80 million Americans (65 percent of the population) went to the movies once a week. Today, the average American sees only five movies per year in the theaters (according to the most recent pre-pandemic poll in 2019)[2]—approximately 10 percent as often as their counterparts of the previous century, though of course today, there are many ways to watch films and other forms of media without going to a theater.

Because of the volume of films needed to satisfy the appetite of the movie-going public, the studios developed a system that was like the assembly lines coming into use in manufacturing during the same period. This system was efficient, streamlined, and somewhat insulated from the possibility of the temperamental manipulations of one creative individual. In other words, it was difficult for one person involved with the production, whether screenwriter, director, composer, editor, or other, to derail, hold up, or change the direction of a production if they disagreed with the others. A new person would simply be brought in from the ranks of the studio staff, and work would continue. The only person with somewhat absolute power was the production executive, compared to whom even the stars had only limited power. If a particularly temperamental actor attempted to sabotage a production, the producer could control them by threatening not to give them any further projects for the remainder of their contract.

Each studio was a completely self-contained film-making factory where every aspect of the process was owned and controlled by the individual studio. The studio employed full-time contracted staffs of screenwriters, directors, producers, actors, extras, costume designers, hairdressers, carpenters, electricians, musicians, publicity agents, and others, spanning every possible job necessary to the making of a film. They had their own labs to develop the film and complete post-production facilities for editing and dubbing. In addition, the individual studios also owned chains of theaters that showed only their films. The studio controlled not only the making of the film in every aspect, but also where, when, and for how long it would be shown. (This ownership of the theaters was deemed illegal in 1949, and the studios were forced to sell off their theaters. It was relatively recently that Sony and others have found a way to own chains of movie theaters without violating U.S. antitrust laws.)

When a film started its journey through this studio assembly line, the producer pulled the strings and guided the process as it went through all the different departments. First, a group of writers would be assigned to create, complete, and polish the script. Note, the operative word here is "group." Even though one writer would get screen credit, often it was a group effort. One person would write certain scenes, maybe love scenes. Another might write action scenes and yet another polish up the dialogue. There might also be a team of directors, each directing various scenes or different parts of the film. Various film editors would work on the project, as would teams of employees from the music, sound-effects, and costume departments. All of these workers were on staff at the studio. They could not work for any other studio, and they were obligated to follow the directions of the executives and supervisors of their departments.

The actors were also under contract to the studio, and especially at the beginning of their careers, had to do what they were told. Many stars were groomed by the studio; at a young age they were discovered, and the studio would plan their careers and create roles specifically for them.

The producer and other studio executives were often involved in the creative process in a hands-on way. They would make creative decisions that might be in accord with the desire of the director(s), or they might be at odds. The producer's decision was the final word. The producer wielded much more power over creative decisions in those days of the studio system than they do today. In contemporary times, the director is responsible for delivering a final version of the film that is approved by the producers and/or studio. During the making of the film, the modern director has much more control over creative decisions than the director of the 1930s and '40s did, although the final cut of the film is still subject to studio approval.

Even though it seems impersonal, many great films were made by this process under the studio system. There were different styles to adhere to in film making: romances, melodramas, epic adventures, etc., and the different creative people learned to adapt to a certain style in order to maintain continuity throughout the film. The music, as well, was produced on an assembly-line basis, and many composers and orchestrators had to learn to adapt to the desired style. This is one of the reasons that so many musical clichés were created in the Hollywood films of the 1930s: the different music departments had to use them to stay within the boundaries of the required style. For example, they produced soaring violins for the appropriate love scenes, and growling low brass or strings for the bad guys.

Another reason that so many clichés were in use had to do with the sheer volume of films produced. There was hardly time to work out fresh, original, creative ideas within the given time constraints. Finally, there was a prevailing attitude amongst producers that existed then as it does today, which is that "if it works, do it again." In other words, there was a general reluctance to try new things, and a conservative desire to use what was tried and proven both in film making and in music.

THE STUDIO MUSIC DEPARTMENT

Starting in the late 1920s, the studios had music departments that were self-contained so that every stage of the music could be done in-house. They each had a staff of composers, orchestrators, songwriters, rehearsal pianists, orchestra musicians, conductors, choreographers, music copyists, proofreaders, music editors (then called "music cutters"), and music executives to oversee the process. These people usually worked under one roof in a music building that contained a music library and a recording studio.

The head of the music department was often a composer or conductor, like Alfred Newman, who headed the music department at Twentieth Century-Fox for many years, during the forties and fifties. The music department head also had to be an executive who interacted with the studio executives, producers, directors, accounting departments, recording specialists, costume directors when musicians were on-screen, and actors when they were singing or playing. They had to have a firm grasp of budgets and time schedules, and be an accurate evaluator of the skills, strengths, and weaknesses of the composers and performing musicians in their department.

The music department head would be aware of the production schedule of a film, and would know when it was about to be ready for music. If the film was a top feature, then they might assign one well-known composer to score the project. However, many of the second level, B-films, would be assigned a team of composers. These composers would screen the film with others on the music production staff. Perhaps the director would be there, perhaps not. They would then have to agree on the musical style of the score—composition, harmony, melodies, orchestration—so that the output coming from different composers still sounded unified.

After the composers began writing, their sketches would go down the line to the orchestrators, copyists, proofreaders, and finally to the orchestra. If there were songs or dance numbers, there were rehearsal pianists on staff to take care of them. Everyone had a specific job; it was all compartmentalized.

The deadlines and the pace of this process in the 1930s was frighteningly rapid, even by today's standards. Composer David Raksin began his career as a film composer working with Charlie Chaplin in 1935, and he related this anecdote about studio composing schedules:

> *We did tremendous amounts of music. For instance, when I composed the score for* Forever Amber, *that had about 110 minutes of music—about 100 of those I composed myself. The rest was music of the story's time. Originally, I had twelve weeks to do that, but they were messing around with the movie, and by the time they got finished doing that, I had eight and a half weeks to do that tremendous amount of music. And I did it!*

The budget and importance of the project would determine quality of the music and the amount of time given to write it. B films were rushed through. If the film had major stars and was high profile, as in *Forever Amber*, there would be one "name" composer who would have more time to write the score. Still, the process that ensued once the score was written remained the same. The music went through the pipeline from composer to orchestrator to music preparation to the studio orchestra.

CHAPTER 4

Musical Styles ~1930 to 1950

It's important to note that though we are focusing on the U.S. film industry here, elsewhere in the world there were other cinematic and film music traditions taking root. However, as each of these could take up an entire chapter or book in themselves, and because of the influence of Hollywood film music globally—especially of the Golden Age period—for now, we are going to keep our gaze fixed on Southern California.

Between 1930 and 1950, an average of five hundred films per year were produced in the United States, and Americans were attending movies more frequently than at any other time in history. For this reason, this time period is known as the "Golden Age of Hollywood." It was an exciting time to be in the movie business. Opportunities were many, and technology and the industry itself were growing to maturity from the infancy of silent pictures, constantly making strides and innovations, both technically and creatively. Film music also grew up during this time, finding its way to a language and a technique that is the foundation for what is still heard today.

The musical film-scoring vocabulary of the 1930s and '40s is still familiar to modern audiences. The easy access to films that we can watch at home, as well as the enduring allure of scores of this kind to set the scene for even modern films, has enabled those of us born after this golden age of movies to recognize the lush, orchestral sound of the early Hollywood film score. Though this sound can seem corny to twenty-first century ears, if we understand where these composers and film makers were coming from, then we can appreciate their artistic accomplishments.

During the silent film era, the musical language that was most familiar to audiences and thus was commonly used in films was that of the eighteenth- and nineteenth-century European classical composers, popular songs by composers such as Irving Berlin and George Gershwin, as well as some well-known folk songs. When sound became a part of films in the late 1920s, there arose a great need for accomplished composers who could write scores that would appeal to the contemporary audience, and be dramatically synchronized to enhance the action on-screen. At this time there was an influx of European born composers who came to Hollywood, many of whom were Jewish and were fleeing political upheaval and persecution in Austria, Germany, and Eastern Europe. They had conservatory training from their native lands in composition, conducting, and performance, and were therefore well versed in classical music styles—especially those of the eighteenth and nineteenth centuries. They had an in-depth knowledge of the operas of Verdi, Wagner, Strauss, and Puccini, and were intimately familiar with the concert and chamber works of Beethoven, Mozart, Brahms, Schubert, Berlioz, and many others.

Of these émigré composers, several were quick to set a high standard for the Hollywood music community. These included Max Steiner, Erich Korngold, Bronisław Kaper, Miklós Rózsa, and Franz Waxman. A brief look at the musical achievements of two of these composers, both before and during their Hollywood careers, will illustrate how the sound of the films during the Golden Age of Hollywood came to be.

Max Steiner (1888 to 1971) wrote over three hundred film scores including *King Kong* (1933), *Gone with the Wind* (1939), and *The Treasure of the Sierra Madre* (1948). An Austrian immigrant who had written his first operetta at the age of fourteen, Steiner arrived in Hollywood in 1929. He was there as film music grew from infancy into a sophisticated art, and was one of the composers that molded its growth. He became known for writing emotional, lyrical themes (as in *Gone with the Wind*), but was versatile and could provide any mood required. In many films, he used *leitmotifs* (themes, specific instruments, or both for a certain character or idea in the story), an idea borrowed from opera composers, especially Wagner. Most importantly, he was originally a composer of operettas, and so was well versed in the marriage of music and drama. It was this dramatic experience that gave him the sensitivity required to write effective film scores. And it was his training and foundation in nineteenth century composition that provided the necessary musical vocabulary.

Erich Korngold was also an Austrian refugee who was trained in the Old World conservatory system. But where Steiner's background was in operetta, Korngold's was in grand opera. Korngold was a child prodigy in his hometown of Vienna, and by the time he was fourteen, his praises had been sung by Mahler, Puccini, and Richard Strauss. By the age of nineteen, he had written three operas and was considered to be one of the shining lights of Europe. He was well known, well liked, and well off financially by the time he was in his early twenties. Mostly, his career consisted of conducting in various European cities while he continued to compose opera and concert pieces.

In 1934, Korngold was invited to come to Hollywood to arrange Mendelssohn's famous incidental music to *A Midsummer Night's Dream*. Although the producer of the project had probably never heard of Korngold, at that time, Hollywood producers scored status points by successfully raiding the artistic world of Europe. So Korngold journeyed to California with his wife and children, and spent several months adapting Mendelssohn's music.

This trip proved successful, and Korngold was intrigued by the possibilities of film music. He was to return to America twice in the next few years, finally coming for good when he realized that the political climate in his native Austria was becoming dangerous for a Jew.

Korngold only scored eighteen films in twelve years, and he worked under the best conditions possible. He had the right to turn down any project, and was given as much time as he needed to write the music. As with Steiner, it was his early training in opera that gave him the ability to come up with appropriate musical solutions for Hollywood films. In addition, the musical vocabulary of his German opera writing and that required by Hollywood films was the same.

There were many other fine composers working in Hollywood during this time, but these two are representative of the ongoing style and trend. The strongest musical influences for them were nineteenth century late Romantics such as Wagner, Brahms, Mahler, Verdi, Puccini, and Strauss. The musical vocabulary of these composers became the most common and fundamental language of the music in early Hollywood films.

Much has been said and written about why this happened. A question often posed is: Why did it take so many years for the more contemporary and modern sounds of Stravinsky, Bartók, Ravel, and Schoenberg to find their way into the dramatic expression of popular films? The answer is twofold. First, the late Romantic period of classical music was the most familiar to the film-going audience. In 1935, they were only fifty years removed from Brahms' *Third Symphony* and many other contemporaneous Romantic works including Wagner's *Parsifal*, Tchaikovsky's *Sixth Symphony*, and Strauss's *Till Eulenspiegel*. The melodic arc, the harmonic structure, and the overall thematic development were musical events that the average film audience could easily grasp. No matter what the dramatic need of a scene, whether it be lyrical or turbulent, it could be expressed musically in a way that was easily understood. This was an important requirement of popular films. They were not aimed at an intellectual or academic audience. They were not even aimed at the most educated audience. They were aimed at the great middle. And although many Hollywood films made philosophical, moral or psychological points in their stories, they were not to be confused with the more arty movies of film makers, such as Fassbinder.

The background of composers like Steiner, Korngold, and Waxman made them perfectly suited to accomplish the musical need of the time. Essentially nineteenth century composers writing in a late nineteenth century and early twentieth-century style, they were able to bring quality music to films. They had an excellent grasp of harmony, melodic development, and other compositional techniques such as passacaglia and leitmotif. They understood form and thematic development so that they could spin out a melody when necessary, or fragment it and tease the audience. And perhaps most importantly, they had thorough knowledge of music dramas: specifically, the operas of the eighteenth and nineteenth centuries.

When movies were silent, the composer or player was simply an adjunct to a moving picture. The music could amplify an emotion, telegraphing danger or sweetening a love scene. But with sound films where the actors were talking, the role of the music changed significantly. The music had to interact with the dialogue of the actors and find a way to create the right mood, and at the same time stay out of the way of the voices. It needed to express and mirror the emotion of the actors as well as sometimes bring these emotions to a ringing conclusion. The music needed to develop as the story developed and move the plot along. The experience of the European composers in writing opera made them ideally suited to this task.

One listen to (or attendance at) a Wagner, Verdi, or Puccini opera would illuminate this point dramatically. The use of music from start to finish, the thinning out of the orchestra during recitative (dialogue), the grand crescendos and emotional outbursts at high points of the drama, and the use of leitmotif in opera are no different in concept from the interactions between music and film during the early days of Hollywood.

In opera, sometimes the same musical idea or phrase might keep returning to reinforce the audience's understanding and response to an idea or emotion in the film. Max Steiner's score to *Gone with the Wind* did just this. There were seven different motives or themes representing distinct characters or situations, and they return periodically throughout the film. Korngold's score to *The Adventures of Robin Hood* (1938) had a theme for the Merry Band, a theme for Marion, one for Robin Hood, and yet another for the Sheriff of Nottingham. (Note that this technique is still used in modern times, but with a more contemporary music language. John Williams' scores to the *Star Wars* and *Harry Potter* franchises, and Howard Shore's scores for the *Lord of the Rings* trilogy are some well-known examples.)

In addition to thematic organization, as more and more scores were recorded over the years, certain conventions or clichés came to be used. This has always been the case and still is today, for it is really prevailing conventions that make up a given style. In the 1930s, those conventions were numerous, and sometimes were born out of necessity. Though all the composers, even those working on "B" films, were highly skilled, the time crunch they worked under was often outrageously short.

Musically, a "convention," as we are referring to it, could be any number of things. For example, it could be a full string section playing a sforzando minor chord to imply something dark or intense, or a certain kind of recognizable harmonic scheme. It could be the use of a flute to impart lightness. In the 1930s, there were love themes with soaring violins—often in octaves, brass in fourths and fifths whenever there were Romans, Greeks, or medieval kings—all themselves frequent subjects of the epic films of this period. String sections were seemingly ubiquitous throughout films, providing a warm, rich, and lush blanket upon which both dialogue and acted-out emotions could sit. But in the eyes and ears of the 1930s audience, these conventions were as effective as the heart-pounding synth and orchestral ostinato hybrids of the modern comic book blockbuster action scene.

We chuckle today at some 1930s conventions, for they seem dated to us now. Unfortunately, some of these musical conventions are not so funny and are the unfortunate result of cultural bias that was pervasive throughout Hollywood for many decades. For example, the use of a parallel fourths motif to represent Native Americans, or a pentatonic scale to evoke Japan or China—both of which are parodies of music from those cultures—originated in the 1930s and persisted for many years. (This will be discussed further in chapter 17.)

The important concept to remember about the development of film music is that every generation of films has had its musical style with different approaches to composition, orchestration, genre, and the kinds of conventions mentioned. The use of these different techniques was and still is dictated by the expectations of the audience of the time, with different audiences of different generations being steeped in and exposed to very different styles of music in their daily lives.

NEW IDEAS IN MUSIC

The nineteenth-century-influenced romantic style of Korngold and Steiner continued to be used in films through the 1950s. But during the 1940s, new ideas were slowly introduced. Composers like David Raksin and Bernard Herrmann were expanding the range of possibilities by introducing elements of jazz and contemporary twentieth-century music. Scores like *Laura* (1944) and *Citizen Kane* (1941) did much to open up the minds and ears of the movie industry to new sounds. For example, Raksin wrote a twelve-tone score for *The Man with a Cloak* (1949).

David Raksin:

> Man with a Cloak *had a twelve-tone row, the first five notes of which spelled E-D-G-A-R. The R became D so it was still Re. I saw Johnny Green (head of music at MGM) the next day and he said, "Gee that's a remarkable score, what's that crazy god-damned tune you've got there?" And I said, "Johnny, it's a twelve-tone row." He was astonished because it sounded so much like a theme and wanted to know why I used a row. I told him it was because in this picture, you don't find out until the last 45 seconds or so that the hero, the man in the cloak, is really Edgar Allan Poe.*
>
> *I had a great time doing what I was doing. Sometimes, I was motivated by jazz, sometimes by contemporary music. You would have to be crazy not to feel the enormous effect of the music of Stravinsky. For me it was Stravinsky and Berg. So I just wrote the way I thought I should be writing.*

Raksin also points out that as film music drew its influences from what musical styles were popular, it also influenced those styles. Contemporary music, or dissonant music that was not accepted by audiences for the concert stage, would be accepted in the appropriate scene of a film. Raksin again:

> *If you have a really violent sequence and you write something that is really dissonant, they wouldn't like to hear that as a [concert] piece of music. But they will accept it if it is the right music for a film sequence.*

New ideas, such as twelve-tone rows and other twentieth-century compositional techniques, were slow to gain popularity in film scores. However, producers, directors, and the composers themselves gradually saw the dramatic value of these methods, and musical styles in films began to change.

CHAPTER 5

Musical Styles 1950 to 1975

In any discussion of artistic and historical styles and eras, it seems to be human nature to want to delineate and mark a specific date, year, or piece that ushers in the new era. But it is never really so cut and dry. Monteverdi did not wake up on the morning of January 1, 1600 and proclaim, "Ah-ha, let us begin the Baroque period of music!" Liszt, Chopin, and Wagner knew they were breaking away from the old classical style of Beethoven, Mozart, and Haydn, but they were not consciously creating a new musical period called "Romanticism." Most new trends are the result of evolution, drawing upon the old and breaking ground for the new. Film scoring styles are no different. The Romantic style of Steiner, et al, remained prominent for about twenty years, from 1930 to 1950. But there were signs of experimentation, and certain scores written during that time seem to point to the future use of more dissonance, atonality, and eventually popular, jazz, and rock vocabulary in scores.

Remember that by the late 1930s, the art of synchronizing music with film was quite new—only ten years old. Although composers, directors, and producers were still heavily reliant on conventions that were tried and proven, there was always the occasional innovation that stood aside from the crowd. In 1941, in the midst of the Romantic style of Korngold and Steiner, a film was released that was to break the mold of the time, innovating visually, structurally, and sonically. This was *Citizen Kane*, a film by Orson Welles with a score by Bernard Herrmann. Many of the more modern compositional techniques used by Herrmann in this film were not in common use until the 1950s. He was about ten years ahead of the pack. *Citizen Kane* pointed to the eventual use of contemporary sounds and textures influenced by Bartók, Stravinsky, Schoenberg, and other twentieth-century composers. In addition, it presaged the rise of American-born composers in the film industry.

By the early 1950s, there were many conservatory-trained American musicians working for the studios as composers, orchestrators, pianists, songwriters, and arrangers. This included Bernard Herrmann, David Raksin, Alex North, George Antheil, Leonard Rosenman, Elmer Bernstein, André Previn, and Jerry Goldsmith. With a firm grounding in traditional harmony, theory, and counterpoint, these composers had not only studied the new music of Bartók, Schoenberg, and Stravinsky—many of them also had a thorough knowledge of jazz styles.

One composer working occasionally in films who was a great influence—not only on film music, but on all of classical composition—was Aaron Copland. By the time he scored his first film, *Of Mice and of Men*, in 1939, he was a world-renowned composer of ballet, symphonic, and chamber music. He only scored a few other films after that, including *The Red Pony* and *The Heiress* in 1949, but Copland left a large musical impression on all who followed. In fact, it was his ability to convey drama in the music to the ballets *Rodeo* and *Appalachian Spring* that brought him to the attention of Hollywood producers. He brought a new and fresh sensibility in his use of instrumentation and harmony. The instrumental textures in Copland's film scores are softer than the big Romantic scores of the time. He used smaller ensembles and avoided the big, overblown orchestral tuttis found in many films. His use of pandiatonic harmonies, polytonality, and controlled dissonance was imitated by many composers.

Aside from musical development and evolution in films, there were several other factors both in the kinds of films released and in American culture itself that must be taken into account when considering the sound of movie music in the 1950s. Perhaps the most important of these is the arrival of the invention of television. There was also the popularity of rebel films—films dealing with youth, rebellion, and the darker issues of life, including alcoholism and drug addiction. The McCarthy committee of the United States Congress, which instigated and led a witch hunt for Communists in many industries—especially the entertainment industry, had an impact not only on who worked and who didn't, but also on the content of the films themselves. The rise of jazz—big-band swing and bebop—created a new musical culture, especially amongst the nation's youth. Add to all of these events and trends the birth of rock 'n' roll music in the mid '50s, and the need for new styles in film scoring can be clearly seen.

THE ARRIVAL OF TELEVISION

Beginning in the late 1940s, television was readily available to the general public. As the cost of TV sets became more affordable, and as more programming was aired by the networks, more and more people made TV a regular part of their lives. At first, Hollywood studios looked down on this technology as someone might look askance at an unwanted relative who shows up uninvited for dinner. They refused to release their catalog of movies to television stations, and did not produce shows for TV. In many cases, the studios hoped and believed television was going to be a passing fad. As we know today, they were quickly proven wrong.

In retrospect, it is not so difficult to see why many Hollywood people had a hard time accepting television. This new form of entertainment arrived only twenty years after the arrival of talkies. The studio system was powerful, smoothly oiled, and profitable, and many people were very comfortable with it. The Golden Age of films was generating millions and millions of dollars in profits from the millions of people that attended movies on a regular basis.

In 1946, an estimated revenue of 1.7 billion dollars was generated by theatrical movies. By 1962, this figure was down to 900 million dollars, just over half the 1946 amount. This was the effect that TV had on the movie business. It threw studios, executives, actors, and all the creative people into turmoil as a new playing field and a new ball game were created.

The period from 1955 to 1970 also saw the demise of the old studio system. Two factors were most important in contributing to this: the advent of television, and a court decision citing anti-trust laws that required the studios to break up their chains of self-owned theaters. This was a true double-whammy. First of all, the popularity of TV meant that many people stayed home and stopped attending movies in the theaters, causing a severe drop in revenues. Secondly, with the loss of the studio-owned theater chains, they no longer had the automatic distribution of a studio-produced film. Previously, a studio could make a film, and no matter how good or bad it was, release it to as many theaters as they wanted, for as long as they wanted to keep it in circulation. Under the new system, if a film was not accepted publicly, the independent theater owner could withdraw it. In addition, because the audience now had the option of staying home and watching TV, if the film wasn't of fairly high quality, or if it didn't strike a chord in the populace, it would fail in the theaters.

With a real pinch in the flow of cash, the studios could not afford to keep thousands of people under contract. So they had to let go of many employees: actors, directors, musicians, and even producers. In the space of a few short years, the dynamic of producing a film completely changed. Producers became independent, using studios to provide financing, a place to shoot, and a distribution network. No longer could the studio control everything from start to finish, though they could still approve or reject the final product. But the process itself often became removed from studio control. Those involved in the production could move from studio to studio as the projects required. This became the norm for all involved in film production, including the composers.

After a few years of refusing to show films originally released in the theaters on television, the studios finally relented, in an attempt to gain at least some profit from the new technology. This gave rise to TV programming of movies from the studios catalogs, albeit frequently edited for length and content, and often interrupted for commercials. This marked the defeat of the anti-TV forces in Hollywood and was the first step toward fully mobilizing the extensive studio machinery to include the production of television shows. It was only a short time before the studios were actively involved in producing sit-coms, dramas, and TV movies.

NEW MUSIC AND THE COMPOSERS WRITING IT

There are many films that contain excellent examples of the different kinds of scores written in the 1950s and 1960s. Several are worth mentioning because they broke new ground, or in some other way stood out from the rest.

One of the young composers making a mark on Hollywood was Alex North. Brought from New York to Hollywood by director Elia Kazan, his score to *A Streetcar Named Desire* (1951) was a landmark musical event. For the first time, a raw, edgy, and modern sounding score with many jazz elements was accompanying a popular film. It was not only the use of jazz but also the use of dissonance (influenced by modern classical composers) that gave this score a unique flavor. This opened the floodgates for other composers to incorporate jazz into their scores, and a whole new musical style began.

In 1953, Kazan again gave an opportunity to a young composer. Juilliard-trained composer Leonard Rosenman wrote a score to *East of Eden*, starring James Dean. Another dissonant, edgy score accompanying a successful film with a popular star did much for establishing that dissonance as an acceptable sound both in the ears of the audience and the minds and pocketbooks of the producers.

Some composers, such as Elmer Bernstein, had the facility to write a contemporary, edgy score like *The Man with the Golden Arm* (1955) and then switch gears and write a Romantic score to an epic or adventure film. Here is Elmer Bernstein speaking about creating the score to *The Ten Commandments* (also 1955) according to the musical tastes of director Cecil B. DeMille:

> *DeMille was a great Wagner lover. His concept of film scoring was utterly simple and very Wagnerian. Every character had to have a theme or motif. In addition to the characters having themes and leitmotifs, certain*

> *philosophical concepts had to have motifs too. God, good, and evil each had to have a theme. The idea was that whenever a particular character was on the screen, his theme had to be present as well. It was all very Wagnerian.*

Because of the leitmotif nature of the score and DeMille's desires, this score was more Romantic than modern in its musical language. That is what was necessary, and yet it didn't prevent Bernstein from being able to create a jazz score to *The Man with the Golden Arm* in the same year.

Another composer to take on scoring several epic films was Miklós Rózsa. A Hungarian-born composer with a doctorate in music, Rózsa had a passion for musicology. For films involving historical subjects, he did extensive research and tried to create a musical sound that was palatable to the average audience, yet based on real historical musical premises, motives, and instruments. His scores to *Quo Vadis* (1951), *Ben-Hur* (1959), *El Cid* (1961), and others are large, grand and well thought out. They established a standard to which many composers writing these kinds of scores had to bear up.

THEME SONGS AND ROCK 'N' ROLL

In every period of movies, there has been the issue of the theme song, pop song, or end-title song. From the early days of sound films, producers realized the financial benefits of having a hit song. Not only could they entice more people into the theater to see the film, but they could sell more records and sheet music. And because they owned the copyright to the song, they could collect on performance royalties if the song became a radio hit. This theme song craze has never really been a craze; it has always been present, only sometimes the frenzy has been slightly greater than others. Every era has had its hit songs, from the 1930s and 1940s onward to today.

A significant wave of theme songs began in the 1950s with the huge popularity of the song, "Do Not Forsake Me, Oh My Darlin'," written by Dimitri Tiomkin and Ned Washington for the movie *High Noon* (1952). However, the popularity of this song doesn't come close to the ongoing success of Henry Mancini's 1961 hit, "Moon River," from the film *Breakfast at Tiffany's*, starring Audrey Hepburn.

Mancini was another Juilliard-trained composer with a strong jazz background. He had his first major success with the theme for the 1958 TV show, *Peter Gunn*. Then came "Moon River" followed the next year by "The Days of Wine and Roses" for the film of the same name. He went on to score dozens of films of every dramatic style, but remains best known to the general public for "Moon River," "The Days of Wine and Roses," and the scores to the Peter Sellers comedy series, *The Pink Panther*.

By this time, the early 1960s, producers could not get enough of the theme song. The producer of the film *Dr. Zhivago* (1965) was so enthralled with Maurice Jarre's melody to "Lara's Theme" that he basically discarded much of the original score and substituted tracks of the song melody. Later in the 1960s, we get "Mrs. Robinson" in *The Graduate* (1967) and "Raindrops Keep Fallin' on My Head" in *Butch Cassidy and the Sundance Kid* (1969).

These songs paved the way for a different use of songs in film. Instead of having the song be sung by a character on screen, or be part of the credits, all of a sudden a pop song, which is seemingly disembodied from the film, became an integral part of the soundtrack. The style evolved where a song was just "dropped in" to the movie soundtrack. Maybe the lyrics were applicable, maybe not. Maybe there was a dramatic reason to have a song, maybe not. For some producers, the only reason to have a song in the film was to hope it became a hit, generated lots of royalties, and caused people to go see the film. And as the popularity of theme songs grew, at least amongst Hollywood producers, more and more films came to rely on songs rather than specifically composed instrumental underscores.

Another factor contributing to this was the rock 'n' roll soundtrack. Beginning with the beach movies of the early 1960s, given a mighty push forward by the Beatles films *A Hard Day's Night* (1964) and *Help!* (1965), and coming to full fruition with the cult classic *Easy Rider* (1969), films consisting completely of rock songs as *song score* (using a song in an underscoring role) became in vogue. As the dark, edgy films of the '50s appealed to that audience, these rock 'n' roll films of the 1960s were aimed at the ever-expanding audience embracing the values of the Woodstock generation. They were pertinent and popular. And truly, the use of songs was completely appropriate. How else to express the tone of those times but through the music of popular songs? The Grateful Dead, Simon and Garfunkel, Bob Dylan, Buffalo Springfield, Steppenwolf, and the Flying Burrito Brothers were perfect for *Easy Rider*. This was absolutely the right music in the right place for certain films.

The problem that arises when this kind of trend hits is that producers and directors jump on the bandwagon rather blindly. When something new works in one movie, there are always several people doing imitations within a short period of time. So instead of choosing a style of music that primarily serves the dramatic intent of the picture, they choose music that they believe is popular and will stimulate the musical taste buds of the audience, causing a positive response to the film or show. This kind of thinking exists today as in the 1960s, the only difference being that in the '60s, a popular song could sell records.

This is not to say that instrumental underscore in the 1960s became a lost art. Although some prevailing trends favored rock songs, and even jazzy underscores (*The Pink Panther*, some of the James Bond movies), there were many excellent orchestral-type scores. Elmer Bernstein's score for *To Kill a Mockingbird* (1962) is a beautiful example of the marriage of compositional structure and dramatic intent. Many other composers of note were active in keeping alive the orchestral vocabulary, including Jerry Goldsmith, Leonard Rosenman, John Barry, Georges Delerue, Maurice Jarre, and John Williams. The trends became parallel. One kind of movie still used traditional orchestral scores, another used pop and rock songs, another kind used jazz-influenced scores, and yet another used more dissonant and avant-garde twentieth-century compositional techniques. The possibilities were expanding even as they were heavily weighted towards songs and jazz music during the 1960s.

CHAPTER 6

Musical Styles 1975 to 2000

During the 1960s and into the 1970s, as films incorporated scores of many different styles, audiences became accustomed to the pop/rock sound and modern dissonance instead of nineteenth-century influenced orchestral underscore. This paved the way in the subconscious awareness of the public to accept what was coming down the road in the 1980s and '90s: the pop flavored orchestral score. But in the '60s and '70s, perhaps the biggest influence on what producers put in the theaters was television.

Many TV themes and underscores were heavily jazz and rock flavored. In an attempt to modernize the shows and make them different from stuffy film scores, the producers incorporated contemporary popular music. Lalo Schifrin's *Mission Impossible* and Neil Hefti's *Batman* themes, both debuting on television in 1966, reflected this use of jazz and rock. In addition, twelve-tone and other methods of atonal composition began to be heavily used by television composers. In television, because the schedules and demands of a weekly series meant the composer had to work quickly and efficiently, twelve-tone became a valuable tool for writing tense or suspenseful scenes. Once again, in yet another way, audiences became accustomed to a new musical vocabulary. In the space of just fifteen or twenty years, from about 1950 onward, a whole new world of musical sounds became possible, and many composers took advantage of this.

One score that is representative of the new kinds of textures used by composers in the mid 1970s was Jerry Goldsmith's *Chinatown* (1974). In this score, Goldsmith used four pianos, two harps, one trumpet, and strings. Some of the pianos were *prepared,* a technique where various objects are put on the strings to change the sound. The piano is intentionally detuned, or the player actually plays the strings inside the piano rather than the keys. This created a uniquely dark and mysterious texture that dovetails beautifully with the rhythm of the film, the way the film is lit, and Jack Nicholson's acting.

In his score to *Patton* (1970), Goldsmith used another technique unusual for that time: *sweetening,* or adding an instrument after the main music tracks have been recorded. In this case, he took a short motif on trumpet and recorded it several different ways with a lot of echo. This little idea was then dropped in to the musical score wherever needed regardless of the harmonic and metrical consequences. It created a disjointed feeling, reflecting the odd and sometimes otherworldly aspect of the character of General George Patton.

These interesting and unusual devices were becoming more common in the 1970s. As nineteenth-century harmony, contemporary twentieth-century techniques, jazz, and rock collided together in the entertainment industry, a myriad of possibilities opened up. Audiences gradually became used to hearing more dissonance, and even came to associate certain impending events with specific musical sounds. Add to this mix the new technology of multitrack recording (beginning in the early 1960s), and the possibilities expanded even more. The film composer's palette was larger and more varied than ever. However, during the 1960s through the early 1970s, orchestral scores, though still used, had fallen somewhat out of favor. It was a succession of two scores—one melodramatic and suspenseful, the other big, dramatic, and traditionally Romantic in style, that were to create a resurgence in orchestral scores.

ORCHESTRAL SCORES RETURN AGAIN

The year 1974 saw the release of the Steven Spielberg film *Jaws,* which was to become one of the classics of suspense and drama. Spielberg and composer John Williams chose to use a more traditional orchestral sound for *Jaws,* and the success of this decision and the resulting score has often been credited with beginning a resurgence of the use of traditional orchestral sounds and a Romantic and post-Romantic musical vocabulary. However, even though *Jaws* was a milestone in the return of the use of a traditional orchestra, there was yet another John Williams score that made movie music come alive in the ears (and the eyes!) of the audience.

In early 1976, the first trailers for the motion picture *Star Wars* appeared in American theaters. Believe it or not, those audiences laughed and jeered at the trailers, causing great consternation for George Lucas and the studio. However, when the film was released, it becamc one of the all-time most popular films, making huge profits not only from ticket sales but from ancillary merchandising as well. Many give the exciting score by John Williams a fair share of the credit for the film's success. From the moment the opening scroll gave the story background, and the bold *Star Wars* theme was heard, the audience knew that something special was about to happen.

According to Williams, when he first viewed the film, it had a temporary music track cut from the 1916 Gustav Holst piece *The Planets*. He originally was asked to edit this well-known classical score, re-record it, and fit it to *Star Wars*. However, he convinced the producer and director that he could do something original in that style and make it fit even better. The result is one we all know today: the wonderful themes for the Rebellion, the dark and ominous Darth Vader theme, Princess Leia's theme, and other fine musical moments are familiar to musicians and non-musicians alike. Using a large symphony orchestra and recording in London with the London Philharmonic, Williams brought back the symphonic score to the ears and eyes of filmgoers.

This was not exactly a return to the Romantic style of Korngold and Steiner. The score to *Star Wars* has many elements of Romantic musical language: lyrical themes, exciting brass tuttis, and delicate woodwind writing. But this new kind of orchestral score was not afraid to incorporate contemporary compositional techniques where necessary. John Williams was schooled at Juilliard and UCLA, and has a thorough knowledge of many different styles of composition, including jazz, twelve-tone, and atonal techniques. So the score to *Star Wars,* and many later scores of Williams and others that followed this lead, fused elements of tonal nineteenth-century writing with whatever textures or effects they wanted to use from the twentieth century: Impressionism, jazz, rock, pandiatonicism, twelve-tone—even aleatoric music.

None of this was completely new to film scoring; examples of all these techniques abound through the 1950s, 1960s, and 1970s. But something happened when *Stars Wars* was released that caused a shift in the way orchestras were perceived, in the acceptance by the audience of the music as a dramatic effect, and in the popularity of this music. It was one more milestone in the constantly developing art of film scoring.

In 1982, another Spielberg-directed film with a John Williams score took the filmgoing world by storm. This was *E.T., The Extra-Terrestrial,* a magical film with an enchanting score that was loved by adults and children alike. Indeed, Spielberg has said, "John Williams is *E.T.,*" emphasizing how important the music was to the emotional impact of that film. Again, as in *Star Wars,* Williams combined a lyrical, tonal style with elements of twentieth-century styles. (For examples of this modern influence, check out the scenes where E.T. drinks the beer from the refrigerator, and when the children take E.T. trick-or-treating.)

The popularity of these kinds of scores opened the door for many other composers to follow suit and incorporate any possible sound they wanted. But the film-scoring industry was about to undergo a massive infusion of new sounds and possibilities, and the whole business of film music was to shift yet again as it absorbed the new technologies of synthesizers and the personal computer.

SYNTHESIZERS AND COMPUTERS: A WHOLE NEW BALL GAME

It is ironic that only a few short years after the resurgence of the orchestral score, the score created entirely, or mostly, using electronic synthesizers became all the rage. Around the late 1970s, synthesizer technology had progressed to where keyboards were affordable. Previously synthesizers had been used in movies, but the ARP and Moog were large, expensive, and cumbersome machines that required a huge amount of expertise to operate. The new technology quickly caught on, and the manufacturers were wise enough to agree together on the MIDI specification (Musical Instrument Digital Interface), a set of technical rules that allowed synthesizers and computers of any manufacturer to interface with each other.

The score that caught the public's attention, and made many producers in Hollywood want the same thing, was Vangelis's score to the 1981 film *Chariots of Fire*. Though the synthesizer technology at the time was primitive compared to today, this score was entirely electronic, with no acoustic instruments at all. All Vangelis had to work with were analog synthesizers, since digital had yet to arrive. There was no sampling, digital editing, or hard-disk recording. The various synthesizer sounds were recorded to a multitrack analog tape machine in Vangelis's home studio.

The impact of this score cannot be overstated. It opened the ears of producers, directors, composers, and the general public to the possibility of using electronic sounds in a lyrical manner. Previously, synthesizer and other electronic sounds, such as the theremin, were used in high intensity dramatic situations and science fiction films. They were usually part of a scary, spooky, or otherworldly musical landscape. Vangelis, in one stroke, showed the world that it could be otherwise.

Not only did this score make a huge impact on the success of the film, but it became a commercial hit, selling millions of records and tapes, and getting serious radio airplay. Of course, many producers jumped on the bandwagon and wanted a similar kind of sound for their films. Since Vangelis clearly could not do them all, it meant that other, more traditionally minded composers would learn the new technology to one degree or another.

The advent of the synthesizer score also opened the first avenue for female composers to gain Hollywood film scoring credits. Some of the trailblazers at the forefront of analog synthesis were Suzanne Ciani on the Buchla and Wendy Carlos on the Moog. Ciani's score for *The Incredible Shrinking Woman* in 1981 marked the first solo composer credit for a woman on any Hollywood studio film. Carlos's hybrid electronic and orchestral score for *Tron* in 1982 followed notable Moog-based contributions from Carlos to several of Stanley Kubrick's films. Though women were working in credited capacities in the U.K. and elsewhere, it took Hollywood much longer to recognize that women could be film composers.

The availability and affordability of synthesizers in the mid 1980s was actually embraced by many composers, both the up-and-coming and established. What open-minded musician could refuse the possibility of adding yet another entirely new dimension of sounds to their palette? Jerry Goldsmith, Maurice Jarre, Elmer Bernstein, and many others began to incorporate electronic sounds into their scores, or even compose scores that were completely electronic. Goldsmith's score to *Hoosiers* (1986) and Jarre's score to *Witness* (1985) are but two examples of traditionally trained, established Hollywood composers writing scores that used electronic instruments exclusively. Up-and-coming composers during this time, such as James Horner, Basil Poledouris, and Alan Silvestri, began to incorporate synthesizer sounds in scores like *Field of Dreams* (1989), *Conan the Barbarian* (1982), and *Romancing the Stone* (1984). Of course, some of this was necessary, as producers were requesting it, but composers found that electronic instruments could aid them in creating new textures.

The rise of this technology was dizzyingly swift. In a few short years, the industry went from having access to only the most primitive electronic sound generators to having extremely sophisticated digital equipment at its fingertips. One downside of this was that for a period of time, many string, brass, and wind players faced a shortage of work. Although there were still many orchestral sessions in L.A. during this time (the 1980s through the early 1990s), there were less than before, because synthesizers were taking the place of the live musicians. In addition, many TV producers, influenced by the success of the score to *Miami Vice*, also switched to completely or partially using synthesizers. The whole world of commercial music was shaken up and altered forever by the arrival of synthesizers and computers.

Another consequence of this new medium was that because of the expertise needed to master the ever-expanding synthesizer and MIDI technology, an entirely new niche and a new kind of film composer was born: the specialist in electronic, synthesizer scores. These composers became experts in synthesizer sounds, sampling, MIDI technology, and *sequencing* (the technique of using computers instead of analog tape to record the synthesizers or samplers). German born Hans Zimmer was one of the first to establish himself in this field, and had many successful scores using either entirely electronically generated music or a combination of electronic and acoustical sounds. Zimmer also ushered in a new business model: working with an expanding team of additional writers and other assistants at his company Media Ventures, which later became Remote Control Productions. Zimmer was able to take on an immense amount of films simultaneously, working in a music factory model.

Even though the synthesizer craze hit hard and made a deep impact—not only on the sound and texture of film scores, but on the recording industry in general—the pendulum always swings back, as we have seen with other styles. In this case, after the initial rush to use electronic instruments, many directors and producers began to recognize the cold and sometimes false sounding nature of these instruments. It was one thing to use synthesizers or samplers to create a new and unusual texture, or combine them with orchestral instruments, but the scores that used them to replace orchestral instruments tended to sound dry and phony, especially in the early days of this period before samples became highly realistic.

The result of this was that composers began to use electronic instruments more as an adjunct to an orchestra, unless the director specified an electronic score. (Here, we are speaking of feature films. For television, cable, and low-budget films, often the film's music budget would not allow the use of an orchestra, and electronic instruments became a necessity.) In addition, many synthesizer specialists began to write scores that incorporated full orchestras. A middle ground was found, and it continues to this day as producers, directors, and composers continue to strive for appropriate uses of both electronic and acoustic sounds.

POP SOUNDS, JAZZ, AND ROCK 'N' ROLL COMPOSERS

For many reasons, the language of rock and pop music has found its way into film scores in general. As we have seen, every style of film music has reflected, to some degree, the film-going audience. For example, in the '30s and '40s, the audience understood nineteenth-century romanticism, and in the '50s and '60s, they resonated with jazz-oriented scores. As pop, rock, and jazz styles became more mainstream through the 1970s, their use in films grew. The influences that rock music brings to the world of film scoring were basically threefold: one, rock rhythms and grooves; two, a certain harmonic vocabulary spanning the traditional blues to progressive pop-, rock-, and jazz-influenced songwriting; and three, pop/rock melodic ideas.

Rock rhythms are the easiest to identify when they are used in film scores. This could be a traditional rhythm section of guitar, keyboard, bass, and drums; a hybrid combination of those instruments; or world music beats. These kinds of sounds have been used in countless scores. In the 1980s, Hans Zimmer used a "world beat" kind of percussion groove in *Rain Man* (1988), Craig Safan used a hip-hop groove for *Stand and Deliver* (1988), and Alan Silvestri used synthesized drums in a quasi-Latin disco beat for *Romancing the Stone* (1984). In the 1990s, Michael Kamen used rock grooves in *The Last Boy Scout* (1991), and Wendy & Lisa channeled hip-hop in *Dangerous Minds* (1995).

Many of the harmonic and melodic ideas used by film composers in this period, and continuing today, draw upon pop melodic and harmonic ideas. This can be heard in the scores of those coming from the record industry as well as those coming from the conservatories. James Horner studied at the Royal Academy of Music in London, and Michael Kamen studied at Juilliard, but they could write a pop hit as well as a traditional sounding score. And this is no different from composers of the previous generation, like Henry Mancini, who did the same thing but with the pop styles current in their era.

The one difference that began in the '70s and '80s was that a composer could be a success in the film industry, and write orchestral scores without any, or minimal, knowledge of the orchestra. This was possible because of two factors: one, orchestrators who assist and prepare a full score from a sketch or a tape, and two, the ease of using synthesizers and MIDI technology. Therefore, a talented rock or jazz musician who had some great creative ideas could realize a score that was beyond the scope of their own orchestral experience.

In order to understand this trend fully, we must also examine the demand side of the economics involved. In the 1970s and 1980s, yet another wrinkle was added to the film scoring community: the desire by some producers and directors to use well-known rock and jazz musicians to create a score for their films. The impact of the popular music of the 1960s and 1970s cannot be underestimated. No other generation bought as many records, went to as many concerts, or looked to rock musicians for philosophical, political, and social leadership as did the generation coming of age in the '60s and '70s. So it was logical that by the late '70s, the same Baby Boomers who were producing and directing films wanted to use the musicians they considered to be icons. The thinking was that these musicians would speak to the audience through the soundtrack as they did in concerts or on records. This was a good idea in theory, but in practice, it could be dangerous for several reasons.

First, a film score requires the ability to create a musical structure that tells a story and remains harmonically and melodically interesting for about two hours. The average pop song is three or four minutes, and many of these artists did not have the expertise needed to sustain and develop their ideas in the way a film demands. Second, film scores need to have a well thought-out texture of sounds, and the experienced classically trained composer will draw upon a wide variety of instrumental possibilities. Most rock and jazz stars, although fine players in their own medium, are only able to execute a much narrower range of sounds and styles. If a film calls for this kind of narrow range, then a rock or jazz artist might be an appropriate choice. Finally, the successful film score comes from a composer understanding their role as a partner to the drama. There is a sensitivity that develops from working with many different pictures and styles of music. The rock or jazz composer who only knows concert performance and the record business was at a severe disadvantage when attempting to work in the unfamiliar medium of film.

All of this is not to say that a jazz or rock musician cannot accomplish a successful film score. Since the 1990s, the contemporary film composer has a support team of anywhere from two to ten or more people accomplishing various tasks, including co-composing, orchestrating, sequencing, synthesizer programming, and music editing. This means that even with less knowledge of traditional composition than a conservatory or university trained composer, the support staff can assist in realizing any creative ideas. And in actuality, this applies to any composer of any background; their team is crucial to making the composer's ideas come to life. (More on this in chapter 11.)

By the close of the millennium, film music was richer than ever. Part of this richness was due to the rock and jazz composers who brought their own special kind of sound. Another aspect was the range of possibilities afforded from traditional symphony orchestras to electronic scores, and hybrids and fusions of the two. At the turn of the century, a film composer could work in just about any sound medium that accomplished the director's vision of the film.

CHAPTER 7

Musical Styles 2000 to the Present

If technology cracked the door open at the end of the twentieth century, then the first quarter of the twenty-first century knocked it clean off its hinges. Synthesis, music notation software, and MIDI sequencing were useful options for composers in the 1980s and '90s, but as the technology became more affordable and powerful, the use of it became necessary and inescapable. Even composers coming from the paper-and-pencil traditions eventually had to either hire a tech-savvy team to handle their notation, mockups, and mixes, and/or embrace the new technologies themselves. By the time of this writing, the number of still-working composers from the end of the twentieth century who are still functioning without using computers in their own writing process can be counted on one hand—even without the thumb!

Composer Kara Talve, who works on the team at the scoring company Bleeding Fingers, describes the centrality of technology in contemporary scoring:

> *The ever-evolving nature of technology in the business is important to keep up with. Being part of a collaborative network means we have the privilege of sharing new plug-ins and sample libraries, synths, you name it, with one another. This constant exchange of ideas and tools allows us to stay at the forefront of music production, always striving to embrace the next breakthrough innovation.*

The use of technology in this period falls roughly into two categories. The first category is the use of technology to make an existing task easier. The second is use for technology's own sake: for the sounds that can only be produced through synthesis, or the manipulation of recorded sound via effects processing. (We have previously discussed this as a late twentieth-century development, but twenty-first century digital technology has exponentially increased the tonal options available.) We'll examine each of these separately.

TECHNOLOGY AS A TOOL

First, let's consider the utilitarian use of technology to speed an existing process. In a way, this is not at all new or unique to this century. The history of music includes many technological advances, beginning with the development of music notation in the Middle Ages. Modern instruments are also themselves the products of increasingly advanced technology. The mechanisms of the piano we know today, for example, would be largely unrecognizable to the pianoforte designers of the late eighteenth century, not to mention those of its predecessors such as the harpsichord. It can, however, be argued that the advent of the personal computer and its rapid development in capability has brought a greater disruption to the scoring field than anything that preceded it. (This particularly rapid development in computing was known as "Moore's law": the observation that integrated circuit speeds doubled approximately every two years over the first few decades of computing, while their cost was halved.)

MUSIC NOTATION SOFTWARE

Beginning with the advent of MIDI in the late 1980s and accelerating particularly rapidly through the early 2000s, the ability to enter music notation into a computer (either by playing it in via a MIDI keyboard controller or step-entering it with a mouse and computer keyboard) allowed incredibly rapid generation of scores and parts compared to the previous hand-engraving process of music preparation. Making edits once a score was in place was also much easier to accomplish when you could simply change a note or rhythm and reprint a part, rather than recopying an entire page by hand.

Notation software also reduced (though did not eliminate) the need for composers to have advanced training in music engraving (the art of setting down music notation in a clear, consistent, and even beautiful way for publication, recording sessions, and live performances). Though composers, orchestrators, and music copyists still need to know the concepts and rules of how best to notate music, the templates and tools provided in high-end music notation programs provide a high degree of automation. For example, previously, each composer, orchestrator, or music copyist would need to know the details of all transposing instruments and be able to quickly transpose parts from concert pitch to transposed and vice versa. Now this process is as simple as one mouse click. (Note: the standard practice in Hollywood today is to produce concert scores with only octave transposing instruments such as piccolo, bass, or guitar appearing in their transposed register, though individual parts must always be transposed.)

DIGITAL AUDIO WORKSTATIONS

Even more impactful was the dawn of the *digital audio workstation* (DAW). In fact, a DAW is actually two pieces of technology bundled together: a MIDI sequencer and an audio recording/editing platform. Originally, each of these tools stood alone. In the late 1980s and early 1990s, you might purchase one software program to record, edit, and mix audio in a studio rather than relying on a tape deck and analog mixing console. You would buy another program to sequence your MIDI data. However, you couldn't record and mix MIDI and audio in the same piece of software until later in the 1990s, when gradually, the software developers began combining MIDI sequencing and audio recording in the same platform. In this century, almost all DAWs deal well with both MIDI and audio, with only slim advantages of quality and workflow when compared with each other. These days, a composer can, at the click of a mouse, add traditional orchestral instruments, instruments from just about any country around the world, and electronic sounds to their sequences. This creates a huge palette of sonic choices all "in the box" (i.e., using a computer).

Though notation software was important—especially early on in establishing a professional customer base of music technology users with digital home studios—the DAW has been even more transformative to the profession, because it proves useful in every type of scoring, whether or not notation even comes into play. And because (as noted previously) Moore's law shows a steep trend downward in cost and upward in computer speed, compared to the fixed and relatively high costs of outfitting a professional recording studio, today's aspiring composer has a much lower cost of entry to the scoring field. Whereas prior to this era it was necessary to have the budget to hire players and an expensive recording studio, to say nothing of music copyists, mix engineers, and so forth, it is now possible to write, record, mix, and deliver an entire score from your bedroom—or even on the road from a hotel room—with only a laptop loaded with a DAW, notation software, and a suite of sample libraries (collections of playable sampled instruments triggered by MIDI data), a pair of high-quality headphones, and a MIDI keyboard.

That said, this so-called democratization of the scoring field brought forth through technological innovation is, in a sense, self-limiting. As there are more composers capable of producing a score, there's a corresponding difficulty in standing out and getting hired. No longer is it sufficient to be able to just write music—to sit alone in a studio with a piano, a pencil, and a pad of music paper. Today, in addition to having a unique musical voice paired with a fluency across multiple music styles, the successful film composer must also have a strong ability to produce music using digital tools; demonstrate business acumen and an entrepreneurial mindset, especially in how to market oneself; and have a high level of ability to tap into the heart of a story, collaborate with filmmakers, and turn in work on time. While it is conceivable that someone can learn all of these skills on their own, it has become increasingly important to have either an educational background specific to scoring and/or to spend time in an apprenticeship or mentorship model, as an intern or composer's assistant, to really break into the field, as we'll explore in depth in the final chapter of this book.

THE RISE OF THE INTERNET

Another key area of technology that came into its own in this era, with huge implications for the scoring field as well as to the rest of modern life, is the internet. Its early stages in the 1990s didn't have a significant impact on scoring. However, in the early 2000s, the focus of the internet shifted towards communication and user-created content. This made it easier to find and stay in touch with collaborators, which became central to the work of scoring, making it possible to work remotely, share files, and receive feed back without having to be in the same room.

Then in the 2010s, the infrastructure became fast enough for streaming of audio and video, transforming the way the media could be consumed. Of particular note for those in the scoring field, streaming video platforms such as Netflix, Amazon Prime Video, and many others proliferated and began to produce their own content. In 2014 came the first Oscar nomination for a film distributed by a streaming service (Netflix) for Jehane Noujaim's documentary feature *The Square* about the Egyptian revolution. Just eight years later, in 2022, came the first Best Picture Oscar win for a film produced by a streaming service (Apple TV+) for Sian Heder's *Coda*; and that same year also saw a Best Director win for Jane Campion for the Netflix-produced *Power of the Dog*. In the meantime, the streaming companies have rapidly filled up the Emmy nomination slots, and these days to the point where it would be more surprising for a traditional broadcast television show to prevail there.

For the film composer, it is important to understand that this industry-wide shift towards streaming services producing content is more of a business consideration than a musical one. Scores still need to be produced in collaboration with filmmakers. However, the sheer amount of media produced by streaming services has impacted musical styles, production, and delivery in ways that we'll return to in this chapter, as well as later chapters.

This quality and speed of streaming data also opened up a worldwide market for orchestral score recording. Previously, to take advantage of lower player and studio rates in another country or city, a composer would have to fly there (adding to the expense). Today, a composer in Los Angeles—or even in a beach house somewhere on a tropical island—can remotely tune into an orchestral scoring session of their music taking place in Eastern Europe or elsewhere. So, though music budgets have continued to decline overall under industry pressures, the ability to record an orchestral score with live players has also become less expensive and more feasible. Nor is remote recording of an entire orchestra the only option; sample libraries have become more sophisticated and subtle. Especially when combined with even a few live players in a hybrid score, they can sometimes be indistinguishable from a fully acoustic score.

TECHNOLOGY AS A SONIC PLAYGROUND

As mentioned, beyond the use of technology as a tool to make existing work easier, it can also serve as a source of new sonic possibilities. Analog synthesis—still in use today to provide unique sounds, especially if a score is meant to evoke the period of the 1980s or '90s—was joined by a huge array of digital synthesizers and sampled instruments. In addition, the creative use of digital signal processing (DSP) allows composers to manipulate and transform recorded sound, resulting in everything from emulation of existing analog effects to highly experimental and boundary-pushing sounds never before heard.

This ability of composers to use technology to morph seamlessly from sounding electronic to acoustic and anything in between further accelerated the trend towards hybrid scores that have a strong component of both orchestra and synthesizers, such as Pinar Toprak's score for *Captain Marvel* (2019), and many of the scores of James Newton Howard, Hans Zimmer, and others. Furthermore, scores began to emerge that blurred the distinction between digital and acoustic to the point where it's not possible to determine which is being used.

One great example of this type of merged hybrid can be heard in Mica Levi's score for the 2014 film *Under the Skin*. To create the otherworldly sense required for the film's story, Levi combined contemporary playing techniques on acoustic instruments with large doses of digital audio manipulation. Another influential example of this type of acoustic-electronic style fusion is Nicholas Britell's score for *Moonlight* (2016). This score uses the orchestra to convey the vulnerability hidden away in the core of the main character, electronically processed using hip-hop techniques of sound manipulation to depict the results of the character's environment on his development as he comes of age.

Though Levi and Britell are both examples of classically trained composers who also incorporate contemporary popular styles into their scores, there were also, as in the previous decades, popular artists who established a strong and unique musical style for which they then became in demand for scores. In the early 2010s in particular, these artists tended to come from the alt rock and electronica worlds. Jonny Greenwood of Radiohead and Trent Reznor and Atticus Ross of Nine Inch Nails are notable examples.

The Reznor-Ross score for 2010's *The Social Network* was particularly influential. Its seeming simplicity, as well as the combination of electronic and acoustic sounds, was much emulated in the decade to come, particularly following its Oscar win for best score. Rather than a melodic, hummable melody, the musical ideas in this film were short melodic motifs and an overall sound focused on texture or sound palette. In the case of *The Social Network*, that sound perfectly captured the precise nuance that the director, David Fincher, sought to convey for the character of Mark Zuckerberg.

Another trend in scoring styles that leans into this kind of textural approach where the line between score and sound design can be hard to discern originated with composers like Jóhann Jóhannsson. As in the scores we've discussed, Jóhannsson combined acoustic and electronic sounds into a lush and sometimes even overwhelming soundscape—particularly those for the films of director Denis Villeneuve such as 2015's *Sicario* and 2016's *Arrival*. Following Jóhannsson's tragically early death, his frequent collaborator and fellow Icelander Hildur Guðnadóttir carried this tradition forward and continued to innovate. Her

Oscar-winning 2019 score for *Joker*, which digs into the head-space of this troubled character as personified by the composer's own performance on electric cello, followed closely on the heels of her intensely creative score for the HBO miniseries *Chernobyl*, which she composed using instruments created entirely from samples of sound from an actual nuclear power plant.

THE GOLDEN AGE OF EPISODIC MEDIA

Though television became widespread in the 1950s, the style of story that could be told was limited due to low budgets, strict time constraints, and the inability of audiences to go back and watch episodes they had missed. In its early days, there was also a stigma of sorts surrounding those who worked in television—often considered a less artistic medium than film. Although some composers like Jerry Goldsmith and John Williams started their careers composing for television before going on to exclusively score feature films, many others made their careers in one medium or the other, and rarely crossed over.

That all changed at the turn of the millennium. First, cable networks like HBO, buoyed by the appetites of audiences for the sophisticated narrative arcs of shows like *The Sopranos* (1999 to 2007) began pumping more money into prestige dramas instead of focusing mainly on cheap-to-produce content such as reality TV programming. Then the streaming networks entered the scene, and all the old rules became obsolete. Suddenly, *show runners* (producers of episodic media who are in charge of the overall story arc and look and feel of a show) could craft story arcs of any length, not just twenty-two episode seasons. Miniseries of any number of episodes were now possible, facilitating the telling of stories that previously didn't fit well in either a two-hour film or an ongoing series. Moreover, each episode could vary in length, since the strict requirements of broadcast commercial television, which relied on having exactly the same amount of content between each commercial break, was no longer a constraint. And as the icing on the cake, episodes could be released simultaneously, allowing eager viewers to binge-watch whole seasons of their favorite shows.

There were also changes in the format of episodes themselves. For example, the ability to skip the introduction or main title of a show on digital platforms has led to some shows eschewing them entirely. In other cases, such as Nicholas Britell's music for shows like HBO's *Succession* (2018 to 2023) and Disney+'s *Andor* (2022), the main title music morphs to become more distorted and fragmented throughout the series, following the arc of their main characters—something never done in traditional television where the main title was expected to remain the same at least through an entire season to set the stage and subconsciously remind viewers what the show was about. There's no reason for a main title to serve that role if a viewer is going to binge-watch a half-dozen episodes in one sitting.

The evolution of the business aspects of streaming were also highly influential on the content that was produced. There was a race on for streaming subscription dollars. Consumers used to paying a bundled cable bill now had a host of individual options of where to spend their hard-earned money, and they tended to choose those services with that must-see show. So the streamers went all out, piling millions of dollars into content crafted to entice and hold viewers.

This ravenous appetite for new content, combined with the fact that many streaming services (such as Amazon Prime Video and Apple TV+) arose from the tech industry rather than from Hollywood, opened the door to composers who might otherwise not have had the same opportunities. As a result, the number and diversity of younger composers increased significantly over previous eras (though, the distribution of composers even in this newer paradigm still isn't representative of the viewing audience).

GENRE BENDING

It wasn't just the boundaries between film and television that were becoming porous; so too were the boundaries between linear and interactive media. Video games, which at the dawn of the new millennium were still considered a relatively niche area primarily marketed to teenage boys, took over from film as the dominant form of entertainment across all demographics. Linear media (film and TV/streaming) naturally sat up and took notice, both optioning game properties to be made into films and shows, and taking influence from game scores. For example, the 2010 film *Scott Pilgrim vs. the World*, based on a graphic novel that itself includes many video game references, uses both quoted music directly from actual games and an original *chiptunes* (deliberately retro-sounding music produced using 8-bit microchips) score. Perhaps ironically, as some films like *Scott Pilgrim vs. the World* have embraced the iconic sound of vintage video games, modern games—especially from the biggest game development studios—have largely taken on the mantle of the golden age of film scoring, often hiring massive orchestras seeking an epic sound.

One last, and notable trend in recent years, perhaps ironic in an age of increased digital delivery and using technology to replace live players, is that film and TV music is increasingly jumping off the screen and into the concert hall. This trend may also owe a debt to the video game music field, since it was live performances of video game music, such as the Video Games Live tour in the early 2000s, that demonstrated the audience interest in this kind of performance. Though there were of course pops-style orchestral performances incorporating film music prior to this point, the idea of showing an entire film with only the dialogue and sound effects, and then hearing all the music performed live in front of the audience was new, and has proven hugely popular. Today, there are live-to-picture tours of many popular movies, as well as some television and streaming franchises whose scores have built up a devoted following, such as Ramin Djawadi's *Game of Thrones Live* tour. In a way, you could say that film music has come full circle from its earliest origins of live music performed to a silent film in a nickelodeon, to an experience of a film in a concert hall with the accompanying resonance and impact a modern orchestra can provide.

PART II

Process

CHAPTER 8

The Filmmaking Process

The making of a major motion picture is an incredibly complex, costly, creative, and challenging endeavor. It requires people with all kinds of skills. One look at the credits of a film gives an idea of the wide range of expertise needed to pull it off: writers, painters, truck drivers, electricians, carpenters, cinematographers, directors, musicians, special-effects designers and technicians, makeup artists, costume designers, publicists, directors' assistants, production assistants, assistants to the assistants, and on and on the credits roll while the music plays (or scroll past on your phone when you look them up on IMDB). The beauty of a production is that these seemingly disparate groups of people are all working in an organized way to achieve a common goal: the release of the film.

What the average filmgoer may not realize is that many of these groups operate separately, yet parallel to the whole operation. For example, principal photography (the shooting of the film) might be finishing up on location in New Mexico and at a studio in Los Angeles, while a team of special-effects wizards is beginning to work their magic in New Zealand, the sound-effects people are working at yet another studio in Northern California, and the composer and their team are in their studio in Los Angeles, staring at the swimming pool, waiting for a cut of the film so that they can start the scoring process.

Actually, this is both far from and close to the truth. Nobody actually waits for a film to be fully completed these days before they start writing the music, because so many films take longer than originally planned and there are so many edits continuing until almost the date the film goes to theaters—sometimes even past that date. But the reality of the filmmaking process is that the music is the very last thing to be done. Before getting into what the composer does, though, let's take a look at the filmmaking process itself.

DECISION MAKERS

There are several people involved in getting a film off the ground: the producer, director, writer, and possibly the talent (actors). These are the people whose creative, financial, and organizational skills actually drive the production.

Producer

The producer oversees the financial and organizational aspects of the film. This person supervises the hiring of everyone from director and actors to the heads of each department—for example, the production designer for the art department and the gaffer for the set electricians. The producer also makes sure there is a workable schedule and ensures that all elements of the production are running smoothly, from the writing of the script to the feeding of the crew. The producer is responsible for the financial bottom line and answers to the executives at the movie studio that will release the film.

In order to raise the funds needed to launch a film, it's often necessary to find and package several different investors. This can include deep-pocketed movie studios, investment banking consortiums, and individuals. The producer will have to pitch the project to these various people and organizations, and create deal structures for them to make a profit if the movie does well.

When a big studio or network is not involved—meaning, the film is an independent production—funding the film can look a bit different.

Independent producer Jane Applegate describes this process:

> *Independent producers need to contribute an enormous amount of sweat equity. Studio and network producers are on a salary.*
>
> *Rarely, except in the form of private investors and public grants, do producers have any significant development money. Savvy producers try to raise seed money and work with organizations providing fiscal sponsorships that provide tax deductions to supporters.*
>
> *Producers often rely on crowdfunding platforms like Indiegogo, Seed and Spark, and Kickstarter to encourage future fans of the film or video project to pay for its production. It's important to note that running a crowdfunding campaign is a full-time job and requires an enormous amount of effort to produce promotional videos, round up perks offered for various donations, and to seek press coverage during the campaign.*

Whether working independently or for a studio, the responsibility for a producer can be enormous, as budgets for feature films climb higher and higher. To paraphrase one producer, a movie can be made for $100 million and last one or two weeks in the theaters. But a huge skyscraper can be bought for the same amount of money and stand for decades.

And the producer does much more than just raise money. The bigger part of the job is to shepherd a project through the maze of production. This involves coordinating all the creative people, the technicians, the marketing experts, and the financial overseers. Therefore, it also involves a heavy dose of managing profit politics, ego politics, and power politics. Even though everyone involved has the common goal of making a successful film, the recipe for success will be different depending on the point of view. The producer is the person coordinating those different approaches and definitions of success; those driven by profit, those driven by artistic standards, and those driven simply by ego gratification.

The organization of the team is one of the producer's main jobs, and the three main components of that team are the writer, the director, and the lead actors. However, it is the director who is the most important day-to-day member of the team. Once the shooting begins, the producer often maintains a respectful distance and lets the director's vision guide the film.

Director

The director is the creative captain of the project with the overall vision for what the film will say and look like. The director must also be able to communicate that vision to everyone working on the project and be strong enough to hold to that vision as the film makes its journey from script to screen. That means coordinating the creative efforts of many people, as well as interfacing with the producers and assuring them that the project is both on schedule and looking good from an aesthetic standpoint.

The director approves the script (sometimes writing it as well), and oversees all the design elements of the film including the cinematography (the camera angles, lighting, and overall "look of the film"), costumes, sets, props, hair, and makeup. The director is responsible for "directing" the actors on the set, deciding when a take is the right one, which scenes will be shot in which order, and keeping to the overall shooting schedule and budget. The director oversees the editing of the film after shooting is completed and presents a version to the producer and studio executives for their approval. Except in the rare case of a big-name director with a long track record who obtains final cut approval, these higher-ups—the execs and producer—have the right to alter the film in any way they see fit.

Writer/Screenwriter

The writer, or "screenwriter," takes a story, an idea, a book, or a play and makes it into a screenplay, or script. This person is responsible for creating a script that fits the director's and producer's desires for the film. This can mean that even if the writer is initially happy with a script, it might not be finished because of rewrites requested by the director or producer. The version of the script that is used in the actual shooting of the film is called the shooting script, and there are often further revisions during and even after shooting that result in new versions.

The writer is responsible for creating an engaging story, making the characters believable, and writing dialogue that fits the characters and the tone of the film. Every line the actors speak, every scene, every part of the plot is considered and mulled over to make sure it is just right. The screenplay then becomes a blueprint for the shooting of the film. Many people, including the director, producer, cinematographer, film editor, and the actors can have input on the script, both during the writing stage and during the shooting stage, and sometimes even after shooting has concluded and the film is being edited. This input can often make it even better, as the collaborative process works its magic, and results in successive revisions of the script.

Sometimes, several writers work on a film because a single author can't achieve the vision of the director or producer. On many films, *script doctors* are brought in to polish up either the whole thing, certain scenes, or lines of dialogue. Even with only one writer, a screenplay will go through many revisions before a shooting script is ready. This process can take as little as a few weeks, or last as long as several years.

PUTTING IT ALL TOGETHER

How does a film make its way from an idea in someone's head, a book, or a play to a multimillion-dollar production showing in your local theater? The beginning of the process, even before the production is a glimmer in a studio's eye, is known as "development." Depending on who comes up with the original idea for the movie, the process can unfold in different ways, and the people described come on board in a different order. There are three basic stages of this process: (1) getting the idea for the film, (2) obtaining financing, and (3) hiring the creative and organizational people to make the idea a reality.

Often, the process is from the top down. The producer gets an idea, receives a screenplay, or buys the rights to a book and then oversees the process from start to finish. However, there are many different ways the process can happen. Here are two possible alternatives to the scenario where the idea for the film originates with the producer.

Scenario 1: A director has an idea for a film, goes to a producer, and pitches a treatment (a short synopsis of the plot) to a producer. The producer agrees to undertake the project and begins arranging for financing. The producer then hires a writer, usually with the director's approval. When the script is finished, the producer and director begin to contact actors for the lead roles. Important roles for the production, such as the cinematographer, film editor, and casting director, are hired at this time. As the script nears completion, a production schedule is created and the rest of the crew is hired.

Scenario 2: An accomplished writer brings the first draft of a screenplay to a director known to them. The director loves the screenplay and agrees to direct it. The story calls for a strong action-hero type, so together they approach a well-known actor who also loves the idea. Next, this trio of proven professionals—writer, director, and movie star—presents a "package" to a producer. The packaged combination of talent, box-office draw, and exciting story line make the project irresistible, and the producer signs on quickly before they pitch the project elsewhere.

There can be many variations of this process, depending on who has the original idea and who that person's contacts might be. Many times, an agent will get involved trying to package together two or more elements: writer and director; actor and director; producer, actor, and writer, etc. In the end, the process can be very political, with who-knows-whom being a big part of it. Sometimes, it simply comes down to a matter of availability—an actor or director is just not available at the time this production requires. And sometimes, a project is pushed through by the sheer will of one of the parties involved because they believe in it. But whether it is one person filling multiple roles or many people dividing the roles, the making of a film is a huge, complicated, and enormously exciting process.

THE STAGES OF A FILM'S PRODUCTION

There are three stages of a film's production: pre-production, production, and post-production. Post-production can be further divided into two parts: (1) editing and assembling the film, and (2) music, sound effects, and the final sound mix.

Keep in mind that this process is a flexible one. Things are always changing and can happen in a different way or in a different order from what was originally projected. But these three main chronological divisions basically stay the same.

Pre-Production

Pre-production begins at the point in the process described in the previous section when a project is "greenlit," or approved for production by a studio. This stage progresses from inception and development of the idea to the planning required for it to become an actual film.

Together, development and pre-production include:

- conceiving the initial idea, or obtaining the rights to a book, play, or short story
- writing the treatment
- obtaining financing
- writing the screenplay
- hiring the principal creative people
- casting (hiring the actors)
- scheduling
- scouting for locations (out-of-studio shooting)
- hiring the crew

Production

Production is the actual shooting of the movie. This can take weeks or months depending on the scale of the production. It is an exciting time, when all the planning starts to become a physical reality. It is also a time when people are under a lot of pressure to meet deadlines, which can sometimes be affected by such diverse circumstances as the weather on the location, an actor's illness, or even a union work-stoppage. Production involves:

- rehearsing the actors
- shooting the film, either at the studio or on location
- screening "dailies" (shots from earlier that day, or the previous day)
- special-effects photography/animation (continues into post-production)
- production sound recording

Post-Production

Post-production can be divided into two segments: picture editing and sound editing. Picture editing involves assembling the film visually, while in sound editing, the dialogue, music, and sound effects are created and placed in the film. These tasks take place simultaneously for the first part of post-production; however, it is not until the second part of the post-production process, after the picture editing is substantially complete, that the most intensive production of the music, dialogue, and sound effects begins. This is because the film must be at least roughly edited in order for the sound elements to be synchronized to it.

Though the digital formats most commonly in use today no longer require actual development of film (for viewing of dailies)—i.e., physical cutting and splicing of film, and assembly of film onto reels—many of these older celluloid film-based terms are still widely in use because of the combined power of habit and the continued utility of the underlying concepts. However, one thing which has changed significantly in the digital era is the ease of making changes compared to the early days of cinema. This has led to many situations where, for example, the music is being recorded and the director remembers having taken out a few seconds of film, and no one told the composer. Or even a situation where edits were made in the film after the final delivery of the mixed music. This creates havoc in the synchronization of music to picture, though it ensures the continuing importance of the role of the music editor, to be explored in more depth later.

Post-Production Part 1: Picture Editing

Editing is when all the footage from production is assembled into a coherent film. This is done by the film editor (also known as the picture editor). Often, a director shoots several takes of the same scene, with different camera angles, that need to be put together in a natural way. This means matching shots, facial expressions, body language, and dialogue. Once the actual photography, or shooting, is completed, the film editor sifts through hours of footage and makes sure the story is being told in a coherent way, that there is no extraneous material, and that the cuts all make sense visually. It is a crucial task, because this process determines the overall pacing and dramatic impact of the film.

The picture editorial phase of post-production includes:

- assembling the *rough cut* (the working version of the film). The rough cut eventually becomes a *fine cut* or *locked picture* (meaning that the timings of the edits are final), and may include a temporary track of music, to be discussed later in more depth.
- screening for studio execs
- screening for test audiences
- visual effects
- film color

From the earliest days of film until the early 1990s, editing a film involved running a copy of the film through a projector over and over again using a Moviola, which is a flat-bed projector. Using foot-pedals, a Moviola allowed the editor to go back and forth over a print of the film while synchronized with the dialogue track. The editor then decided where to make the edits, physically cut pieces of film, and spliced them together—hence the expression that a scene or line of dialogue ended up "on the cutting room floor." Once this version of the film was approved by the director, producer, and studio, a negative was cut and spliced in the exact same way. That negative was sent to the lab and copies were made for the theaters.

The method of film editing that uses Moviolas is now extinct. In today's world, even if the shooting happens on celluloid film, editing is done digitally using non-linear editing software (known as an NLE). All the various takes are loaded into a computer, and the editor then cuts and pastes as needed. This also allows the director to easily view several options of a scene.

Once the film is edited to at least a rough-cut stage, it enters the process involving the composer and the rest of the music crew, as well as the sound-effects crew. Simultaneously, the picture will continue to evolve as visual effects teams create CGI characters, composites are made to enhance backgrounds, and color is adjusted to create the final look of the film. As previously mentioned, in a perfect world, the composer and sound team would not begin working until there is a locked picture to avoid changes in the edit that would affect the synchronization of the music and sound, though it is rarely, if ever, possible to get a true locked picture that will not be changed, so it's common to start the music creation process with a rough cut. The exception to this is if music is involved to which the actors sing or dance on-screen. Then, the music is usually recorded before shooting begins (prerecorded) so that the final version of the song or arrangement can be played on the set.

Post-Production Part 2: Sound Editing

The audio post-production process itself involves three areas being worked on simultaneously by largely separate teams: music, dialogue, and sound design.

These areas include the following steps, which will be explained in more detail in the next few chapters:

MUSIC	DIALOGUE	SOUND EFFECTS
• Spotting session • Music composition, with input from the director on mockups of cue versions • Orchestration, copying parts, and recording of music (if using live ensembles) • Mixing music • Song clearances • Music editing	• ADR • Dialogue editing	• Field recording for sound effect creation • Foley (sound performed and recorded live to picture) • Backgrounds and designed sound effect creation and editing

These three areas of audio are each submixed into *stems*—that is, submixes of several tracks sharing a particular characteristic. For example, one music stem could be all of the strings; another, all of the percussion. A stem of sound effects could be several individual tracks combined to make the sound of a car crashing.

These are among the very last elements in the film's production, and once complete individually, they are mixed together on the dub stage, in a process known as "dubbing" or "rerecording mix." At that point, the film is ready for the audio and picture to be married together, given a final check, and then distributed. Note that distribution is its own process and not considered one of the three stages of production, as it takes place once the film is complete.

One thing that cannot be emphasized enough is the pressure that can be placed on the composer because of the fact that just about everything else needs to be finished before the music can be scored to picture. Films are often behind schedule in production, but the release date cannot change. The composer may have less time to complete the score than originally scheduled.

This goes double for films that change composers late in the process—a disturbing (for composers) situation that can occur when there are creative differences that surface between composer and director, or when a film is not getting positive responses from test audiences and a director believes that changing the music will change the audience response. Since music is one of the last things to be completed, it's also one of the few things that can be changed at this late stage to try to improve audience perceptions. Composer Haim Mazar shares this example:

> *I'm finishing a film right now: the movie had a composer that was fired, and then I got to score it. Originally, they only gave me four weeks, and I'm now kind of sneaking in my fifth week, chasing the dub.*

The stages of film production outlined here are not set in stone; this whole process involves a great deal of flexibility. For example, editing could overlap production. If enough footage for the beginning of the film has been shot, while the director is off shooting the ending of the picture, the film editor might assemble the first few scenes. Or parts of the script might be reworked even while the movie is being shot. The process is fluid, and the successful people are those who learn to honor that fluidity, and even harness it to improve the project.

DIFFERENCES IN EPISODIC PRODUCTION

Most of the processes described here hold true whether the production is for a film or a television, streaming, or other episodic series. However, there are some differences worth noting in both the roles and schedules for episodic productions.

First and most important to understand is the difference between the producer and director roles in an episodic series. Unlike in film, where the director is the one whose vision everyone follows, in a series it is generally the producer, or "show runner," who is the creative captain. Directors on a series may change episode by episode, so they are usually focused on the production itself, on set or on location. The show runner or producer will oversee the arc of the entire series, as well as its look and feel. Another key aspect of keeping a series consistent is the use of a "bible" that covers character arcs, color palette, costume, set, and prop decisions, and goes far beyond a treatment in setting out the world of the show for everyone to refer to.

For episodic network television, new episodes air every week. In the production process, the composer will often have about that amount of time to write the music for each episode. For streaming, the timeline is largely the same, even if the shows all drop at once—though in that case, the weekly schedule can have some flexibility. As a result of these relatively compressed timelines in comparison to feature films, some steps in the process described above may need to be shortened or eliminated. For example, there may only be time for a very brief music spotting session, and that might only take place between the picture editor and the composer—at least, once a show is underway and the show runner's intentions are clear.

Even given these differences, it's important to note that there is less distinction now than ever before between the people working in film and television. Multiformat producer Jane Applegate shares a story:

> *In 2004, I attended a big documentary conference and ended up being offered a job to oversee production of five Discovery Health specials for a medical animation company in New York City. My life-changing moment hit when I wrote, directed and produced a six-figure World War II battlefield scene for a Discovery Health documentary. It was the first time I ran a set and worked with a professional film crew.*
>
> *On a frosty fall night in upstate New York, I stepped outside the production trailer for a breath of fresh air. I looked up at the moon at declared aloud, "I'm going to produce films someday."*
>
> *When I walked back into the trailer and shared my declaration, a snarky dude laughed. "No way. You're a TV*

> *producer. We're film people. You'll never be able to work on films."*
>
> *Of course, today every film person is working on TV shows.*

As we've seen, whether the medium is film, television, or something else yet to be devised, producing an immersive multimedia story requires collaboration, skill, and the vision of a creative director or producer. As the credits roll, the magic that arises from varied talents following a shared vision becomes clear.

CHAPTER 9

Post-Production Sound

Before moving on to music—our main focus—let's take a deeper dive into the other areas of post-production sound, to more fully understand the frame within which music will function. Let's unpack those extra-musical areas of film sound that were listed in the last chapter.

SOUND EFFECTS

The work of post-production sound can be divided into subcategories of backgrounds and ambiances, hard sound effects, and Foley. Each of these may be generated by different teams, and then assembled together into one sound stem by yet another team of sound editors, and finally mixed on the dub stage along with the other audio stems: dialogue and music. Because there are multiple teams working on this at the same time, there is usually one person hired as the *post sound supervisor* (sometimes called the "supervising sound editor") to organize this entire effort. This role is roughly analogous to that of a producer on the film as a whole—generally not getting involved directly in any one area, but enabling everyone else to get the job done in the optimal way.

The post sound supervisor/supervising sound editor will also have at their disposal the *production audio*—audio that was recorded on set or on location by the production sound recording team. Though it's not uncommon for all of the production sound to be replaced in post-production, serving only as a *guide track* —an indication to the sound team what the original sounded like, some of this production audio track may remain in the final soundscape and may require clean-up and editing to select the best mic option and fill in gaps with *room tone* (recorded background sound of a particular space with the set and actors in place but making no sound).

SOUND DESIGN: EFFECTS AND BACKGROUNDS

Perhaps the most creative role in the post sound department is that of the sound designer. Though sound has been a key part of the experience of film since the first talkies, it wasn't until 1979's *Apocalypse Now* that the title was coined. The title was first given to Walter Murch to recognize the outsized role that his heightened and subjective sound played in this film, such as using the sound of helicopters while the main character is looking at a ceiling fan to give us a first-hand sense of the character's trauma. Prior to that film, though this role existed and was important to the experience of films, the person filling this seat would be credited as sound editor or sound montage.

Sound design is also the most musical area of film sound aside from the actual music. The sound designer generally starts with recordings of isolated sounds (either from a pre-existing library of such recordings or custom recordings made for a particular film) and layers them together, much as a composer might double individual instrument voices to create a richer texture through orchestration, to find the right sound for a particular moment. They generally do this with the same kinds of tools as composers, using computers running some of the same DAWs that you might find in a film composer's studio, as well as sampler plug-ins to load sounds in a way that they can trigger them with a MIDI keyboard. Then, after layering, manipulating, and synchronizing sound into a scene, the sound designer may leave in multiple options for a particular moment that the director can choose from later in the context of the full soundscape at the dub mix.

Though sound design can be realistic and provide a sense of realism to a scene, sometimes in order to feel right to an audience, it actually has to be heightened from what something would sound like in reality. For example, pulling a sword from its sheath in real life doesn't produce much sound at all, but we would be disappointed not to hear the characteristic "brrrrring!" we've come to expect in a film. Some franchises have a sound world all their own. Think for example of the different sound worlds of *Star Trek* and *Star Wars*. Just hearing the sound of a door opening in one of these two universes would tell you precisely which you were watching.

When we think of sound design, we're likely to picture gunshots, explosions, and creature effects in our mind's ear. However, there is another key area of sound design that, when done well, isn't noticed at all: background or ambient sounds. While a "hard" sound effect like a dinosaur's roar might bring a particular moment to life, a well-designed ambient sound will pull you right into the film's world. Like other areas of sound design, backgrounds generally have many layers of orchestrated sound, assembled in a DAW. Like hard sounds, they can aspire to realism or to something more fantastical, depending on the filmmaker's overall approach. Whether the film is set in a woodland glade, an erupting volcano, or a suburban kitchen, to really make the audience believe in the world of the film, the backgrounds have to sell the sound of that space. The work of the sound designer in creating ambience can be unsung and is often unrecognized, but is hugely important to the audience's experience of the film.

FOLEY

One final—and key—area of sound that is not handled by the digital sound design team is called "Foley," which is a process in which individuals known as Foley artists (or "Foley walkers" due to the importance of this technique for footsteps) create sound effects through live recording while watching a projection of the film. This particular technique was named for its originator, Jack Foley, and therefore is always spelled with a capital F. Because Foley is performed live while watching the film on screen, as opposed to crafted in a computer, it is best suited to the most realistic and detailed sounds—very difficult to create manually, but natural if performed live. An analogy that might be helpful in understanding the distinction between Foley and other sound effects is that Foley is akin to practical visual effects, like puppets and model shots, where digital sound design is more like CGI (Computer Generated Imagery). Foley uses props or the Foley artist's own body to record unique performed sound for the film.

Foley can be as primitive as simulating horses' hooves by clapping two coconut halves together, as in the old radio days, or it can be something like breaking windows or other glass to create the sound of a crash, actually walking in different kinds of shoes on different surfaces in a Foley pit, or rustling cloth or other materials as the characters move in various costumes. Foley artists are essentially actors, with their medium being sound. Though not every sound will be exactly the same as that seen on screen, they do generally seek to be very authentic to what is seen, so they will use a variety of costumes, props, and surfaces for the ultimate verisimilitude. The amount of Foley you hear in a finished scene will change depending on the medium and genre of the production, but in all cases, it's serving an important purpose in helping the audience be immersed in a particular location.

DIALOGUE

You might imagine that most dialogue is recorded on set or on location, as part of the production audio recorded on set or on location, but in reality much of this is actually done in post-production through *ADR*, short for either Automatic Dialogue Replacement or Additional Dialogue Recording. ADR is when the actors go into a studio to redo any lines that were not recorded well or have extraneous noise on the production track. They will also record any new off-camera lines added after shooting, as well as narration. Often, the dialogue that is recorded on the set of a film is muddy, unclear, or marred by unwanted sounds on the set. This is especially common with shooting outdoors, when it is impossible to control noise such as airplanes, lawn mowers, sirens, and wind. In addition, the actor may have garbled the line, the boom operator may not have gotten a good angle, or if wearing a body mic (known as a "lav," short for "lavalier"), the actor may have brushed it against an article of clothing. In ADR, the actors go into a studio, listen to and watch their original performance on a loop (with visual cues called "streamers" letting them know when each line will start), and redo the line or lines until they are synced up exactly. This is so common that in some films, every line you hear in the final version was actually replaced through ADR.

Whether recorded through ADR or part of the production audio, all the dialogue is eventually edited by the dialogue editor, and assembled into the dialogue stem for the dub mix. The dialogue editor will apply EQ and reverb, if necessary, and balance every line of dialogue (whether production sound or ADR) with all the lines in that scene as well as the sound of the dialogue in the entire project.

THE FINAL DUB

The *dub* is where the sound effects (abbreviated SX), dialogue (DX), and music (MX) stems get mixed together into the final soundtrack. Reel by reel, scene by scene, line by line, and sometimes crash by crash, the dubbing team mixes, filters, pans, and generally tweaks these three sound elements to blend them together. It's important to emphasize that the word "dub" has a different meaning colloquially than it does in film post-production. In everyday speech, we might say a film is "dubbed" when its dialogue has been replaced with a different language (e.g., "This copy of *My Neighbor Totoro* has been dubbed from Japanese into English"). This isn't what we mean by "dubbing" in post-production on a film. The two uses of this term refer to completely different things—in fact, dubbing a film into another language is closer in process to ADR than it is to the dubbing mix in film post-production that we're discussing here.

We can think about the complete soundtrack as though it were a landscape painting:

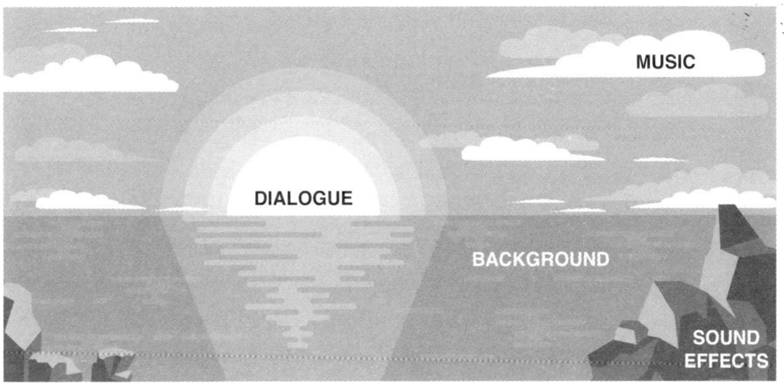

FIG. 9.1. Parts of a Soundtrack

All of the elements in this image—the ocean with rocky crags along the coast, the sun, and the clouds—form a single image. In the same way, the layers of sound discussed above—sound effects and backgrounds, dialogue, and music—are mixed together into the film's final soundscape.

Not all of these elements are equal, however. Just as the sun both draws the viewer's eye and illuminates the rest of the scene in our seascape, so must dialogue come through the rest of the soundscape—at least, in most films—so that no matter what else is going on in the sonic space, the dialogue is clearly audible. If clouds (music) block the sun (dialogue), the result will be an unclear image—or in the case of the soundscape, a confusing story. In the same way, sometimes sound effects need to take precedence over the rest of the soundscape. In most cases, when there is a need to choose between sound elements at the dub mix, the dialogue will be the first priority, then the music or the sound effects, depending on the context of each scene.

The most challenging thing to resolve is when two sounds happen in the same frequency range. For example, a high, sustained note in the violins could be canceled out by the whine of a jet engine. Or a percussion track could get lost in a rain of gunfire. It is the job of those on the dubbing stage to make all of these things sound like one continuous whole while still maintaining the sonic integrity of each sound element. A sound palette that sounds natural and lets each voice or sound speak where necessary is the ultimate goal.

Dubbing happens in two stages. The first is called "predubbing." At about the same time that the music is being recorded and mixed, the dialogue engineers clean up the dialogue tracks and get them to sound strong and clear, independent of the sound effects and music. (Each voice and each component of a sound effect has its own separate audio track that can be controlled independently. Music usually has two to eight tracks of stems, depending on the format.) Concurrently, the sound-effects team are doing the same thing in their own studio. One of the reasons predubbing is so important is because of the complexity of some of the tracks. Sound effects alone can have over one hundred separate tracks!

Dubbing is the next to last stage in the entire filmmaking process, and it is actually the final stage of the film's creative process. Nothing can be changed or altered after the dub, so in many ways dubbing is the point of no return for the director. For this reason, it is a detailed, painstaking process, and the feeling of completion is profound for all. Dubbing engineers are juggling dozens of tracks, and this is why the various sound elements are grouped into stems. The total of music, sound effects, and dialogue could easily take up hundreds of tracks—definitely unwieldy and likely unmanageable. With stems, this becomes much more efficient, though the process of dubbing for a feature film usually takes one or two weeks of twelve- to sixteen-hour days. Finally, it is important to note that although the sound experts—engineers, music editors, dialogue editors—all have input on the dubbing stage, it is the director who has the final say.

Now that we've seen the way the rest of the sound comes together, let's dive into film music, our primary topic, and see how it comes into being and joins its sonic partners.

CHAPTER 10

The Scoring Process

Film composer Mason Daring describes two phone calls that are most composers' favorite parts of the scoring process: the first is your agent calling to say "I want to talk to you about a movie," and the second is your mom calling to say she's seen your name in the credits. Though both of these events are in themselves crucial for a scoring career, and we'll come back to them in more detail when we get to business topics, for now let's look at what happens between these two phone calls, during the actual scoring process.

KICKING OFF THE COLLABORATION

Once the composer or composers (there are often collaborative pairs or teams who are hired jointly) have won the gig, the first step is generally not so much musical as it is political. That is, it's crucial to identify who the real client is. Often, as previously discussed, that will be the director in the case of a film, and the producer in the case of an episodic show. However, what if there is more than one director? Might there be a producer with creative input that the composer hasn't met yet, or perhaps an executive producer with final sign off authority? Or could it be that the director or producer has empowered the picture editor or music supervisor to weigh in on the original music score? It's important for the composer not to make too many assumptions at this stage, and instead to ask questions, pay attention, and read the room during meetings. Knowing whose directions to pay most attention to will save a lot of time and heartache later.

Once the composer figures out who they're reporting to, then they should move on to building a rapport with them. Alan Silvestri has wonderful relationships with several directors, and understands the pressure the director can feel, and how that pressure affects their relationship with the composer.

> *You've got to remember what you're doing here. You're working for somebody, and you, the composer, are not going to be the one called on the carpet when the movie was supposed to make $40 million this weekend and it only made $150,000... You're probably off on your next movie, but there's somebody out there who's sitting in a chair right now... having a real bad day. That person's called the director! So if you think for a minute that the director is not going to have a whole lot to say about what kind of music goes into their film and how it sounds, you're kidding yourself.*

Keeping your empathy open for your director can be key—not only to working with them again in the future, but also to creating the best possible score for their film. It's also helpful in taking the next step: establishing the overall concept for the score. This might be thematic, involving melodic motifs attached to characters or ideas, or it might be a particular sound palette consisting of selected instruments and other timbres, or a particular rhythmic signature. It could also be a combination of these. Ideally, the composer can articulate the score's concept verbally, as well as demonstrating it musically through demo cues or a music suite. We will return to this step in depth in the Aesthetics section of the book, but for now, the key thing to understand is that like most aspects of scoring, there must be agreement between the composer(s) and the director or other creative lead.

Sometimes, the scoring concept comes organically from the film, even as early as the script stage when the characters and plot are taking shape. In other cases, especially when the composer is hired later in post-production, there is almost always a temp score—pre-existing music edited into a film in progress—or at least some *reference tracks*—pre-existing audio that the director provides outside of the context of the film as examples of the type of music they think could work well. Since "talking about music is like dancing about architecture," having a musical reference point that can be pointed to even by a non-musician to indicate the mood, genre, or pace can help tremendously in narrowing down the scoring concept from the entire universe of sound possibilities.

SPOTTING

Of the many activities that go into creating the music for a film, one of the most important is spotting. *Spotting* refers to where the music goes and what it will sound like. One could have fabulous themes, sparkling orchestration, great players, and a terrific creative relationship with the director, but if the music comes in and out at the wrong places, it can ruin a film. If a particular instrument enters in a way that is obtrusive, it can destroy the dramatic impact of a scene. If the overall sound and texture of the music is light and bright, but the film is dark and brooding, clearly that will not work. Psychologically, if the music does not fit like a glove in the way the costumes, lighting, and sets do, the audience can get distracted consciously or subconsciously. Therefore, the music's starts and stops, swells and retreats, and specific instrumentation and textures are carefully crafted to fulfill specific dramatic functions. This cannot be overemphasized. The point of the music is to further the story, to move the drama along, or tell us something about the characters or situation. In order to accomplish this, the music must be placed sensitively. When music is present in the film, it must be there for a reason, or it is probably not necessary.

The beginning composer should understand that effective spotting is a skill that comes with experience, so patience is in order. Many composers just starting out make the familiar mistakes of writing too many cues, overwriting the individual cue, and starting a cue too strongly (for example, using strings in a thick chord when a gentle unison would be better). Learning when to bring the music right in on a cut, and when you can be early or late, is a skill that comes with experience. In addition, as you become more experienced after scoring many different kinds of scenes, your insight will become more finely tuned to what is on the screen and the intentions of the director. There are some general concepts that can guide this process:

1. **You are a partner in mixed media.** In most cues, music accompanies an actor's lines, creates a bridge from scene to scene, or gently helps to enhance the drama in a subtle way. In these scenes, the music is truly in the background. In a few situations, the music gets to stand out on its own—montages and main titles, action scenes, love scenes, and grand vistas of mountains or oceans. And these scenes also require sensitivity to how the music fits dramatically with what has happened and what is about to happen.
2. **Does there need to be music?** One must be absolutely sure that a given scene needs music. This surety can come in the form of a gut feeling, a plot driven need, or the director's request (whether or not you are in agreement). Points to consider include the dramatic needs, as well as what music has come just before or just after the scene in question.
3. **If there is music, what are you trying to say with it?** Asking this question helps keep the composer focused on an intent that gives an overall guideline for the emotional impact of the music. This goes beyond happy, sad, light, dark, etc. Similar questions are: Are you moving the drama forward? Are you expressing this character's thoughts or feelings appropriately? What instruments will accomplish these goals best?

Remembering these points helps keep the music a carefully considered element of the film, not just a composer's creative whim. If the composer is clear on why the music is there and what it is trying to accomplish, then the job of scoring the film is that much easier. The music then becomes a whole organic piece, not just a series of short musical sequences. On the other hand, if a composer writes music for a scene without knowing what the purpose is of that music, it can certainly fill up sonic space but feel random and dramatically unnecessary.

Though originally, spotting was a discrete activity conducted in a single spotting session after the picture was locked, these days, the tendency to keep editing the film up until the last minute has made spotting more of a rolling process. Whether there is a single spotting session or a series of them, at some point, the composer will sit down with the director (in the case of film), music editor, and sometimes a producer and/or the film editor, to review the film and discuss where the music will go, what it should sound like, and which dramatic situations to emphasize (or de-emphasize). At these meetings, the film is discussed scene by scene to determine the need for music, and to discuss what the music should sound like—what style, instruments, and emotions are musically necessary. The music editor takes notes for the composer regarding specific timings of cues and dramatic hits (see chapter 12). Even in cases where the picture is never fully locked, there will generally be one or more such meetings to spot whatever sections of the film are ready to be scored. Sometimes, if a major edit has taken place, a follow-up meeting will be scheduled to re-spot the affected reels. (*Conforming* is when a previously recorded cue is reworked to fit a picture change.)

In the case of television, the process is similar except that the producer generally replaces the director as the creative lead, and the picture editor is likely to play a bigger role. (For episodic television, the director is often not involved in post-production. They just oversee the weekly process of shooting.) When a series gets into later seasons, there is often less need for in-depth spotting sessions, as the team gets tuned into the patterns of the show. In those cases, it's often possible to skip actual spotting sessions and spot based on temp music placement and written notes about the spotting from the creative team, except for unusual or important scenes which may require a meeting to discuss.

Recently, instead of having to sit in the same room to spot a film or show, it's become possible to do this work remotely. This shift, already starting to take place in the 2010s, was greatly accelerated by the COVID-19 pandemic and resulting lockdowns, which prevented in-person meetings for over a year.

Composer Kara Talve remembers:

> *Prior to the pandemic, we used to have in-person spotting sessions for* The Simpsons *(a show that I've had the privilege to work on for a few years now). However, with the shift brought about by the pandemic, we seamlessly transitioned all our interactions to virtual platforms like Zoom. Surprisingly, this adjustment proved to be incredibly effective and convenient for everyone involved. It's remarkable how technology has enabled us to adapt and continue our collaborative work in a virtual setting.*

Whether in person or remote, spotting sessions are the time when different approaches should be discussed, e.g., to play through a certain piece of action, to emphasize it, or to foreshadow an event (or not). The music can begin right on a cut, a few seconds before it, or even right after it. It can start immediately after an important line of dialogue, or it can wait and let that line sink in. It can foreshadow a dangerous situation or play it more neutrally. Keep in mind that most directors have no formal musical background and must speak in layman's terms, not musical terms. The composer must find a way to understand the director's desires and translate words into musical ideas. The best way to do this is to discuss the scene dramatically, focusing on emotion and pace.

Spotting must be done carefully, sensitively, and with the understanding that the music is a partner with the drama, as the composer is a partner with the director. Sometimes, this partnership is smooth, with excellent give and take. There can also be considerable friction if the director (or producer) requests a certain style or musical idea that the composer finds objectionable. As mentioned previously, it is in these situations that the composer must decide whether to push back or to go along with their client's wishes. Ultimately, the composer's job is twofold in nature: one, to please their client, and two, to maintain their own musical integrity. Being a film composer involves an enormous amount of flexibility and sensitivity, with a handful of diplomacy thrown in for good measure. One must be a good communicator, and especially have the ability to listen and transfer into musical terms what a director is saying.

SKETCHING AND MOCKUPS

Once the score concept is approved and an initial spotting session has taken place, it's time to actually start writing. Each composer has their own unique composition process; however, there are some common threads. In approaching a cue, composers will almost always begin with some kind of *score sketch*. If they compose using notation, this might be a literal sketch with pencil on paper, or it might be a lead sheet or condensed score created using notation software. If they compose directly into their DAW (the most common approach, given tight deadlines and the relative ease of making changes in a DAW), they might record a pass of the cue using just piano or a string pad sample—even if they don't necessarily plan to use those instruments in the final version—just to get their ideas in place and check that their musical idea works dramatically in the scene. Once they're satisfied with this sketch, then they'll color it in musically with orchestration.

It would be rare, however, for this kind of sketch of a cue to be heard by the director. Though it used to be the case that directors would listen to a composer play their sketch at the piano (when that was the only way a composer could demonstrate themes and moods), with the advent of realistic-sounding sample libraries, the expectation is now solidly in place among directors that they can hear more or less exactly what each cue will sound like before live recording (if any) takes place. Thus, composers must create *mockups* of each cue—sequenced versions of the draft cues using sampled instruments and synthesizers. If the composer has sketched on paper or notation software, they then must translate their cue into a mockup in a DAW. Even though notation software can also generate pretty good-sounding MIDI renderings, these days, the amount of control and finesse afforded by the MIDI editing and audio production capabilities of DAWs is preferable—especially the ability to record each part individually via a keyboard or other MIDI controller. This allows the mockup to have a more human, performed quality than can be approximated by step input (at least, as of this writing).

Though MIDI sequencing tools and sample libraries are truly impressive these days—so much so that the mockup may be the final version, as opposed to a step towards replacement with live players—there are still significant limitations in using MIDI for some instruments and genres. Mason Daring explains:

> *You'll mock up cues if they're orchestral. If it's rock and roll or if it's pop music, you've got a problem, because you really need some real players even to demo it. Then you're going to start having small recording sessions just to get an idea of what works.*

Inherent in the very name "mockup" is the understanding that the cue at this stage is subject to review and revision. It's rare that the first version of a cue will be the one that makes it into the finished film. Between two and five versions is much more common, and sometimes, the version count can climb to double digits! Daring describes this process:

> *You'll be playing these [mockups] for the director. And at the same time you're doing that, you're bringing in rewrites. In other words, by the time you're into the second week, you'll be rewriting cues from the first week, based on the reaction of the director. So, past the first few days, every day you'd be well advised to do a combination of writing new cues and rewriting old ones, because you want to show the director that you care. You want to show the director that you're listening to their feedback, and you're capable of understanding it and correspondingly altering the nature of some of these cues because you didn't understand what was necessary. Or perhaps the melodies aren't strong enough. Perhaps they're too strong. There's lot of ways to go awry in this world! So you're going to go through weeks of writing and rewriting.*

The post-production timeline will constrain this process. For example, on a television show, there simply wouldn't be time for more than a couple of revisions in most cases, while in a film with a long time horizon, there might be room to experiment. It's also good practice not to consider a cue final (let alone naming the file that way!) until it's in the film. Even then, it's possible that alternate cuts will happen down the road that require additional changes to a given cue.

Another common reason a cue might need to be changed has nothing to do with a meeting of the minds with the director, and everything to do with a change to the timings of the film's edit. In a digital world, it should be expected that a film will continue to be edited even after the composer has started scoring, so it's inevitable that sometimes an editorial change will affect a scene with a cue that was meticulously timed to the previous cut. In these cases, the composer must tailor, or conform, the cue to this new cut. Some conforms happen after the score is mixed and delivered and therefore must be accomplished by the music editor through audio editing. However, if the need for a conform is identified before final music delivery, it's generally preferable for the composer to handle the conforming process via MIDI sequencing, because the possibilities for rewriting and adjusting the music are so much broader than with an already mixed track. Whether done in audio or MIDI, conforming is a necessary process that most composers get used to, even if it's not their favorite activity.

RECORDING SESSIONS

If a cue is going to remain in the box (that is, a fully digital production), then when a version has been approved by the director, making a final music mix is the only remaining step before it goes to the dub stage. However, if there are going to be any live players involved, there is another series of steps that take place. For many film composers, there is nothing like walking onto the scoring stage and seeing dozens of musicians gathered there to play your music. Composer Lolita Ritmanis describes walking into a Hollywood scoring session this way:

> *You forget, and sometimes you have to pinch yourself and realize, "Oh my goodness, this is amazing!" These are the best players, definitely the best sight-readers in the*

world. Absolutely the best sight-readers. And the mistakes-quotient is: there is hardly ever a mistake.

Present at a scoring session are the composer, conductor (if the composer is not conducting), director (and sometimes producer), music editor, musicians, recording engineers, and all kinds of assistants and on-lookers. Someone with good ears and score-reading abilities—usually an orchestrator but sometimes someone given the dedicated role of *booth reader*—sits in the control room with the recording engineer and follows the score to check for errors that the conductor might not hear. This person also assists the engineer by announcing which instruments are about to play (especially helpful if there is a solo of some kind). The music editor usually sits behind the conductor or in the control room, ready to jump into action if last-minute changes are needed.

In the days or weeks before the sessions begin, the composer will hire a *music contractor*. This person (often simply called the "contractor") books the studio, hires the musicians, takes care of union paperwork and payroll (if applicable), and oversees the sessions to make sure everything is on time. In their initial conversations, the composer and contractor discuss the numbers of players and the breakdown of the orchestra—how many strings, woodwinds, brass, rhythm section players, etc., are needed. They also discuss any specific musicians—based on their playing ability and certain instruments that the score calls for. For example, a woodwind chair might need an individual who can play flute, piccolo, and recorder. It is up to the contractor to find the appropriate players.

Sometimes, a film requires the entire orchestra to play on every cue. However, often, there are smaller groups that play various cues throughout the film, such as strings only, or a small group of strings, guitar, and oboe that are featured in several cues. In this case, the composer records all the cues for the larger group at one time, and then lets most of the players leave while the smaller group records. This is efficient and cost-effective. The larger group is known as the "A" orchestra, the smaller combinations the "B" orchestra, the "C" orchestra, etc.

Since the early 2000s, many large scoring stages in L.A. have closed, creating greater competition for fewer spaces. Many composers find it efficient, both from a studio booking standpoint as well as a musical and/or mixing standpoint, to record orchestral sections individually. For example, on different days, they might record just strings in one studio, brass in another studio, woodwinds in yet another, or various permutations of that process. One of the upsides to this is that you get better isolation of each section. A downside is that you never create that group dynamic and energy of everyone in the same room at the same time. Because of the complexity of scheduling this many sessions, there is often a need to hire a *score coordinator,* who will take care of the scheduling of studios. On a simpler or smaller project, the composer might handle this themselves, but on a large film with a bigger budget and shorter timeline, there is likely to be someone hired specifically for this task.

Hiring musicians can be done in either a union or a non-union environment. Before the turn of the century, most recording sessions for studio films and network TV were under a union contract negotiated with the American Federation of Musicians (AFM). However, with the advent of digital recording and internet communication protocols opening up a world market, that has changed significantly.

If a production is recorded under the union contract, then there are specific and comprehensive rules for how musicians get paid, as well as regulations to follow during the sessions, like taking a ten-minute break every hour, a meal break after a certain amount of hours of recording, etc. The contractor, who is the liaison to the union in such sessions, attends the session and assists the composer in keeping track of these rules.

In a non-union session, there may not be any formal rules other than whatever is agreed upon case by case. However, even in these circumstances, the AFM guidelines are a helpful starting point and indication of fair treatment for session players. Because of the way the laws regarding unions differ by region, the rules that apply to session recording vary state by state within the U.S., and do not apply at all outside the U.S. It's not uncommon for recording sessions to take place in states or countries that allow non-union sessions, even if the production is based in Hollywood. Furthermore, remote recording either of individual players or full orchestras is increasingly chosen by composers for both cost and time reasons. Finally, a composer might choose to record abroad in order to access a particular player (especially of an instrument unique to one part of the world) or the sound of a particular orchestra.

A remote session will be largely the same as one where the composer is in attendance on site, except that when attending remotely, the composer will usually connect through special software designed to maximize audio fidelity. The composer will then make comments to the session producers in real time over a microphone, as well as by text or voice chat between takes. These comments can then be relayed to the conductor.

When recording an individual soloist remotely in their home studio, the session might be *asynchronous* (when a player records without real-time input from the composer). In this case, the composer will deliver a mockup, tempo map, and part to the player who will record themselves and deliver audio files back to the composer, who can request changes if needed (for example, to playing style) after trying the parts out in their DAW. The capability of musicians to handle this kind of remote recording request increased exponentially following the COVID-19 lockdowns, during which time it was the only way that was possible to work.

Session cellist Ro Rowan, who was one of the pioneers of remote recording prior to the pandemic, notes that though some players initially worried this would provide more competition, they realized that it was actually a boon to them as well. They were able to build a community of remote recording musicians that support each other. In addition, more composers became comfortable with this way of collaborating with musicians and were therefore more likely to continue including live players in their sessions instead of staying "in the box."

Rowan further reflects:

> *The rise of remote recording during the pandemic shifted the film-scoring community's perception of the validity, effectiveness, and benefits of remote recording. I think that, while most composers will understandably continue to prefer recording in person, remote recording has now established itself as another tool that can be used. One niche area I have benefitted from is tailoring my brand to the composer who is short on time. They send me some audio files and their MIDI file. I create parts, record, comp, and clean all stems before delivery so that all they need to do is drop them into their session. This saves them time and money so the composer can continue writing. It's not uncommon that a composer says they couldn't have gotten it done if I wasn't able to create parts and deliver polished stems. I find that more and more scoring situations are continuing to explore and utilize remote recording.*

Whether in person or remote, the recording session is usually an exciting and rewarding moment for the composer. Music representing weeks of work is finally heard and its effectiveness evaluated. Flexibility is a key attribute to have at the session, for changes are often requested. Sometimes, the director wants a little more dissonance or less musical activity in a cue. Sometimes, a cue needs to be lengthened or shortened. Sometimes, everyone, including the composer, is in agreement about a certain change, and sometimes the composer disagrees. The bottom line is that the composer needs to be able to make changes quickly without being overly attached to what was already written. Making movies is a team exercise.

MUSIC MIX

Once recording sessions are completed (if applicable) and the cues have been approved by the director, the music needs to be mixed—including any parts recorded live along with synth and other MIDI sequenced parts that are remaining in the final cue. This will either happen in a mixdown studio, or the composer might mix the music themselves back in their own studios, if on a limited budget. Depending on the project, the producer will ask for the music to be delivered in a specific format or formats, such as stereo and/or surround sound (5.1, 7.1, or other surround format). A good film-score mix engineer can mix ten minutes or even more per day. Compare that to the pop-music record mix, which is going very well if one or two four-minute songs per day are completed.

The mix of the music for films is usually done in stems. *Stems* are basically sub-mixes of different groupings of the entire orchestra. For example, a mixdown engineer might make five stems, which would be pre-mixes of the woodwinds, the strings, the brass, percussion, and everything else. Stems are a compromise between delivering a stereo or surround-sound track completely mixed versus delivering all of the many individual tracks unmixed. With stems, when the music is mixed in with the dialogue and sound effects, there is some flexibility to control these various sections of the orchestra without the complication of dealing with all the individual music tracks, or the restriction of dealing with an already mixed stereo track.

FINAL STEPS

Once the music is mixed, it is delivered in the correct formats to the dub stage. Though the composer may be invited to the dub, they usually stay home and instead leave it to the music editor to advocate for the music. This kind of advocacy is necessary, because during the dub, the composer's carefully crafted music is often brought down in volume until barely audible, remixed from the stems, edited in a way that went contrary to the original scoring intent, or even replaced by a cue from the temp track or a different location in the film. In the end, it's all about the story and what the director thinks the film needs, not about what the composer originally planned. Yet, having the music editor be an effective voice at the dub session can be helpful to the director in understanding the composer's intention for the music.

Meanwhile, back in the composer's studio, there are a bunch of important clean-up tasks to do such as carefully archiving the project's files, and administrative tasks such as creating or reviewing the *cue sheet* (we'll come back to this in the Business section) and filing any contract paperwork.

Finally, though not technically part of the scoring process, it's important to remember that each score might be the springboard for the next one. So, it's important for a composer to attend the premiere, take part in publicity for the film as needed (including posting on social media and seeking out press opportunities), consider releasing a soundtrack album or behind-the-scenes video about the scoring process, and nurture and maintain relationships with the director and other collaborators so as to get set up for future success.

CHAPTER 11

The Composer's Team

In the popular imagination, the word "composer" conjures up visions of a solitary figure feverishly scribbling musical notes onto the page, playing them at a piano, or creating a track surrounded by computers, keyboards, synthesizers, and racks of electronic gear. This enduring myth perpetuates the idea of composers as singular geniuses, capable of conjuring entire musical worlds on their own. However, the reality of film scoring, a realm where time is of the essence, is a different story. Behind every memorable film score lies the collective effort of a team of skilled professionals. Instead of the solo composer paradigm, today's scoring teams may consist of multiple composers, orcehstrators, electronic music specialists, MIDI transcribers, and many other possible configurations. As composer and orchestrator William Ross has said, "In today's world, film composing has become a team sport." In this chapter, we look at the reality behind the myth, revealing the web of expertise that converges to create a film score.

CO-COMPOSERS

To start replacing that mental image of the solo composer, let's begin by looking at some of the many co-composing teams out there. Some collaborations begin with band members who know each other well, as with Trent Reznor and Atticus Ross whose scoring careers began with *The Social Network*. Others have met in college, like Sonya Belousova and Giona Ostinelli, co-composers of Netflix's *The Witcher* (Season 1) in 2019 and *One Piece* in 2023. And some start as mentor and mentee, as with

Blake Neely and Sherri Chung, whose first co-composed show was *Supergirl* beginning in 2017. No matter how they find each other, effective co-composers discover complementary strengths in terms of music background, interpersonal or technical skill-sets, or even just the ability to work across more than one time zone to effectively create an extended work day. As with any business or even personal partnership, there are pitfalls that can occur if a composing team has a personal falling out or professional disagreement. However, long-standing teams often swear by this approach and find solutions to any difficulties that come up.

Ben Bromfield, who has co-composed with several different composers on different shows, finds that this process generally benefits his own growth as a composer:

> *Co-composing is great because you can trade tricks with another good composer and pick up some things that they do differently than you. It's an opportunity to keep learning. And even when you are a professional, we're all obviously still learning all the time.*

When co-composing a score, sometimes composers will split up the cues, perhaps on the basis of a particular theme or story arc, and at other times might work more closely together, even collaborating on a single cue. Composer Kara Talve, who works on the composing team at the scoring company Bleeding Fingers, describes an example of the latter:

> *One notable project that shows this collaborative spirit is* Prehistoric Planet, *a composition endeavor involving myself, Anže Rozman, and of course, Hans Zimmer. Throughout the creative process, we shared pivotal moments of discussion with Russell [the score producer], exploring innovative ways to craft an otherworldly and distinctive score. It was during these collaborative sessions that the concept of our custom instruments took shape, playing a pivotal role in shaping the entire sonic landscape of our score. In some instances, Anže and I even had moments where we were completing each other's cues,*

and that adds an exciting layer of creativity as you build upon someone else's initial idea.

Bleeding Fingers in particular is an example of a relatively newer business structure in Hollywood in which instead of one lead composer with perhaps one or more assistants, there is an entire team with a hierarchy and more or less defined roles, which functions as an end-to-end music production house with most or all of the roles we'll look at next rolled into a single, in-house team. The head of the company will generally get the work and assign it to one or more composers on their team, who in turn will bring in junior composers and tech assistants to get all the music done.

Though relatively new to Hollywood scoring, this type of company structure is more common in Asia. In South Korea, for example, the main scoring credit is often "music director." Unlike in most American scoring companies, in which the lead composer is still likely to at least write the main themes, in the Korean model, the music director generally doesn't compose at all but rather manages their team and the interaction with the clients, and delegates scoring roles for each film or show within their company. Composer Woody Pak describes:

In South Korea, the top music directors want to make sure everyone's taken care of and supported. So it becomes a real company, where there are managers, and then assistant managers, and so on down to the people who get the coffee and interns.

Still, in the rest of the world, the majority of media scoring still takes place in smaller studios with some amount of outsourcing of roles. Let's examine these roles and see how they can come together, whether in-house or freelance, to form a complete scoring team.

COMPOSERS' ASSISTANTS AND ADDITIONAL MUSIC WRITERS

Assistants are critical to most composers' teams. This job has grown in the past twenty to thirty years from someone who was primarily an administrative aide into—most commonly—a junior composer with skills in scoring technology, composition, music editing, and/or orchestration and music preparation. A composer may have a single assistant who works side-by-side with them and is on call to take on whatever task is needed, or may have several assistants, perhaps of varying seniority, to take on different tasks.

Because of the shortened schedules in modern post-production, most composers must rely on their assistants to get the score from conception to the screen. This means having reliable people to assist with the myriad details of sequencing, orchestrating, copying, booking musicians, and so forth. The goal is to create a space where the composer can focus on composing, and everyone else works diligently to accomplish that. While in some teams there might be a designated administrative assistant, technical assistant, score coordinator, and so forth, it's more common for assistants—like the composers they often aspire to become—to be nimble and versatile, ready to step into any of these roles as needed.

One of the most coveted and important roles an assistant might perform is that of additional music writing: composing individual cues for a film under the direction of a lead composer. Sometimes, a composer will set up their assistants or freelance additional writers with scoring rigs identical to their own so that their cues sound the same in terms of mockup and mix. At other times, the additional music composers work more independently, especially if they are creating cues of a particular type or music genre. For example, if the underscore is orchestral but there are some source music cues in the style of a 1940s big band, an additional writer with specific skills in that music style might be hired just for those cues. Although someone may be hired specifically as a freelance additional music writer, especially once established in the field with several years of credits, it's also common for a composer's assistant to make the progression from primarily technical and/or administrative duties, to being entrusted with additional music writing once fully immersed in the composer's workflow and musical style.

Because the assistant role is next to the action, the skills involved in both assisting and being a composer are similar. The opportunity also exists to build up additional music credits on larger films. In addition, watching the process unfold is an invaluable learning experience. Therefore, it is desirable and common for aspiring film composers to start their careers as assistants to more established composers. Looking into the origin stories of many of today's top writers, you will find assistant work in their résumés. That said, this role is not without its issues, as composers are generally not trained managers, and there are few safeguards to enforce fair crediting, payment, and working conditions for assistants. We will revisit the pros and cons of this path in the Business section of this book.

ORCHESTRATORS

When writing for a large ensemble of instruments, a full score must be created. This is the version that has one line for each instrument—flutes, oboes, clarinets, French horns, trumpets, violins, etc.—that will be used by the conductor at the recording session. However, making this final score is time consuming and detail-oriented, and requires a great deal of understanding of the orchestra and of music notation. So instead of filling in all the notes on a full score page, the composer generally creates either a *score sketch* or a *MIDI mockup* and hands that off to an orchestrator to handle the final notation.

It used to be that a composer would quickly notate a score sketch using pencil and paper with anywhere from just two to eight or ten staves, but these days, that is increasingly rare. When used, this kind of sketch can be brought to varying degrees of completion. It might contain complete information for every melody, countermelody, and even designate individual instruments, as in

John Williams' score sketches; or it might be a bare-bones, single-line melody or lead sheet with some harmonic indications, the rest to be filled in by the orchestrator.

However, in today's workflow, the sketch is most commonly a MIDI mockup, which will be delivered to the orchestrator as both a standard MIDI file that can be imported into notation software, and an audio file of the mockup for reference. Since the mockup is generally already a close representation of what the composer hears in their head and what the director has approved, the job of the orchestrator becomes less about making decisions about orchestration per se and more about making sure that what is recorded in the session sounds as close as possible to the mockup, taking into account the characteristics of real instruments (as distinct from their sampled versions) and what indications a player may need to see on their part to generate the intended sound.

FIG. 11.1. Notated Score Sketch

FIG. 11.2. Full Orchestrated Score Page

Orchestrator Òscar Senén, who has over a hundred credits from films and television shows in both Hollywood and Europe, describes his role this way:

> *It's not only about distributing the voices, but also deciding what will make it sound exactly like the mockup. Especially dynamics, expression, and articulations. All those things that seem like small nuances actually help on the scoring session because they can save many, many takes just saying "a bit louder," or "more marcato," or all those character things, if they are already in the score.*

It is important to note that many composers, especially if classically trained, are also excellent orchestrators in their own right. Some composers may even insist on having enough time on the film to be able to do their own orchestrations. Even in these cases, however, the composer-orchestrator may still complete a sketch or mockup first and then orchestrate from it.

Orchestrators themselves can be from any background in music, but they must have studied composition and orchestration in depth in order to be able to execute what is required of them in a film score. Obviously, a full knowledge of many instruments is required: their high and low ranges, where they sound strong and where they sound weak, which rhythmic gestures sound natural on an instrument and which ones sound awkward, whether there are any troublesome notes, and how they balance, overpower, or blend with other instruments. A thorough knowledge of composition is also required, since an orchestrator might be required to write a counterline, fill in a harmony, or voice-lead a series of chords.

William Ross is a composer, orchestrator, and arranger who has worked on hundreds of films, television shows, and record dates. He explains his role when orchestrating:

> *My job as an orchestrator is to assist the composer in getting the job done. Because of today's post-production schedules, it's very difficult for anyone to compose and orchestrate their own music. An orchestrator is a problem*

> *solver. Your best skill as an orchestrator is your ability to solve a problem, whether it's musical, psychological, economic—whatever it is. That's the mission: to solve these problems.*

Orchestrators like Òscar Senén and Bill Ross work as independent contractors; they are basically freelance and go wherever their services are needed. There are also instances when a member of the composer's immediate team (one of the assistants) will be tasked with orchestrating. The pay scale for an orchestrator is determined by the musicians' union if the score is being produced under an American Federation of Musicians contract, in which case the orchestrator's rate is calculated by the number of pages scored (four measures per page) and the number of staves on the page. Depending on the texture and complexity of the cue, this could take a few hours or an entire day, though the difficult cues and the easier ones tend to balance each other out in the long run. On non-union scores, an orchestrator might be hired on a similar per-page basis or they may charge an hourly rate.

One final thought on orchestrators. It is sometimes said that an orchestrator or team of orchestrators has saved a composer. At times, this can be true. But the bottom line is that the composer has a vision of the finished music, and even if their sketches or mockups leave out musical details, the composer is still the driving force behind a score. So if the composer's musical concept works for the project, then the orchestrator's job is to realize and amplify this concept. If the score concept is poor, then no amount of help by the orchestrator can make it succeed.

MUSIC PREPARATION

Once the orchestrator completes the full score, it goes into *music preparation*: the process of preparing parts from the full score, and printing both parts and scores. In the old days of Hollywood, every studio had its own music preparation office where everyone was under contract and worked only for that studio. So, the music would go down an in-house assembly line, from composer to orchestrator to music preparation to orchestra, and never leave the studio lot. Nowadays, everything is contracted out to individuals or small companies that have offices in various locations.

When an orchestrated cue is handed off to a music preparation team, it is checked off on a master chart. This chart indicates which tasks are completed/not completed for each cue. There can be as many as fifty or more individual cues for a single film, so there is a lot to keep track of.

Once the final orchestrated cues are delivered, the head of the music preparation office assigns one or more copyists to work on each cue. The term "copyist" comes from the days when parts were prepared by hand and actually copied from the score, note by note. Since orchestration these days is done in notation software (Finale, Sibelius, or Dorico), copyists or music preparers now automatically extract each part from the full score file. This extraction involves making sure the transpositions are correct, that accidentals and enharmonics are logical, that the part is easily readable—the notes not too crunched or spread apart—and that any page turns are do-able at the session.

Once the copyist finishes extracting and laying out a part for a cue, say the viola part, it goes to a proofreader. This is to ensure that errors are not discovered on the scoring stage where they would take costly minutes to fix (time on a scoring stage can cost several hundred dollars per minute). The proofreader is never the same as the original copyist, as proofreading requires a fresh set of eyes. Once the proofreader completes a part or a stack of parts, they're returned to the supervisor of the music preparation office who then goes to the master chart and checks off those parts that are complete.

The next person in line, also in the music preparation team, is the music librarian. This is a crucial job. The music librarian sees that every musician in the orchestra has the proper music on their music stand at the start of each session. The composer is in communication with the music preparation office to say what cues to record on which days, and to find out which cues are actually ready. The music librarian consults the master chart to make sure the desired cues are completed, takes the music to the scoring stage, and places the music on the stands of the musicians in the proper recording order. After the session concludes, the music librarian collects the marked-up scores and parts and, in some cases, maintains an actual archival music library for future use or study.

By this point in the production process, the film is often behind schedule, and all these music people can be working under enormous time pressure, increasing even more in recent years. It is common for the music preparation office to be in full swing all night leading up to a big session. Veteran music preparer Thanh Tran describes:

> *Projects in past years containing 60 minutes of music would allow the music preparation team 4 to 6 weeks from part prep commencing to wrapping production, but in recent years, the time frame for this amount of music has reduced drastically to 2 to 3 weeks, with extreme cases of orchestrators having 2 to 3 days, music copyists having 48 hours, and music production having 24 hours to turn around 60 minutes of music.*

As you can see, this role requires great patience, attention to detail, and flexibility in dealing with many stressed out people leading to their portion of the workflow.

Finally, it's important to note that it's common for music preparation companies to also handle orchestration in-house for composers seeking a one-stop shop. Furthermore, in locations outside Los Angeles and even on lower-budget projects in Hollywood, composers may collapse several of these roles together—for example, having their orchestrator also handle music preparation, or even doing some or all of these steps in-house (personally or delegated to an assistant).

OTHER ROLES

The roles discussed above are the most common and important in almost every composer's workflow, but there are of course a great deal of other roles that can be part of a composer's team.

First of all, there are many people that contribute to the recording of the music in a scoring session. These include the score coordinator who organizes and schedules the sessions, the music contractor who books the musicians, the conductor (often the orchestrator or composer, but sometimes someone hired specifically for their conducting skills), one or more recording engineers, and a Pro Tools operator/recordist. Then, once the music is recorded, there is generally another person or team who handles the music mix. We've explored all of these roles in the previous chapter.

Another role that might be outsourced is the *MIDI programmer* (sometimes known as "synthestrator," a portmanteau of synthesis and orchestrator). Though the time constraints and number of revisions per cue required in most films make this job more likely to be done by the composer or an assistant, there are still some composers who hire a dedicated MIDI programmer to create detailed and realistic mockups if they really want their demos to shine, or don't have that expertise in-house. Similarly, there are some freelance sound designers who might be hired specifically for their synthesis and sampling abilities, either to create a custom instrument for a particular film or a palette of custom sound libraries for a particular composer.

Whether outsourced or handled in-house by a larger composition company, what should be clear by now is that it takes a lot of people to create a score, and one or more composers leading the charge. And that's before we consider the other roles that are essential to the use of music in a film that are not considered part of the composer's team. Next, we'll turn our attention to those roles: music editing and supervision.

CHAPTER 12

Music Editing and Supervision

The last two roles we'll explore are key to the success of a film's score, but do not report to the film's composer. Rather, both the music editor and the music supervisor are hired directly by the studio, and may have more or less direct contact and interaction with the composer depending on the circumstances of each project.

THE MUSIC EDITOR

The music editor is one of the unsung heroes of film music, responsible for making music work in films in many ways that few outside the field know about. The music editor is responsible for everything from assembling the temp track to editing the final music files and placing them in synchronization with the final version of the film, as well as in many cases serving a pivotal role in organizing the entire music score, including both original and licensed music. They must have excellent music skills, thorough technical knowledge, and be a cool, calm, and collected diplomat in the service of both the composer and the director.

Music editor Eric Reasoner:

> *As a music editor, the more you know about music, the better off you are. However, there are still a lot of music editors that have an instinctive sense—not that they studied music, but they really know and have quick instincts about cutting music. They are also good at*

dealing with pressure and handling a lot of different kinds of individuals, which is a big, big part of it.

Music editors are almost always hired by the studio or production company making the film, but they may also work closely with the composer. This unique divided loyalty has led to two categories of music editors in today's practice: some, considered a "composer's music editor," have a primary connection with one or more composers, and will generally be hired at the request of that composer to work on any films they score. The other is the "studio's music editor," who may not work directly with the composer at all and instead often works in the film studio along with the rest of the audio post-production team. Lena Glikson shares this example of her role as a studio's music editor:

When you're working for the director or the studio, then your main goal is to facilitate the picture's needs. In that case, if the studio decides to fire the composer, to change the approach to have a different score, then you'll have to be creative, and you'll have to figure out what's going to happen with that. One example of this was a situation where a movie had a score written and recorded by a particular composer chosen by the director, but the producers and the studio didn't like the score at all. They hired our music editorial team to temp the entire movie in two weeks and find a new sound for it. Based on our temp track, the team chose a new composer who recorded a fresh score that now the producers and the studio were happy with—but not the director! Simultaneously, the producers approached some electronic musicians who demoed for the project, and loved some of their compositions. So we [the music editors] ended up trying to make a score out of music from four different composers, with some music scored to picture and others being licensed from electronic music. We had to come up with something creative that would have all the best pieces from all four of them, and create a score that's going to sound like one continuous concept as opposed to separate pieces by different people with different ideas.

Shie Rozow is a prominent example of the other kind of music editor, having served as music editor for several composers on all their films. As he explains:

> *Most of my work is from people who know me and want me specifically. Sometimes, it's the composer. For example, I've been working with Pinar Toprak for the last six years. She's now at the place where they just say, "Who's your music editor?" and she says me. Other times, it's the director. I worked with John Singleton for sixteen years until he passed away. John would send me scripts long before things were in production. He brought me on before he even picked a composer. But I'd say, most of my work comes from composers asking for me, and then the number two thing is either studio execs or a director or producer who has worked with me and likes me.*

Many of the tasks of the music editor remain the same regardless of whether they owe their primary loyalty to a composer, director, or studio. However, there are some differences that we'll point out later in this chapter.

TEMP TRACKS

Generally, the first involvement the music editor has in a film is during post-production. At this time, as the cut of the film is becoming solidified but the original music is not yet composed, the film will need a *temp track*. This is a temporary track of music laid into the film in order to give studio executives and test audiences an idea of what the film will be like once the final score is completed. Without any music at all, the film can be dry and lifeless, especially in action scenes.

Sometimes, the picture editor will cut music in as they're working, and the music editor will help finesse their edits or replace tracks with better options. At other times, the director gives the music editor guidelines as to what kind of music to use, and the music editor cuts these pieces to fit.

A good temp score will work with the film not only dramatically, but also rhythmically and harmonically. In the old days, magnetic tape and film had to be spliced in order to accomplish this. Today, Pro Tools is used.

The music for the temp track can come from anywhere—from other soundtracks, from classical, pop, or jazz albums—anything the music editor can find is fair game. No royalties need to be paid and no sync licenses obtained because this temporary music will not be used in a version of the film that is shown to the public commercially. It is only used in-house, or at special test screenings that are free for volunteer test audiences, to give the director and editing team a sense of the film with music, and to show to producers, studio executives and test audiences to get their reaction.

Most contemporary films have temp tracks until the final scoring is completed. If one listens closely, often it can be discerned what the temp track was if the composer had to closely imitate it in order to please the director. For example, the temp track for *Titanic* (1997) was built from music recorded by the Irish singer Enya. Composer James Horner then had to adapt this kind of flowing, ethereal, New Age style to fit the action. Another good example is the temp track for *Star Wars* (1977). This temp track was Gustav Holst's 1917 classical piece *The Planets*. If the movie is a sequel, it's an easy call. For example, the temp track for *Lethal Weapon IV* (1998) was taken from *Lethal Weapon I, II,* and *III*. But no matter what the source of the temp track, music editors must work hard and long to edit a temp track to fit a picture, and they must have command of a huge selection of music from which to choose.

Music editors often use the term "tracking" to describe either the process of creating the temp track or the task of laying-in preexisting music to a finished film. Either way, the use of music that is not written by the composer specifically for a scene, but instead taken from another source, is usually called "tracking." Eric Reasoner discusses the process of creating temp tracks:

> *It depends on the relationship between the director, picture editors, and you [the music editor]. You may set up a traditional spotting session where you look at the*

> *film and discuss ideas for the temp track. Or you may just screen the film on your own and then converse with the director about styles and things like that, and then just begin searching for music. Sometimes, you have a really wide creative range to pick music that's appropriate, and you can just go your own way.*

If a composer has already been hired by the time the temp score is assembled, the music editor might try to choose temp music from that composer's prior work. Some composers feel this makes it easier, since the temp is already in their style, while others feel it constricts or pigeonholes them. Shie Rozow explains:

> *I'll have a conversation with the composer, and I'll ask: "Would you like me to use your music in the temp, or do you want me to avoid your music in the temp?" Some composers absolutely hate hearing their own music in the temp, others love it. But I always try to make a temp that the composer should be able to easily beat, while at the same time the temp has to do its job of being a blueprint, setting the tone and the direction. If I do it well, then the composer will say: "You hit all the beats, you caught all the moments. It's doing all the right things. I can just do them better!"*

Note that though the music editor will assemble the temp track in films with adequate budget to hire a music editor, in episodic shows and in lower-budget productions, it's often the picture editor who cuts the temp in as they are working directly with the flow and pacing of the picture.

SPOTTING NOTES AND MASTER CUE LISTS

The music editor's next responsibility, after cutting the temp track, is usually to go to the spotting session and take spotting notes. Spotting notes contain a description of where the music begins and ends for each cue, along with any special instructions discussed between the composer and director for each cue, such as bringing in a theme at a certain point or hitting a specific moment of the action.

Figure 12.1 (though from 1997) is a good example of spotting notes. Notice how short some of the cues are—short cues being characteristic of music in *The Simpsons* that often was used for comedic effect.

THE SIMPSONS #5F02 "**Treehouse of Horror VIII**" · Music Spotting Notes — Page 1
Composer **Alf Clausen** / Music Editor **Chris Ledesma** — 9/29/97

CUE #	START	STOP	LENGTH	DESCRIPTION
1M1	01:00:35:17	01:01:04:03	:29	Main Title starts as sword appears; low, change on stabs; play thru title and couch gag to out
1M2	01:01:19:03	01:01:22:14	:03	Open Act 1 - Homega Man - Sci-Fi; tail under Brockman dia
1M3	01:02:12:25	01:02:15:05	:02	Start on cut to military antique store; Homer goes to buy a bomb shelter; tail under next dia.
1M4	01:02:40:11	01:02:44:25	:04	On cut to estab shot of Paris; musette; happy until settle on military compound, then dark on settle; tail under next dia.
1M5	01:02:59:09	01:03:07:28	:09	On cut to Eiffel Tower splitting open; launch missile; ominous and threatening; out on cut to outer space
1M6	01:03:11:08	01:03:23:00	:12	On EOL "What the hell was that?"; through snickering aliens; out on cut to missile headed for earth
1M7	01:03:24:17	01:03:42:10	:18	on cut to missile flying over Springfield; G.P. on comic book guy; resume on POV missile and out on explosion
1M8	01:03:55:14	01:03:59:00	:04	Spooky and creepy on overhead shot of car in traffic, out on cut to back of Homer head leaning out of car
1M9	01:04:20:28	01:04:23:27	03	Sting the push-in on newspaper, out on cut to Homer
1M10	01:04:27:13	01:04:46:21	19	Eerie as Bart ghost appears; thru entire family until Maggie and others are out of frame; then sad as Homer cries; out just before "No, no, no!"
1M11	01:05:02:20	01:05:05:02	02	On cut to estab movie theater: happy Homer; tail on cut to int
1M12	01:05:23:25	01:05:35:12	12	*SOURCE* -- Homer sings along with a boom box: "War" CD master
1M13	01:05:38:19	01:05:40:10	02	Start on cam settle on mutants; scary/dark; out as Homer shrieks
1M14	01:06:08:19	01:06:28:09	20	As Burns: "And now you must die"; dark and scary; then chase as they run after him; tail on cut to dead chauffeur; thru reveal of coffin and out
1M15	01:06:35:13	01:07:03:13	38	On cut to ext. on car: Car chase; tail on cut to int. house on relieved Homer
1M16	01:07:09:27	01:07:10:14	01	Sting on push-in on mutants: out on cut to reverse angle on Homer
1M17	01:07:22:04	01:07:24:26	03	Start on cut to back of Homer going to hug kids; tail under the mutants: "Awww."
1M18	01:07:56:23	01:08:00:03	03	Sincere Marge as cam pushes in on her during her speech; out to clear "NOW!"

FIG. 12.1. Spotting Notes from *The Simpsons*. Used by Permission

From these spotting notes, the music editor also creates a *master cue list*: a list of all the cues and the corresponding places they appear in the film but without the actual notes for each cue describing music and dramatic approach. The master cue list shows every cue, assigns it an appropriate number, indicates how long it is, and gives the SMPTE time for when it begins and ends. Cues are also called "starts." Therefore, the master cue list shows every start. Notice how this master cue sheet lists every instrument and which cues they play on.

Simpsons 5F02
Alf Clausen

Mon 10/6/97 2:00 Pm O'Henry

				STRINGS				WOODWINDS				BRASS				RHYTHM						
CUE	CLIX	TIME	TITLE	Vln	Vla	Vc	Bs	1	2	3	4	Hns	Tpt	Tbn	Tba	Pno	Syn	Harp	Guitar	Drums	Perc	Arr
1m1	9 - 4	00:28	Halloween VIII	10	3	3	1	Fl	Ob	EbCBC	CB	2	2	2		Syn	Syn	1	-	-	2	AC
1m2	10 - 1	00:08	The Homega Man	10	3	3	1	AF	Ob	Fl	Fl	2	-	2		Syn	Syn	1	-	-	1+El	DH
1m3	12 - 5	00:07	The Withstandinator.	10	3	3	1	Fl	Ob	Cl	Bn	3	2	2		Pno	Syn	1	-	-	2	DH
1m4	9 - 7	00:05	Cordon Bleu	10	3	3	1	Fl	Ob	BC	CB	3	-	2		Syn	Syn	1	Gtr	1	1	DH
1m5	16 - 1	00:09	Rocket In The Pocket	10	3	3	1	Fl	Ob	Cl	CB	3	2	2		Syn	Syn	1	-	-	2	DH
1m6	21 - 0	00:12	Kang & Kang	10	3	3	1	-	-	EbCBC	CB	-	-	-		Syn	Syn	1	-	-	1	AC
1m7	9 - 3	00:18	Missle Whistle	10	3	3	1	Fl	Ob	Cl	Bn	3	2	2		Pno	Syn	1	-	-	2	DH
1m8	13 - 2	00:08	A Disarming Discourse	10	3	3	1	AF	Ob	Fl	Fl	2	-	2		Syn	Syn	1	-	-	1+El	DH
1m9	11 - 0	00:03	Oh, My Dog Sting	10	3	3	1	Fl	CB	Cl	Bn	3	2	2		Pno	Syn	1	-	-	2	DH
1m10	15 - 2	00:19	Just Cos	10	3	3	1	-	EH	-	-	-	-	-		Syn	Syn	1	-	-	2	AC
1m11	11 - 6	00:07	The Last Man Alive	10	3	3	1	Fl	Ob	Cl	Bn	3	2	2		Pno	Syn	1	-	-	2	DH
1m13	16 - 6	00:02	A Mutation Sensation	10	-	-	-	-	-	EbCBC	-	-	-	-		Syn	Syn	1	-	-	1	AC
1m14	10 - 6	00:20	Hearse Castle	10	3	3	1	Fl	Ob	Cl	Bn	3	2	2		Syn	Syn	1	-	-	2	DH
1m15	9 - 5	00:28	Cloakie And Dagger	10	3	3	1	Fl	CB	Cl	Bn	3	2	2		Syn	Syn	1	-	-	2	DH
1m16	13 - 4	00:01	Sting Da' Mutants	10	3	3	-	Fl	Ob	Cl	Bn	2	2	-		Pno	-	1	-	-	-	DH
1m17	13 - 3	00:08	Brings A Tear To Your Eye Socket	10	3	3	1	Fl	Ob	Cl	Bn	3	-	2		Pno	-	1	-	-	1	DH
1m18	19 - 4	00:03	Sharing Their Vision - Not	10	3	3	1	AF	Ob	Cl	Bn	2	-	-		-	-	1	-	-	-	AC
1m19	11 - 3	00:11	That's The Marge I Married	10	3	3	1	Fl	Ob	Cl	Bn	2	2	2		Pno	Syn	1	-	-	2	DH
2m1	14 - 3	00:06	Fly vs Fly Theme	10	3	3	1	Fl	Ob	Cl	CB	3	2	2		Pno	Syn	1	-	-	2	DH
2m3	15-1	00:06	I Must Warn You	10	3	-	-	AF	EH	Cl	-	-	-	-		Syn	Syn	1	-	-	2	DH
2m4	13-6	00:08	The Cat's On His Way Out	-	3	3	1	AF	-	Fl	Fl	-	-	-		Syn	Syn	1	-	-	2	AC
2m5	10 - 1	00:11	Oh Dog, A New Look	10	3	-	-	-	-	-	-	-	-	-		Syn	Syn	1	-	-	2	AC
2m6	14-0	00:11	A Superfly Fantasy	10	3	3	1	Fl	Ob	Cl	Bn	3	2	2		Pno	Syn	1	-	-	1+El	DH
2m7	18 - 4	00:17	Flee, Fly, Flo, Fun	10	3	3	1	Fl	Ob	EbCBC	CB	2	2	2		Pno	Syn	1	-	-	2	DH
2m8	10 - 0	00:05	Big, Fat & Ugly	10	3	3	1	Fl	Ob	Cl	CB	3	2	2		Pno	Syn	1	-	-	2	DH
2m9	9 - 5	00:05	A Little Night Music	10	3	-	-	Fl	Ob	Cl	Fl	-	-	-		Syn	-	1	-	-	2	AC
2m10	14 - 2	00:04	Another Sucker Spidered	10	3	3	1	Fl	Ob	Cl	Fl	-	2	-		Syn	Syn	1	-	-	2	DH
2m11	15 - 7	00:05	Big, Ugly	10	3	3	1	Fl	CB	Cl	CB	3	2	2		Pno	Syn	1	-	-	2	DH
2m12	16 - 1	00:06	Fly-By Nite Visitor	10	3	-	-	AF	-	Cl	-	-	-	-		Syn	-	-	-	-	1	AC
2m13	8 - 6	00:08	Ew, Gross!	10	3	3	1	Fl	Ob	Cl	Bn	3	2	2		Pno	Syn	1	-	-	2	DH
2m14	16 - 1	00:17	Big Mistake, Flyboy!	10	3	3	1	Fl	Ob	Cl	Bn	3	2	2		Pno	Syn	1	-	-	2	DH
2m15	17 - 1	00:12	Don't Trifle With Them	10	3	3	1	Fl	CB	Cl	Bn	2	-	2		Pno	Syn	1	-	-	2	AC
3m1	11 - 4	00:10	Easy Bake Coven Main Title	10	3	3	1	-	Ob	Cl	Bn	3	-	-		Pno	Syn	1	-	-	1	DH
3m2	9 - 5	00:04	The Smoking Lamp Is Lit	10	3	3	1	AF	Ob	EbCBC	CB	3	2	2		Pno	Syn	1	-	-	1+El	DH
3m3	16 - 6	00:06	Which Is Witch?	10	3	3	1	-	-	EbCBC	CB	3	-	-		Pno	Syn	1	-	-	2	AC
3m4	15 - 5	00:15	Falling Every Witch Way`	10	3	3	1	Fl	Ob	Cl	Bn	3	2	2		Syn	Syn	1	-	-	1+El	DH
3m5	17 - 3	00:08	Witch Is Which!	10	3	-	-	AF	EH	Cl	Bn	-	-	-		Syn	Syn	1	-	-	1+El	AC
3m6	11 - 1	00:21	Bats Entertainment	10	3	3	1	Fl	Ob	Cl	Bn	3	2	2		Pno	Syn	1	-	-	2	DH
3m7	12 - 4	00:09	Frame Spotting	10	3	-	-	AF	EH	EbCBC	Fl	-	-	-		-	Syn	1	-	-	2	AC
3m8	12 - 5	00:21	Witch Excitement	10	3	3	1	Fl	Ob	Cl	Bn	3	2	2		Pno	Syn	1	-	-	2	DH
3m9	13 - 4	00:01	Crossed-Witch	-	-	3	1	Fl	Ob	Cl	Bn	3	-	1		Pno	Syn	1	-	-	2	AC
3m10	15 - 6	00:05	That's Owl, Folks	10	3	-	-	-	-	Cl	-	-	-	-		Pno	Syn	1	-	-	2	AC
3m11	16 - 0	00:26	The Story Of Caramel Cod	10	3	3	1	Fl	Ob	Cl	Bn	3	2	2		Pno	Syn	1	-	-	2	DH
3m12	3m12	00:11	Which Witch Is Which?	10	3	3	1	Fl	Ob	Cl	Bn	3	2	2		Pno	Syn	1	-	-	2	DH
3m13	8 - 2	00:40		-	-	-	-	-	-	-	-	-	-	-		Syn	Syn	-	-	-	-	AC
3m14	10 - 6	00:03	Gracie Logo	-	-	-	-	-	-	-	-	-	-	-		-	Syn	-	-	-	-	AC

FIG. 12.2. Master Cue List and Orchestra Breakdown from *The Simpsons*

Eventually, the composer gives every cue a title, like "Billy Splits Quick," or "The Big Kiss." But at this stage, which is before the composer has begun writing, the music editor assigns every cue an alphanumeric designation, like "4M23," which indicates the reel and its location within the film. (As previously mentioned, even in a digital world, a film is often still broken down into smaller pieces, or "reels.") The first number is the reel number, "M" stands for music cue, and the last number is a sequential number indicating where that cue is placed in the film. In this instance, 4M23 means the fourth reel, music cue number 23. It should be noted that in the old analog world, where the film was physically divided into reels, the music cues were numbered sequentially within each reel and began again with "1" in the next reel. Hence, a typical numbering could have been 1M1, 1M2, 1M3, 2M1, 2M2, 3M1, etc. In today's world, the numbers simply continue from reel to reel and represent the cue's placement within the entire film. So, that same example would be 1M01, 1M02, 1M03, 2M04, 2M05, 2M06, and so on, going all the way up to, say, 11M53 (or however many cues and reels there are in the film). Note that a leading zero will be included in cue numbers less than 10 in this new numbering system (e.g., 1M01 instead of just 1M1) so that file names using these cue numbers will be listed in the proper order in a digital folder. This is because a computer's file system will otherwise alphabetize cue 1M10 between cues 1M1 and 1M2.

In television, there are other variations of this numbering system. Because the shows are generally divided into acts instead of reels, the first number may correspond to the act number. (An act is each segment of the show, divided by commercials if made for broadcast.) Other times, the first number refers to the episode number, with the hundreds digit indicating season number. The code 214M07 in that numbering system, for example, means the seventh cue in the fourteenth show of the second season. As long as the entire team uses a consistent numbering scheme, confusion can be avoided.

Modern tools employed by many music editors and composers might combine spotting notes, master cue list, and even workflow status and other information into one place. Software tools such as CueDB have become fairly ubiquitous for this purpose, though some music editors have created their own custom databases and spreadsheets that they or their composer's team prefers. In any of these cases, it's not necessary to create separate spotting notes and master cue lists in a formal way as used to be considered de rigueur, as long as all the same information comes easily to hand when needed.

SYNCING AND RECORDING

The next job, if the music editor is assisting the composer, is synchronizing the music to the film during recording sessions. Though the composer generally already has a tempo map in their DAW that can generate the *click track* (digital metronome) needed to keep everything in sync during the recording session, the music editor makes sure that the music and the picture are locked and that the click track is all correct and workable. Also, at the session, the music editor keeps a log of every take of each cue known as "take notes." If a cue needs to be moved, whether by a few frames or even by a few seconds, the music editor assists the composer in making the timing changes. This can involve changing tempos, moving bar lines, and/or adjusting meters.

In cases where visual *punches and streamers* (streamers are lines that move across the screen at a constant speed to indicate the approach of some event for synchronization, and punches are dots that flash at the moment of synchronization) are used to give the conductor cues of coming *sync points* (moments when a musical and picture event are synchronized with each other) and tempo changes, the music editor is also generally in charge of creating those—though the use of punches and streamers to sync a score to picture during a recording session has greatly diminished. It generally takes longer to record a cue conducted this way, and the ability to do so has become less prevalent among composers. At the same time, budgets have become more restrictive and scoring timelines are getting ever shorter. Even when there might be adequate time and money to record more freely using punches and streamers, the overwhelming majority of music recorded for films is done with a click track. This is because using a click allows easier overdubbing as well as *punching in* (recording just a section in the middle of a cue).

In addition, if after the recording session the director asks for significant changes in the music, or wants to place a cue originally slated for an early reel into a later one, it will fall to the music editor to accomplish this task. Also, as mentioned, conforming a cue to a new cut of the film will also fall to the music editor, rather than the composer, in cases when the film cut happens after the music has been mixed and delivered. Although this usually happens at the dubbing stage (see the next section of this chapter), sometimes the music editor will move, edit, conform, or rebuild a cue earlier in the process. This is a time when the music editor's job gets especially interesting and creative. Taking material meant for one scene and reworking it to fit another requires both technical and musical skill. In addition, diplomatic skills come in handy, because at this point, the music editor is answering to the director, who may or may not have the ability to communicate musically.

DUBBING AND CUE SHEETS

Once the music is recorded, it is mixed to whatever format the film requires—stereo, surround-sound, ATMOS, etc. The music editor then prepares the cues for the dubbing stage. The music editor attends the dub sessions and assists the dubbing engineers in placing the music at the proper spots, as well as providing input on the levels and EQ of the music.

It is at the dub session where a composer's music is most likely to be moved around. A director might change their mind after having signed off on a cue at an earlier stage of the process and will try a different cue in place of the original. Again, this is the filmmaker's prerogative. Many cues from the best composers have been moved around on the dubbing stage. The composer does not often attend the dubbing sessions so the responsibility of speaking up on behalf of the music is generally given to the music editor. This can be a challenging part of the process.

Eric Reasoner describes the process:

> *It's extremely tedious. You're going back and forth, back and forth, over the same area of sounds with a different focus each time, and if your area of sound isn't of concern at the moment, you'd like to get out of that room. You may very well spend a 12- or 16-hour day mixing one reel of film—that's a 10-minute segment of film. In action films, when they're really loud, you walk out of there and your ears are just completely fatigued. I can remember*

> *going home from the dubbing stage on* Die Hard with a Vengeance *after an action reel. I got up the next morning, and got in the car to go back to the dubbing stage. I started up the car, and the radio came on with the volume up to 11. I was thinking, oh my god, I was listening at this volume last night when I drove home! It just kind of shows you what your ears and your body can do, shutting down after a bit.*

Once the dub is completed, there is one more task for the music editor: preparing a finalized list of all the music in the film. This is called a "music clearance sheet," or (again) a "cue sheet." (Note: "Cue sheet" is a term that has several different uses; in this case, we are talking about the kind used to determine music performance royalties.) This list is submitted to the appropriate organizations for licensing the music so that performance royalties can be paid—a topic we'll revisit in depth in the upcoming Business section.

As Prescribed

Music Cue Sheet

Cue Sheet Classification: Original
Date Prepared:

Initial Airdate:
Category: Movie
Version: Theatrical
Network/Source:

Program/Show Duration: 95 min. 26 sec.
Total Music Duration: 33 min. 47 sec. (auto calc.)

Program (series, film, etc.) Title: As Prescribed
Program Title AKA(s):
Episode Title:
Episode Title AKA(s):
Episode Number:
Production Number:

Production Company: Gobbo Films, LLC
Mailing Address: 29 Sumner Street, Great Barrington, MA 01230
Cue Sheet Prepared By: Alison Plante
Email Address: alison@treblecove.com

Usage Codes: BI = Background Instrumental | BV = Background Vocal | VI = Visual Instrumental | VV = Visual Vocal | MT = Main Title Theme | ET = End Title Theme | Logo

Seq. #	Cue Title (Song/Track Name)	Usage	(optional) Time In h mm ss	(optional) Time Out h mm ss	Duration min. sec.	Role	Composer/Writer First (and Middle) Name	Composer/Writer Last Name	Publisher Name	PRO Affiliation	% Shares
1	Lori	BI	0 00 00	0 00 58	0 58	Composer	Alison Linda	Plante		BMI	100.00%
						Publisher			Trimountaine Music Publishing	BMI	100.00%
2	Main Title - Geraldine's Theme	MT	0 01 13	0 03 28	2 15	Composer	Alison Linda	Plante		BMI	100.00%
						Publisher			Trimountaine Music Publishing	BMI	100.00%
3	Meet Sam	BI	0 07 20	0 08 16	0 56	Composer	Alison Linda	Plante		BMI	100.00%
						Publisher			Trimountaine Music Publishing	BMI	100.00%
4	REPRISE Meet Sam	BI	0 09 35	0 09 52	0 17	Composer	Alison Linda	Plante		BMI	100.00%
						Publisher			Trimountaine Music Publishing	BMI	100.00%
5	Meet Amy and Scotty	BI	0 10 54	0 11 35	0 41	Composer	Alison Linda	Plante		BMI	100.00%
						Publisher			Trimountaine Music Publishing	BMI	100.00%
6	Amy's Routine	BI	0 16 00	0 16 52	0 52	Composer	Alison Linda	Plante		BMI	100.00%
						Publisher			Trimountaine Music Publishing	BMI	100.00%
7	Scotty's Symptoms	BI	0 18 35	0 19 07	0 32	Composer	Alison Linda	Plante		BMI	100.00%
						Publisher			Trimountaine Music Publishing	BMI	100.00%
8	Sam's Panic Attack	BI	0 19 07	0 19 37	0 30	Composer	Alison Linda	Plante		BMI	100.00%
						Publisher			Trimountaine Music Publishing	BMI	100.00%
9	Hearing 1	BI	0 21 46	0 22 27	0 41	Composer	Alison Linda	Plante		BMI	100.00%
						Publisher			Trimountaine Music Publishing	BMI	100.00%
10	Legislative Failure	BI	0 26 11	0 27 02	0 51	Composer	Alison Linda	Plante		BMI	100.00%
						Publisher			Trimountaine Music Publishing	BMI	100.00%
11	Support Group Letters	BI	0 27 17	0 28 01	0 44	Composer	Alison Linda	Plante		BMI	100.00%
						Publisher			Trimountaine Music Publishing	BMI	100.00%
12	Meet Matt	BI	0 28 38	0 30 01	1 23	Composer	Alison Linda	Plante		BMI	100.00%
						Publisher			Trimountaine Music Publishing	BMI	100.00%
13	Under Construction	BI	0 31 47	0 32 29	0 42	Composer	Alison Linda	Plante		BMI	100.00%
						Publisher			Trimountaine Music Publishing	BMI	100.00%
14	Sam Tries to Taper	BI	0 34 01	0 34 24	0 23	Composer	Alison Linda	Plante		BMI	100.00%
						Publisher			Trimountaine Music Publishing	BMI	100.00%
15	Sam is Homeless Part 1	BI	0 35 09	0 35 46	0 37	Composer	Alison Linda	Plante		BMI	100.00%
						Publisher			Trimountaine Music Publishing	BMI	100.00%
16	Sam is Homeless Part 2	BI	0 37 52	0 38 37	0 45	Composer	Alison Linda	Plante		BMI	100.00%
						Publisher			Trimountaine Music Publishing	BMI	100.00%
17	Geraldine's Tree	BI	0 39 39	0 40 19	0 40	Composer	Alison Linda	Plante		BMI	100.00%

FIG. 12.4. Music Cue Sheet

As a final note, "thinking like a music editor" is cited by some composers as an emerging part of their own scoring process. Ben Bromfield describes:

> *After my first draft, I try to think like a music editor as much as possible, because there's a lot of [filmmakers'] notes I can address with the stems. This is the process I developed that has been really good because it keeps me attuned to the fact that I'm a player in a production. I'm not just a composer, I'm the whole music department. I'm here to make the show good.*
>
> *I think that being at dub mixes is part of what inspired me to do things like this. When I'm on the dub stage, I hear what they do on the fly to solve their creative problems. It's not polished, it's not perfect. It just has to do what they want it to do. And so, being the composer, and then after the first pass thinking more like a music editor, makes me into a music editor with superpowers! Because a music editor can't add new notes. They can't add new music. But I can also add a new violin part. I can add multiple new instruments, I can add new compositional ideas. And that has served me really well in my career, thinking like that.*

The music editor performs an interesting, important, and often unheralded role in the making of a film. An ability to work quickly and accurately under pressure, and also to work with grace under people who are not always kind or gracious, is a must. But the role of music editor is an exciting one that is also crucial to the successful completion of the score and the film itself.

THE MUSIC SUPERVISOR

The music supervisor is another extremely important role, with a job description that can vary from project to project. Oftentimes, the tasks of the music supervisor include interfacing with both the music editor and composer.

Music Supervisor Evyen Klean puts it this way:

> *Ego aside, you need to know: what does the project actually need, and how much support do the filmmakers need? How much support does the composer need? And if there's an artist on camera, or you're in the studio with an artist, what do they need?*

In the early days of Hollywood scoring, the title "music supervisor" described someone who oversaw all the music in a film. This included assigning a composer and orchestrators, setting deadlines, interfacing with the producers and director, overseeing the music editing process, making sure everything came in at or under budget, and holding final responsibility for recording sessions of underscore and songs. Up until the 1960s, this person would be under contract to a specific studio, and ultimately was beholden to the studio executives. In the Golden Age of Hollywood, the music supervisor would have been a trained musician, often able to compose, orchestrate, or conduct if necessary, or if they desired. As the industry developed and the studio system gradually dissolved, the music supervisor became an independent contractor hired to work on a film-by-film basis, and the role morphed into someone who retained some of the previous job description, but not all of it.

In the late 1960s, as discussed in chapter 5, songs became more and more prevalent as a crucial element of a film, bringing extra revenue streams to film studios. As the desire for a hit song and the use of songs in a film became more prevalent, the need for someone to oversee the acquisition of rights, as well as the production of the song, became necessary.

Broadly defined, there are essentially two types of music supervisors today: someone who is mostly a business person overseeing the choosing and clearance of songs as well as the logistics of getting the music recorded (budgets, deadlines, etc.), and someone who is musically trained and can produce a recording session or participate in the actual music creation. In essence, that means that there are those that are strictly business people with some creative input and those who can combine both musical and business roles. This is, admittedly, a generalization.

Here are some of the many roles a music supervisor might fulfill during the making of a film. Depending on the needs of the filmmakers and the abilities of the music supervisor, either just one or even all of these may be one person's job description:

- **Helping to pick the songs.** This is often the largest part of the music supervisor's job. Which songs are chosen depends on many factors, including the budget, the director's wishes, the producer's wishes, instructions from the executives at the movie studio, which artists and publishers agree to allow use of their songs, and which artists are available for recording. It can be a difficult and politically complicated labyrinth to negotiate.
- **Getting clearance for songs.** Before a song is used in a movie, permission must be obtained. First, the publisher must grant sync rights (the right to synchronize the song with the movie). If the producer or director wants to use the original version of a song, then a second permission must be granted by the owner of the original master recording—usually the record company. The music supervisor either handles the negotiations for these clearances directly, or hires a music clearance company to do that work. We will discuss more of the details of how this works in chapter 20.
- **Creating and monitoring budgets.** Since the music supervisor is often doing some of the actual business negotiations on behalf of the producer, they usually assist in creating a music budget for the film. This can involve budgeting only for the use of songs, and can also include overseeing the finances of recording the underscore and hiring the composer. It is usually the music supervisor's job to oversee the day-to-day budgets in the recording studio during production of any songs.
- **Record producing.** Whether it is an old song being rerecorded or a new song commissioned for the film, the music supervisor may produce the recording session. This job

can be done by the film composer if they wrote or co-wrote the song, and sometimes an outside record producer is contracted. But even then, the music supervisor makes sure these sessions go smoothly and stay on budget.

- **Recommending the composer.** Because the music supervisor is often involved in the project at an early date, often they are asked to recommend a composer they consider appropriate for the film, and who fits the budget.
- **Overseeing the temp track.** Often, the music supervisor is part of the team, with the music editor and director, that chooses the music and builds the temp track.
- **Overseeing music performed on camera.** If there is a scene where the actors are singing or dancing, the music supervisor will be present to ensure that everything is going well. This means making sure the playback is correct and that the lip-syncing or shots of musicians playing are accurate.

Evyen Klean talks about being on the set for *Behind the Candelabra* (2013), a biopic about the flamboyant pianist, Liberace:

> Behind the Candelabra *is a good example of being on the set for an on-camera performance and all the beats that go along with it. With multiple on-camera performances, there was a need for prerecording multiple songs for playback on the set. That process included booking recording studios, recreating arrangements, and hiring musicians, copyists, a Pro Tools operator, and an engineer. Not to mention the critical act of rerecording all of Liberace's amazing piano performances, which was handled by virtuoso pianist and composer Randy Kerber. For* Behind the Candelabra, *we had to hire music coaches for the actors, cast hand and body doubles, and work with the department heads, including casting, props, set design, choreography, wardrobe, sound and playback, etc. I was on the set for all on-camera playbacks to ensure that all the music performances went smoothly and accurately.*

> *Working with the music editor and playback operator, we made adjustments and edits on the fly to accommodate the director's needs. We were solving problems in real time.*

The role of music supervisor is also particularly variable in different world markets. For example, in Japan, this role doesn't yet exist and instead is covered piecemeal by others involved in the production. Ayako Tsuchiya, music executive for Amazon Studios in Japan, notes that this is one of the greatest challenges in her role:

> *Due to the lack of music supervisors, I always struggle to find someone dedicated to managing the music for a single project. Given this position, Prime Video is making efforts to establish the presence of this role in Japan, aiming to promote its adoption.*

As you can see, the role of music supervisor in the twenty-first century is difficult to define, as there are many possible dimensions to it. The bottom line is that the music supervisor operates in a creative world that overlaps filmmakers, composers, songwriters, publishers, and music editors. The music supervisor must be a skilled communicator and people person, as well as an excellent negotiator, organizer, and possibly trained musician and/or music producer. It can be an exciting and gratifying role where each day has a different set of tasks that contribute to the success of a film.

PART III

Aesthetics

CHAPTER 13

Music and Story

As long as humans have existed, we have told stories. Stories help us to understand ourselves and the world around us, as well as to imagine things that go beyond reality. Evidence for this exists in cave paintings in Indonesia dating back 44,000 years, notably one representing a scene with figures made up of both human and animal characteristics, showing that even at the dawn of human history we had an imaginative capacity.[3]

Though we've moved from cave walls to movie screens, at its heart, filmmaking is a form of storytelling, and storytelling is at the heart of film scoring.

As film composer great Alan Silvestri puts it:

> *For me, a great film composer is always someone who not only has musical talent, but also a talent for telling a story with music. This is what makes film scoring a unique musical expression. It's all about how the composer can assist the telling of the story as well as writing great music.*

ELEMENTS OF STORY

In all the many storytelling traditions around the world, there are some common elements that go back to the most ancient recorded stories. These include character, setting, plot, and often a moral or lesson that the story teaches.

These can be mapped onto the familiar "5 W" questions: Who? What? When? Where? Why?

- who = characters
- what = plot
- where and when = setting/world-building
- why = morality/ethics/central dramatic question

Composers must become intimately familiar with all of these elements in any film they score. They should get to know the characters well enough that if called upon to write a musical theme for one of them, they can represent that character's traits and development through music. They should be ready to evoke the setting and enhance the sense of being carried away to another time and place, whether it's imaginary, as in James Horner's score for James Cameron's *Avatar* (2009), which imagines what an orchestra on the world Pandora might sound like, or real, as we'll explore in depth in chapter 17. Above all, it's crucial to be able to look at a film with an eye to the important story moments rather than being too focused on purely musical concerns. This is where constructive collaboration between composer and filmmakers becomes invaluable. *X-Files* (1993 to 2018) composer Mark Snow describes how he learned to let his scores be guided by dramatic considerations:

> *I learned so much from [directors and producers] who know nothing about music. It didn't matter that they weren't musicians; they were talking about the drama and the emotional elements of the story. They would say, "Take this out, oh no, that's fine, but take out the piano, or try it without the bass," and I would say to myself, "That won't work." Then I'd look at it again and say, "Oh my God, they're right, that's great!" So these people who came in and told me; "I don't know anything about music, but ..."—it never ticked me off. I always thought I could learn something from them.*

STORY STRUCTURES

Once we understand the elements of a story (its content), we can then examine the structure (its form). Composer Michael Kamen described this in terms of identifying the architecture of the score:

> *I often can see what the architecture of a score will be by talking about it with the director, or the producer, or whoever I'm spotting with. I learn more as I'm working on it, and sometimes, I change my mind. But it's really the architecture of a score that you're talking about, and that is a very complicated—and yet quite simplistic—design. Nobody goes to the theater to listen to the score. The score is assisting them in watching the film. The score is a component of the story and of the characters.*

Many films, especially Hollywood blockbusters and others meant to have broad audience appeal, use the following three-act structure:

1. **Beginning (Setup):** We are introduced to the characters, story world, and premise of the story.
2. **Middle (Conflict Development):** The plot plays out as set up in the first act, often introducing some further complication or unexpected development in the central conflict.
3. **End (Resolution):** The story builds to a climax, and then wraps up loose ends.

These types of stories, termed by film theorist Robert McKee as "the archplot,"[4] are centered on the path of a hero or protagonist, and their conflict with some external force or antagonist, ending with the protagonist having been changed.

Unlike in a staged play, there are no actual breaks between acts in a film. However, screenwriters, as well as directors and others involved in filmmaking, tend to think and talk about their script structure as being divided into acts. For example, a film having trouble landing its ending after a strong start might be said to have "third act problems." It's important for film composers to be able to identify these invisible divisions in a film's story structure, so as to be able to point them out musically, giving the audience a subconscious reinforcement of the story structure. Then, the composer can address the underlying character and dramatic developments in each section by bringing in musical themes and textures according to the flow of the story. For example, a character's theme might be introduced in Act I in a straightforward and clear way, be transformed in Act II by using various compositional techniques such as augmentation and diminution, harmonic and rhythmic modulation, and so on, to represent the development of the character, and then brought back in full but with a more robust orchestration or return to a tonic key center in Act III to represent that character's growth and the completion of their plot arc.

It is important to note that these three acts are not necessarily equal, in terms of screen time. Typically, the setup and resolution are shorter, with the middle development section (conflict) taking up the bulk of a film. There is not usually a symmetrical balance, and composers must take all of this into account when planning the score.

Of course, not all films and stories follow this structure. There are many filmmakers who want to present a story in their own unique way, even a non-linear fashion. Pulitzer prize winning playwright and screenwriter Suzan-Lori Parks, for example, draws from structures of "repetition and revision" inspired by jazz forms, rather than linear structures.[5] Here, we see not only an example of a different kind of dramatic form, but also the feedback loop that takes place between storytelling and music. Story influences music, then music influences story, and so on, in its own pattern of repetition and revision.

Whatever form the story takes, it behooves a film composer to understand the structure of the film they are scoring, get to know its elements and story beats, and reflect all of these in their compositional choices so that the film and score work together seamlessly to tell the same story.

DIEGETIC AND NON-DIEGETIC MUSIC

When something in a film is present in the world of the story, it is referred to as "diegetic," or part of the "diegesis" (story world). For example, if one character says something to another character, that speech is diegetic. However, if there is narration over a film sequence, even if voiced by one of the characters, that is "non-diegetic" or "extra-diegetic" because it is not heard in the world of the story—it is only heard by the audience.

SOURCE

Music that is diegetic is referred to as "source music" because it comes from a source, seen or implied, in the film. For example, if a character turns on a radio and then we hear music mixed as though it is coming from that radio, that is a source cue. So too is the music in a dance scene where we see a band performing on stage. Even if we don't see the source, we can often infer that music is a source cue from context. For example, if we hear music in a restaurant scene, and it fits the period, is mixed quietly under the dialogue and ambient sound, and does not seem to respond to the emotions of the characters or events on-screen, we can conclude that it is a source cue.

Often, source music is mixed in the film at barely audible levels; it is frequently part of a room's ambient sound, far in the background. However, there are times when source music can play an important dramatic role in the film. For example, in the film *Tár* (2022), the music played by the orchestra conducted by the title character plays a large role in the story. As the world seems to close in around Tár's character, the way that the source music from the orchestra is mixed contributes to the sense of foreboding and dread, reflecting the subjective experience of that character.

In addition to dramatic usage, source music often establishes a time or place. By using source music that is indigenous to a culture or specific to a time period, the feeling of that culture or time is placed in the mind of the audience. The underscore can then also use elements of that cultural or period music, or it can be a completely different entity. For example, in the Pixar film *Coco* (2017), when the main character Miguel runs into the plaza where the talent show is taking place, we hear various authentic Mexican musical ensembles as source cues, all of which were recorded and produced in Mexico by Germaine Franco, who also provided additional music, orchestrated the underscore, and co-wrote five of the six songs in the film. There are also countless films that have used source music to establish a time in history. We'll return to a thorough examination of how music can serve to channel a time and place, and questions of how to accomplish this with the appropriate level of authenticity, in chapter 17.

UNDERSCORE AND SONG SCORE

Most of what we think of when we talk about film scoring is underscore. *Underscore* is any music in a film that is extra-diegetic—that is, it is not heard by characters in the film. It exists only for the audience, and serves one or more dramatic functions in the storytelling that we will explore in depth in the following chapters. Underscore is generally not panned or mixed to sound as though it is emanating from a particular source in the scene, and it often wouldn't make sense if it were present in the story world. It might be anachronistic to the period, come from an ensemble that couldn't physically be present, or respond to the story in a way that wouldn't make sense in real life.

When a music cue is non-diegetic and is a song (with lyrics), rather than an instrumental piece, it may be referred to as "song score." This distinction doesn't have anything to do with the way that cue is being used in terms of the storytelling, however, and both underscore and song score are extra-diegetic uses of music in film. However, since song scores have some unique properties, we will explore them in more depth in chapter 20.

SOURCE SCORING

Because the distinction between diegetic and extra-diegetic music is so powerfully tied to the film's world-building and sense of reality (or unreality), this distinction can be played with by imaginative composers and directors in ways that deepen or comment on the very substrate of the story of the film. Though they are not nearly as common as purely diegetic or non-diegetic cues, sometimes music takes on characteristics of both source and underscore in ways known as "source scoring" (sometimes collapsed into the portmanteau "scource").

One form of source scoring is when the cue is clearly diegetic, but has sync points with the picture that wouldn't make sense in real life. A famous example of this is the final scene of Alfred Hitchcock's *The Man Who Knew Too Much* (1956), in which Arthur Benjamin's "Storm Cloud Cantata" (arranged for the scene—and conducted on camera in the film—by the film's composer, Bernard Herrmann) is being performed by an orchestra as part of the story while the main character desperately searches the theater for a would-be assassin. Many cuts in the film and moments in the action hit precisely on beats in the music, as though the orchestra is underscoring the action, leading to the climactic moment in which the assassin will fire his gun and the orchestra's percussionist performs the piece's sole cymbal crash. Another example of this form of source scoring is heard in Edgar Wright's *Baby Driver* (2017), in which the protagonist listens to music on headphones that also seems to almost supernaturally align with the action on screen.

Another way source and underscore can be blurred, despite the music still remaining fully diegetic, is when there is a subtext to the music that is only obvious to the audience. An example from the Netflix show *Bridgerton* is various dance scenes in which the source music is a contemporary pop song from the time the show was created (2020) that is arranged for string quartet in the style of the story's period (the early nineteenth century). The audience for this show is meant to perceive the humor in the anachronism, and if they recognize the specific underlying song, they will understand the additional commentary on the scene in the form of the song's title and even unsung lyrics. For example, in a scene in which suitors to the main character are successively turned down, the quartet plays a rendition of Ariana Grande's "Thank U, Next." This type of source scoring can also take place when a source cue uses a musical theme established in the underscore, or vice versa—as when in Hitchcock's *North by Northwest* (1959) composer Bernard Herrmann introduces the love theme as a source cue in a train dining car when the main characters first meet, before developing that theme in the underscore as their romance deepens.

When diegetic and non-diegetic music are mixed there are even more variations possible for source scoring. For example, a cue may be ambiguously diegetic. Perhaps we see the source, or are explicitly told that we are hearing music produced in the scene, but then it is mixed or arranged in ways that would not be possible as a source cue. Or sometimes, the source will be joined at some point by underscore so that the resulting music cue is both source and underscore in equal measure. For example, in *The Last of the Mohicans* (1992) there is a love scene at the fort and a source music cue is gradually joined by orchestral strings that add an element of underscore to the building romantic tension in the scene. Or in *Everything Everywhere All at Once* (2022), as we cut between multiple different realities of its parallel universes, Debussy's "Claire de Lune" is played by a character on the piano in one universe and joined by underscore layers by the film's composers (the band Son Lux) to serve an underscoring function across several levels of reality in the story.

Finally, the distinction between diegetic and non-diegetic music can sometimes be played for laughs. A famous case of this is in the Mel Brooks Western parody *Blazing Saddles* (1974), when we hear a big band cue as the camera slowly pulls back from the main character on his horse and follows him as he begins to ride away across a desert landscape. This seems to clearly be an underscore cue until the camera pans over far enough to reveal the Count Basie Orchestra playing there in the desert, as part of the diegesis, with Basie himself high-fiving the sheriff as he rides past. The apparent absurdity of this being a source cue is itself the joke in this scene.

As we've seen in all these examples, whether a cue is source, underscore, song score, or source scoring, it may be composed specifically for the film (by the film's original music composer or by someone else), be licensed from a pre-existing instrumental work or song, or a combination. What matters in terms of the storytelling is how it's used in relation to the story world (diegesis). Furthermore, all of these categories of cues are important in telling the story, either from within as a source cue, from outside the story world as underscore or song score, or something in between as in source scoring.

CHAPTER 14

Scoring Concept and Approach

There are times when the most intimidating experience a composer can have is looking at a blank sheet of paper or computer screen. And there are other times when that same blank space can be an invitation to fill it with wonderful, exciting ideas. This is the reality of the creative process; there are ups and downs, there are times when the ideas just keep coming, and times when the stream is dry. For a composer working in films, there is usually no luxury of waiting until the ideas start flowing, so you must be able to find a way to turn on the faucet yourself.

THREE CORNERSTONES OF FILM SCORING

There are several important yet simple concepts that can help in actually controlling and sometimes even jump-starting the creative process: first, having a foundation of craft and knowledge of music; second, knowing what you want to say dramatically, emotionally, and psychologically; and, third, knowing your own strengths, weaknesses, and capacity to produce. These cornerstones hold true regardless of musical style, film genre, and writing approach. In the film-scoring business, these are all extremely important. As we have seen in other chapters, because the composer often comes in at the end of the filmmaking process, the pressure to produce in a timely manner is enormous. So a composer relies on these three pillars to deliver the score on time.

CRAFT

It is important to have developed your craft so you have as much technique as possible. If you write great romantic melodies, but that is all you do well, then what happens if you need to score a horror scene? If you are great at action/adventure films, what will you do if the project you accepted requires a lyrical approach?

The more you know about music, and the more different kinds of music you have analyzed extensively, the more tools you have at your disposal. Your musical vocabulary becomes larger, and you can speak in many musical languages. Traditional orchestral, atonal, jazz oriented, electronic, or pop-music derived soundtracks will not intimidate you if you are familiar with how these styles work.

Gaining this breadth of expertise is a lifelong process. For every composer, there are variations on the theme of musical learning and development. When you begin a project, if you can draw upon many different kinds of musical expressions, you are much better off. You will know the kinds of harmonies, rhythms, and melodies to write. As you watch a scene, or when you sit down to write, your familiarity with a style may start to suggest possibilities. Or if you are stuck, your knowledge of what it should sound like can bail you out. For example, if you know the director wants a particular scene to be heroic, there are certain rhythmic and melodic devices that you can draw from to create something of your own. On the other hand, if your background is narrow, and you are asked to write something outside of what you know, it can be difficult and time-consuming—if not flat-out impossible—to create something appropriate.

Study requires discipline and curiosity. If you are not interested in a particular style—if it doesn't make you sit up and take notice, curl your ears, or give you goosebumps—then study that style as an academic exercise. This can be a necessary part of the path of the aspiring film composer.

Alf Clausen, Emmy-winning composer for *The Simpsons* for many years, strongly believes in the need for musical curiosity and study. He spoke about this issue in relationship to writing songs in different styles:

> *[Students'] questions are always very pointed about, "How do you do this, how do you do that, how do you write these styles, etc." My response is to ask, "Have you dissected the popular songs of all the eras to find out what makes them work? Have you analyzed them to find out what the chord progressions are, what the melodic tricks are, what chord tones on what chords created a certain sound in a certain era? And can you sit down and write a song in that style because you have spent hundreds of hours dissecting those songs?" And they say, "Not yet." Well, I have. I have spent thousands of hours dissecting and playing those songs. It's a matter of craft, it's a matter of study.*

DRAMATIC INTENTION

The intent of your music—knowing what you want to say—is crucial. There is such a large range of emotion and feeling that can be expressed by music that it often takes a lot of thought and contemplation to figure out what to do with a particular film or scene. But to start writing without knowing what you want to say is like trying to swim without knowing the strokes. When you get in the water, you would just flail around and desperately try to stay afloat. It is important to take in a whole lot of information: the flow of the drama, the look of the film, and probably most important for the composer, the inherent tempo of the scene. Every film and every scene has its own musical implications, and the composer must know what a film or scene means before beginning to write.

Elmer Bernstein composed the scores to over two hundred films, and was quite familiar with this process:

> *The first thing I do is to spend a week just looking at the film without prejudice. When I say without prejudice, I say to myself, I'm not even going to try to think music during this week. I just want to look at the film until the film talks*

> *to me and the film tells me things. What I want the film to tell me is what it's about, and that's not always on the surface. What is the film about? What is the function of music going to be in this film? Why are we having music in this film, what's it going to do? So I start with those kinds of thoughts. It's a kind of intellectual process rather than a composing process.*
>
> *Now, I had a big problem with that in* To Kill a Mockingbird, *because if you look at the film without music, all you're looking at is a film with a lot of kids in it. But you're also seeing a lot of adult problems—problems of racism, problems of injustice, death and violence, violence to children. So it took me the longest time to find where the music was going to go, how it was going to go, and what its specific use would be in the film. I determined after a long time—it took me six weeks—that the film is about the adult world seen through the eyes of children. All these problems, what we call adult problems, are seen as the children see them. Which led me to childlike things. For instance, playing the piano one note at a time, music box sounds, harp, bells, things of that sort. So what really got me into the film was the realization—at least, my realization—that it was a film about adult things seen through the eyes of children.*

Taking six weeks, as in *To Kill a Mockingbird,* to think about the approach to a film is a luxury most film composers don't have today. But even on a condensed timeline, it's crucial for a film composer to start from that dramatic sense, and approach the score as a storyteller and a member of the filmmaking team. This mindset is a crucial component of what sets a film composer apart.

KNOWING YOURSELF

Dick Grove, a well-known music educator in Los Angeles, used to say, "We all think we're writing music to make money, or to move people. But what we're really doing, if we just take a look, is finding out about ourselves." When we sit down to write music, many things about ourselves come into play: How disciplined am I? How much do I trust my training and ability? How much do I believe in myself? Am I actually enjoying writing music and having fun, or is it a chore? Am I following the instructions of the client, or is my ego too big to listen to anyone other than my own inner creative voice? On the other hand, am I too concerned with what people will think of me to stand up for my opinions, especially if someone asks for something I know is musically a bad idea?

These questions, and others, can come into play every time a composer accepts a gig. At some level in every writer's consciousness, there is an expression of one or more of these questions, whether they have acknowledged it or not. For example, are you the type that procrastinates until the last minute? If so, you'll need to seek out proven strategies to combat this tendency, because a film with sixty minutes of music won't get written the night before. Do you have a problem taking direction and/or feedback? Lose it, because as soon as you sign the contract, you are effectively somebody's employee. Do you know you can write quickly and appropriately? Nurture that and utilize it. Are you very organized and structured? Stay organized, but don't forget to stay flexible.

When you sit down and start to write, it is essential to be brutally honest about these questions. You must know how many minutes a day you can produce, how many days there are before the recording session or final delivery, which cues seem to be suggesting musical ideas, and which cues are tougher. There is very little time for second-guessing and extensive rewriting of any one cue, so confidence in your technique is crucial. Being clear in your communication with the director and having a willingness and ability gained through experience to translate the director's requests into music are fundamental to this process.

DEVELOPING THE CONCEPT FOR THE SCORE

In speaking with composers, the one thing that comes through again and again is that the most successful scores have a concept that drives the music. Then, once the concept for the whole score is set, each individual cue presents a particular problem to be solved. For example, just because the main concept for a film is big, orchestral, and Romantic doesn't mean that there cannot be a piano solo if the drama calls for it. But that piano solo must still feel like part of the rest of the score. In today's world, almost any musical language is part of the composer's palette, so choices abound. But keeping to the overall concept keeps the sound focused.

Elliot Goldenthal is an accomplished composer of film scores, ballets, theater, and concert works. He has found a way of approaching a score that produces a unique sound for each of his projects:

> *Before I approach anything, I have a very strong concept of what I want to pull off, whether it works out or not. That might include limiting the choice of pitches or a very clear choice of orchestration. So, I don't go into something and just start improvising, I find that if I do that, I just sort of waste my time. I stay away from the piano, away from the computer, away from the pencil. I think about the scene, and I say, How can I achieve the dramatic effect that is necessary for the scene and have it still sound fresh? How can I make it sound like you haven't heard that before, you haven't lived that before?*
>
> *Sometimes, the answer can be surprisingly simple. In* Alien 3, *for example, I used a solo piano to underline the scene with the little girl because I thought that having a piano way out in space would remind you of the most domestic of all instruments; it would remind you of home. Just things like that. That's a concept.*

Sometimes, a composer's concept for a film can be generated from a feeling or an idea that, in itself, is not musical. Many composers are artistic in the way they look at the world; that is to say, they see the world in terms of emotional responses that eventually get translated into music. Clearly, this is a very valuable way to see things from the standpoint of writing music for the visual medium of film.

In *Forrest Gump*, Alan Silvestri had to come up with an opening music cue that would embody the whole film. He first discussed the opening shot, of the feather floating down from the sky and almost landing on Forrest, with director Robert Zemeckis:

> *[Zemeckis] didn't really go into a whole lot of detail, but the gist of what we did talk about was somehow, "This is the start of the movie. This is the start of this whole incredible odyssey we're about to go on." My take on it was... I've got a couple of things to deal with now. One is, I've got physical things to deal with. I've got some events; the feather floats from the blue sky, makes an entrance into this town. It winds up almost landing on somebody's shoulder, then at the last moment, it's blown off. It's very symbolic, you know, if you're looking at this as something descending upon someone's life. That guy is not chosen right now. Then eventually, the feather lands on Forrest; he's the chosen one.*
>
> *So now we've got some physical things in terms of the image, and we've also got some events that are episodic in a sense. Coming from nowhere, blue sky, into this town, what does it mean? It's just a feather, then it almost lands on somebody, blows off. Now, there's some kind of dramatic context.*
>
> *So now, what do you do? The invisible aspect of this is that somehow, whatever you do also has to essentialize and embody this entire film. Right now. This cannot be "feather music." This cannot be "falling down music." This cannot be "missed opportunity music." This music somehow has to take everything, sentiment wise, that this film is about, and somehow essentialize it and present it. I'm thinking, at this point, if I can find that, I've got the key to this film. This theme will be all over the movie, and there*

will be a tremendous sense of cohesiveness for the overall tone of this film.

Now of course all of this is going on under the surface because I'm not sitting there making lists and treatises on 1M1. I know I've got to do something here. So I sit down at the piano, and I'm thinking, "This music has to deal with Forrest," and I start doodling at the piano. Literally in twenty minutes, it's done! It's childlike, and it's simple, and yet it's not baby-like. It's innocent. It's what I'm feeling from Forrest. I look at this moment, where the feather moves away from this other guy. I make a key change there—an immediate unprepared key change there. We already planned that we're going to bring the orchestra in, with more sense of scope at this point.

That was the mission in Forrest. It had to be an honest attempt. Musically, as an actor, as a writer, as a cinematographer, don't get cute with this movie, or you'll sink the ship.

This anecdote embodies many of the principles outlined above with Silvestri's own personality and musical sensibility bringing it to its ultimate destination. He had a clear idea of what he needed to do, and what not to do, dramatically. And having this understanding, he was able to sit down and create the theme that was just right for this film. (Ironically, this theme was eventually used in only one other spot in the film: the ending where we see the feather again. Every time he tried to use it elsewhere, it just didn't work.)

Where this process may diverge in scoring a film versus a series is that in the case of something with multiple episodes and possibly multiple seasons, the concept may need to start off as more of an outline or set of constraints and then be refined as the story itself progresses. Emmy-nominated composer Ben Bromfield describes his initial scoring concept for television and streaming as the "sound of show":

Strong themes tend to be more important in film than television. There is, of course, a lot of room for that in TV as

> *well. But I find that the single most important thing when I'm doing a film is coming up with a good theme that I can use all the time, and for TV, it's one of many important things. I find that "sound of show" is a good shorthand to describe to filmmakers what you're doing. What does this show sound like? It's not just the instruments—you could also have some genres in there. It's so important to find a good sound of show, if you can, and sometimes really difficult. This is part of why the beginnings of projects are so hard, because you're still trying to find that stuff.*

Composer Haim Mazar also describes this initial process of finding the right sound as more fluid than just creating themes, even in his film work:

> *Sometimes, you set out to write a theme, and you write the theme, and then it's successful. But many times, the themes almost happen as an accident. The thematic material can be a very simple one-note gesture, or a sound. Basically, I try to come up with a cool piece of music, and I write like five or six. I just call them ideas. Then I kind of play this game of "where can I fit this"? Each idea has, I call it a "schtick," and what that means is that it's the one main thing that this idea is doing.*

One of the joys of film composing is this process of discovering a concept. Unlike writing concert works or pop songs, the film composer is responding to the visual images and the story on the screen. These images and story-lines suggest musical ideas and provide a framework within which the music can fit. Many composers have said that once they find the initial concept, the rest of the score writes itself. The trial and error, the thought, and contemplation often result in the stimulation of the composer's imagination. Then they experience the satisfaction of completing the director's vision of the film in the language of music.

CHAPTER 15

Dramatic Functions of the Score

Once a composer arrives at an overall concept for the score, it's time to begin writing individual cues. A film can be anywhere from a short subject of just a few minutes to a full-length feature of over two hours. Either way, as the story unfolds on screen, the music must continually develop so that it stays interesting. Themes develop, instrumentation develops, and the overall emotional thrust of the music has an arc that matches the arc of the film itself. Conversely, the music can affect the way the film is put together. It can smooth out cuts, transitions, or dissolves. It can also help the audience understand shifts in location in time or place. Every cue has an impact that the composer and director are considering when placing it in the movie. It's never the case that a piece of music is simply written to sound good, without taking into consideration the needs of the film. As Michael Kamen once wisely noted: "Nobody goes to the movies to listen to the score. The score is simply assisting them in watching the film."

The first question that faces the composer is "What is this cue's dramatic function?" In other words: why is this cue here, and what is it doing? For the purposes of this discussion, we've divided the various functions of film music into three broad categories: physical functions, psychological functions, and technical or practical functions. It's important to understand that this is just a framework that can be applied in analyzing a score. They're not hard and fast rules, or even concepts a film composer is likely to be consciously considering when spotting or writing. Just as harmonic analysis arose to explain existing practice in musical styles, it's helpful when studying film scoring to understand this kind of framework, especially when first approaching a score analytically. However, don't confuse this with the composition process itself, for which each composer approaches the task from a different angle. Sometimes, a composer will intellectually analyze a scene and determine its musical requirements; at other times, they will write from instinct. Also, the real world isn't always clear-cut or cleanly divided. Often, several functions we'll describe here will overlap in the same cue, because every situation is different and can have more than one dramatic implication.

PHYSICAL FUNCTIONS

Physical functions refer to what can actually be seen on screen, in which music impacts or comments on the physical action or location of the scene. This includes:

- **Setting the location of the film.** If a movie takes place in an exotic location, often this setting is reflected in the music. For example, a movie that takes place in Ireland could use Uillean pipes and a pennywhistle. A movie that is set in the Appalachian Mountains of the United States might call for banjos and fiddles. The composer and director might decide to have the score sound authentic to the location, or simply incorporate one or two elements of the culture's music into an orchestral score. See chapter 17 for more on this.

  The setting also might be less specific to a particular, real place, and more evocative of a type of location, physical setting, or atmosphere. For example, an urban street might employ a busy ostinato, or an aerial shot of a mountain range might use ambient synth pads or a lonely flute to put the audience in the mindset of that type of setting. Just as films often start with an establishing shot (often an aerial or wide shot to establish the location of the scene), beginning with a cue that puts the audience in mind of the setting of the story is helpful in immersing them in that world.

- **Setting the time period.** If a movie takes place in another historical era, sometimes music of that time will be used. For example, if a film is set in eighteenth-century Europe, a harpsichord can be used to give the audience an immediate association with that time. For movies set in medieval times, there are various ancient instruments like shawm, sackbutt, or psaltery that can be used. As in setting the location, the composer may use a lot of these sounds, or just a hint. Again, chapter 17 will explore this in much more depth.
- **Bringing the audience's attention to something seen onscreen.** This is the first of three examples of sync points—when a musical event occurs at the same time as a picture event. For example, if a character passing in the background who might otherwise have gone unnoticed is important to the scene, the music might have a sync point at the appearance of this character to draw the audience's attention to them.
- **Underlining the action.** When there's a series of sync points, the music can be said to be underlining the action seen on screen. This musical technique is commonly used in action scenes: chase scenes, fights, and intense arguments between characters are all heightened with appropriate music. By composing music that closely follows the action onscreen, music accentuates what is seen, as opposed to bringing a different emotional element to the scene.
- **Mickey-mousing.** When the score goes beyond simply underlining the action and begins mimicking every little action on screen, it is called "mickey-mousing," a term that comes from Mickey Mouse cartoons where this scoring style originated. There is a key difference between mickey-mousing and simply hitting various sync points. Mickey-mousing is reserved for hitting the majority of the on-screen actions, not just one or two moments, and also providing a musical version of the action—e.g., a

downward glissando as a character falls down the stairs—functioning almost like sound effects. It is often used as a comic device, and continues to be most common in certain genres of animation.

PSYCHOLOGICAL FUNCTIONS

Music can assist the psychological and emotional impact of the film in many ways. Sometimes, it can be parallel to the drama and say basically the same thing as what is viewed on-screen. This is known as playing "with" the drama. At other times, the music can add a new dimension, thought, or idea that is not expressed by dialogue or action. This is called playing "against" the drama if it runs counter to what's evident, or can simply be an additional layer of commentary. Some of these psychological functions of film music are:

- **Creating a mood.** In almost every scene of every film, setting the mood is important, and that is something that music is particularly good at doing. There are countless examples of a change in the music altering the impact of a scene or an entire movie. The composer must continually be aware of the result of any musical moods they're setting with their compositional choices. Even an individual note or harmony might have an emotional charge to it that will color the scene. And in some cases, it can even be important to avoid setting any particular mood, but rather maintain a sense of ambiguity.
- **Revealing the unspoken thoughts and feelings of a character.** Often, a director wants the audience to understand something about the character that is either not expressed verbally or not entirely clear from the visual action. The music can help to communicate these things because it can represent another dimension of the character's inner world—their thoughts, feelings, and deepest emotions.
- **Revealing the psychological makeup of a character.** Sometimes, a cue is less about the specific thoughts and feelings of a character in that moment and more about

the underlying psychological makeup of the character in a deeper sense. Character themes, like score concepts, generally try to reflect or unearth something central to who that character is, and developing that theme over the course of a film can reveal a lot about that character's development through the story. A character theme can also be used to stand in for a character even when they're not present in that scene, or even if they're not present in the story—for example, in the Pixar movie *Up* (2009), the theme for the main character Carl's wife, Ellie, is established in the first few minutes of the movie before she passes away. But even though she's no longer a physically depicted character in the story from that point forward, her influence on Carl motivates the rest of the plot, as evidenced through the development of her musical theme.

- **Revealing unseen implications.** How many times have we watched the hero draw their gun and slowly walk down a deserted alley in search of the villains? Then, the low strings come in with a sustained, swelling note, and we know they're out there somewhere! This is also known as "foreshadowing." The music can tip us off to what is going to happen, either in a suspenseful way, or in a way that hints at the resolution of a situation.
- **Deceiving the audience.** Drawing on the same techniques as revealing unseen implications, but twisting them to create a surprise, the music can set us up to believe something will happen but then a different event takes place. Sometimes known as a "reversal," in this case, the music can play with the scene so as not to give away a twist, as when in a horror movie the score plays the suspense as the main character slowly opens a closet door where they hear scary noises, only to discover that it's just a cat. Or it can add another dimension to a scene that is visually neutral. This is most often used in suspenseful situations.
- **Playing against the scene.** As mentioned, sometimes a cue will run completely counter to what is happening in the story. This is often done to comment on the story or make

a philosophical point—for example, a scene of seemingly heroic battle, underscored with a child soprano singing a lament, might be commenting on the horror of war.

PRACTICAL OR TECHNICAL FUNCTIONS

Practical or technical functions are when the music aids the overall structure of the film:

- **Covering an audio problem.** Sometimes, music is simply needed because there is no (appropriate) sound in the scene. In a *montage sequence*, for example, where time and/or space is compressed by cutting back and forth between different shots, it can be impractical to hear the synchronized sound in each shot. Instead, the score steps in to provide consistency.
- **Pacing.** Try this experiment: watch a scene from a film with the audio muted, and guess how many minutes long the scene was. You're likely to find that watching a film this way makes it seem to take a lot longer than it actually does. This is because one of music's hidden effects is to make time seem to go faster—or sometimes slower, depending on the nature of the music and the context of the scene.
- **Building continuity from scene to scene.** (Also known as "making a transition.") Music can help the viewer make a transition from one scene to another. This is a result of the way the human brain processes information. If we watch a scene that ends, and then we cut to another scene in a different location, obviously, the eye is very aware of this change. Many times, an abrupt visual change is appropriate, but sometimes, it is desirable to soften this change. Music can help achieve this by beginning in the first scene, and carrying over to the second. In this way, both the eye and the ear are engaged. The eye takes in the abrupt scene change, and the ear hears a continuous piece of music. The total effect is one that is smooth; the music effectively overrides the visual aspect.

- **Building continuity of the entire film.** By using themes and textures that return throughout the film, the music can create a continuity of sound. By continually developing one or more elements of the music further, such as certain melodies or instrumentation, the composer can create a dramatic build. This is rarely the only reason that a consistent theme or sonic palette is used, of course. In addition to unifying the score, developing a theme or recognizable musical texture over the course of a film can help tell the story.

MUSIC AS NARRATOR

One powerful way that music can be deployed to serve many of the above functions in combination to tell a story is to establish and then develop a musical theme attached to a character or idea. As explored in the history section earlier, this idea arose from opera and the concept of *leitmotifs*, popularized by Wagner in the 1800s. Since a melodic or rhythmic motif can be transformed musically by modulation, augmentation and diminution, playing it in different instruments and orchestrations, and so forth, they can be very powerful storytelling tools, serving almost as a nonverbal narrator, of sorts.

The film composer perhaps best known for this approach is John Williams. In *E.T., The Extra-Terrestrial* (1982) for example, Williams presents fragments of what we know as the flying theme throughout the first half of the film in various scenes. It is not until the climactic flying scene about one hour into the movie that these fragments come together in a complete musical statement. This is an example of the music developing with the plot. The basic musical idea is similar in several situations, but the audience doesn't hear it as a complete idea until the story line is also complete.

It's not only melodies that can be developed in this way of course. In *Marcel the Shell with Shoes On* (2021), composer Disasterpeace employs a low, whistling sound in the score, that is only at the end of the film revealed as coming from a particular source that's important to the story. Synthesized variations of this sound are developed throughout the score so that when that moment of revelation occurs as to its underlying meaning, it has already taken on a strong subconscious association for the audience.

As we've seen, the storytelling functions of film music are broad-ranging and powerful. The role music plays in a given film overall, or a specific scene, is always front of mind in a film composer's work. There are, however, a lot of other considerations that come into play when scoring a film, and we'll explore them in the next chapter.

CHAPTER 16

Technical Requirements of the Score

There are many composers who can write excellent music, but not all are sensitive to the language of film or a director's vision. Along with the storytelling ability required to discern what function the music serves within the arc of the story, an understanding of film-making itself and the technical requirements of a film is necessary in crafting an effective musical score. Some of the technical choices that need to be made when writing each cue are:

- Tempo. What is the rhythm of the film editing? How are the individual shots cut together? What is the overall pacing of the movie? Are there musical tempos implied by this? Does one go with the implied tempo, or play against it?
- Sync points. Are there many? Just one or two? Or is the music meant to just wash over the scene?
- Is there source music or a song at the beginning or end of the cue that needs to be taken into account in terms of key, tempo, etc.?
- What is this cue's placement in relation to the whole dramatic arc of the film?
- Where is this cue's placement in terms of other cues? Are they close in time? Do the keys have to match?
- Is there dialogue or sound effects, and are they likely to be mixed louder than the score in the dub?
- Are there thematic or motivic ideas that need to be stated in this cue, either verbatim or as a variation?

This list can go on, for the composer must answer many questions and make many choices. But this process is not always a conscious one. In fact, the more experienced a composer gets, the more instinct takes over. Whether instinctual or unconscious, to make the film work, the composer must break down every scene from many angles in order to really make the music fit.

HOW TO APPROACH EACH CUE

You may be wondering, "Once I've got my dramatic concept, how do I start writing?" Which notes to choose is something that cannot be taught in a book. It will be the sum of your musical and personal experience—your ability as a player and composer, how much music you have absorbed over the years through listening and study, your musical philosophy, your life experiences, and your personal outlook. No one can dictate taste and musical choices; that is what gives every composer a unique musical expression. The way to find yours is by doing it—by writing scores, playing gigs, listening, studying, making choices along the way, and learning what works for you. That said, the nuts and bolts of approaching a given cue usually involve the following steps (possibly with some variation in their order):

1. Determine the instrumentation and musical material (theme or texture) to be used in that cue.
2. If writing using a DAW (the most common approach), get that session file set up with the movie file spotted correctly to the music start time for that cue, and the relevant virtual instruments and other elements of the template loaded.
3. Watch the scene several times to determine the most important moments (especially noting any called out in the spotting session), and drop markers into the sequence at those points.
4. Determine an appropriate starting tempo for the scene based on any rhythmic elements in the action or the cutting, or simply your dramatic intuition.
5. Create meter and tempo changes as needed to hit any desired sync points with a musical beat or a bar down-beat. Tempo is the composer's main tool for aligning a beat with a timecode event in the film since tempo is itself

a relationship between beats and clock time, as expressed in its units of "beats per minute." Meter changes effectively allow the conversion of an unaccented beat into a downbeat. For example, if you want to hit beat 2 of bar 2 in 4/4 meter, you could make bar 1 a 5/4 bar, thus converting that important moment into the downbeat of bar 2.

6. Sketch the cue in full, often using piano, string pad, or some form of light orchestration, so that writing can take place fluidly without having to stop frequently to decide many individual orchestration moments.
7. Orchestrate the cue and polish the MIDI, recording acoustic instruments when possible and desirable, so that it's ready to present to the director.
8. Get change notes from the director, and make revisions as necessary until the cue is approved.

The most common variation on this process is to improvise the cue to picture at step 5, rather than starting with a tempo map, and then create the tempo and meter changes needed to match what was played freely. This is more musical and creatively freeing in some cases, especially for composers who have a strong improvisation background. Composer Ben Bromfield for example, who spent five years as a pianist playing live with the famed improv comedy troupe Second City early in his career, describes his approach this way:

> *Before I sit down to write a cue, I have markers in place, and a starting tempo, and a general sense of where things should change. But I find that when I just start improvising, I illuminate new things. Like, I'll make a little space for a joke to land. The way I see it, it's all theoretical until you start writing, so you might as well start writing!*

Some composers prefer to write in notation (whether digital or on paper) rather than directly into a DAW. This is the exception, not the norm, these days, if only because the timelines involved make it much easier to make changes quickly if a cue starts in the DAW and only goes to notation (if at all) once approved and ready to be prepped for a scoring session. However, even composers writing directly into their DAWs might pause from time to time to view their MIDI in notation view to look for patterns, or may work out a tricky modulation or counterpoint on paper before sequencing it.

As you have seen, there is never only one solution to a creative problem, and every composer has their own viewpoint and method of working. There are many variations on the same theme. When writing a score with many cues, there is a lot to consider. Some composers plan every cue for thematic content and key center. Some create as they go, and their basic musicianship enables them to make a unified musical statement as the movie unfolds. Whether you plan everything out or do it on the fly, understanding how the music functions in any situation is crucial to creating a successful score.

SCORING SCENES WITH DIALOGUE AND SOUND EFFECTS

Writing for a scene with a lot of dialogue or sound effects is one of the trickiest things for a composer. There is no one way to do it, for every situation is different. The approach to writing music that plays nicely with these sonic cousins is determined by any number of factors, including the mood of the scene, the pacing of the scene, the amount of sound effects or dialogue present, and the importance of that sound or dialogue to the plot. Ultimately, the music will probably be dubbed, or mixed in, very low under the actors' lines, and may or may not be covered by sound effects. This is the natural fate of film music, for it is meant to accompany the action, and only infrequently does it take a starring role.

There are different schools of thought on the use of music under dialogue. Some believe that it is good to have the music be active when the actors pause and sustain when the actors are speaking. This technique has been used by many composers over the years. It originated far before the advent of film music: the technique of scoring operatic *recitative* (a kind of blend of speech and singing meant to advance the plot) also follows this pattern, from the Baroque through the Romantic periods. Some composers write only sustained tones during dialogue. This is an effective technique in some films. Overall, it is best to consider every situation to be different, having its own musical requirements.

In order to determine the appropriate music for dialogue scenes, there are melodic, harmonic, and orchestrational factors to take into consideration. How active should the melody be? How thick should the chords be? What instruments should play? Here are several questions to consider when writing under dialogue:

- **What is being said?** If the actors are declaring their undying love, or if some important element of the plot is being revealed, then the music must support that mood—and at the same time, stay out of the way. One way to do this is to write a transparent texture that allows the voices to cut through. (A "transparent texture" would be one that has just a few voices spread over one or two octaves, or is centered mostly in the upper-mid and higher registers.) However, sometimes a rich texture is appropriate. The theme could soar into the stratosphere with fully voiced chords going into the lower registers while the actors are speaking, in which case the music will be mixed very low underneath the dialogue. The kinds of intervals used, the tempo, and the overall busyness or simplicity of the melody also contribute to the degree of conflict with this dialogue. Large melodic intervals, quicker tempos, syncopated rhythms, and busy melodies tend to draw the audience's attention to the music and away from the dialogue.
- **Who is speaking?** There are times when a particular register of a certain instrument conflicts with the actor's voice. For example, cello or French horn played between C4 (middle C) and C3 share the same range as most male voices, and they might fight for attention with the dialogue. Instruments between G3 and G4 might fight with a woman's speaking voice. However, counterintuitively, the most important frequencies for understanding dialogue are actually independent of who is speaking. To make out consonants (which aren't voiced) and the formants that let us recognize vowels, the most important frequencies

to avoid in the score, regardless of the dialogue's speaker, are those between 1 kHz and 4 kHz. Put musically, that's between the C6 and C10. These are very high pitches for most instruments, so the successful composer or orchestrator underscoring dialogue will be wise to take especial care when using the highest register of the violins, flutes, oboes, clarinets, and pitched percussion.

- **What is the pacing of the dialogue?** Are the lines spoken quickly, with urgency, or are the actors taking their time? Are there pauses between each line, or do they come rapid-fire, with each line overlapping the previous one? These considerations will help determine how fast the music moves. For example, the composer can accentuate quickly spoken lines with active music, or instead provide a cushion (sometimes called a "bed") for those lines, with long sustained tones.
- **What is the pacing, or tempo, of the film editing?** How the film is edited can provide another clue to finding appropriate music under dialogue. For example, as with the pacing of the actors' lines, the composer can write music that mirrors a lot of fast cuts, or it can soften those cuts with a melody line of long tones.

Perhaps the most important point to make about writing music for dialogue is that the music should not draw too much attention to itself. Ninety-nine percent of the time, the dialogue reigns. If the music draws too much attention to itself, two things are likely: the cue will be rejected and the composer asked to redo it, or it will be dubbed very low in the mix. The best music under dialogue is that which reflects the dramatic situation, can be heard through the speaking, and allows the voices to be in the foreground without any aural conflict. This requires great sensitivity and a good deal of experience on the part of a composer.

When it comes to sound effects, the relative sonic position of the music can be more variable. In cases of Foley and other subtle or atmospheric sounds, it may not be important to hear every detail, and the composer might be able to safely ignore it when writing. However, if there's a big explosion or other foreground sound effect, the composer ignores that at their peril. Sometimes, there is no way to fully avoid the sound effect in terms of frequencies. An explosion, to take that example again, fills the entire frequency space. In such cases, it is generally advisable to leave room for that sound in the score and not try to compete with it. (Or, understand that the music will disappear during that explosion.) In fact, dropping the cue out completely for a moment or two of silence before and during a loud and important sound effect, called a "negative accent" in scoring, is often satisfying dramatically, as well as technically realistic.

In other cases, especially when there is some inherent rhythmic quality to some prominent sound design, the composer can adopt an "if you can't beat 'em, join 'em" mentality. In some cases, the composer actively treats the sound design as though it were part of the rhythm track in their cue. This is especially to be found in some fight scenes. The thwack of punches or clang of swords hitting can sound a lot like drums or cymbals.

One more factor that makes scoring difficult around sound effects, especially, is that the sound design is usually being created at the same time as the score is being composed. The composer may have only production sound, or partial or temporary sound design, and may not be aware of what all the final sound will be. It takes a good deal of forward thinking, imagination, and communication with the director—and when possible, the sound team—to avoid having the sound and music filling the same sonic space or dramatic role in the film. This is especially true if there might be pitched sound effects. Hopefully, in such cases, the composer and sound designer will decide together what key they'll work in, to avoid unintended dissonances. And if there is a conflict between the music and sound effects, a great deal of time will be spent on the dubbing stage to isolate those conflicts and either fix them in the mix or delete a music or sound effects stem.

THE MAIN TITLE

The music that is played at the beginning of the movie or show, when the show's title and main credits are on screen, is called the "main title music," or simply the "main title." (The main credits would be director, producers, composer, screenwriter, etc., with the secondary credits of the larger team or crew at the end of the film.) The goal of the main title music is to set the mood and tone of the film or show. The audience needs to know what kind of story they are about to experience, and the music should tell them that in a succinct way. There are several different approaches to this music, which will be determined by the director's vision. If there are simply credits rolling, with or without location footage, then the music will probably be featured. However, if there is dialogue while the credits are rolling, then the music takes a more subservient role; it will not be so much in the foreground, and act more as an underscore.

It is important to understand that the treatment of credits, and hence the main title music, has changed over the years. For example, during the Golden Age of Hollywood, the main titles were big orchestral statements, often two to three minutes long, with enough time to present one, two, or even three thematic ideas in the style of an opera overture, while almost all of the credits rolled—creative team as well as the crew. During the 1960s, rock or jazz main titles were common, and we began to see the division of credits into the creative team in the beginning and the rest of the team at the end of the film. In the 1990s to 2000s, orchestral styles came back, though with the added dimension of extended ostinatos or synthesizer grooves. And during that time period, another style emerged: one where filmmakers began to opt to not have any credits at the start of the film, saving them for the end only, as the film would start right in on the action.

This paradigm of saving the credits for the end of the film continues to this day in both films and streaming/cable shows. If a director chooses to go with that approach, then if there is music right at the beginning, the composer may start the film with a dramatic cue and not present any important motific material, as they would with the other style of main title.

Some episodic shows maintain the longer main title format (especially historical dramas, like *The Crown* or *Victoria*), but now that viewers can choose to skip the main title with a click, the length of main titles has trended shorter and shorter—as short in some cases as ten or twelve seconds. In these cases, almost like writing a haiku, the composer must choose distinctive and recognizable musical gestures that also serve to sum up the story in some way, putting the audience in the right frame of mind to jump back into an ongoing story. As noted in chapter 7, some composers have started to develop the main title music from episode to episode rather than leaving it the same for an entire season, so that it becomes part of the storytelling as much as the rest of the score. Audiences who reflexively skip it are missing out.

Finally, it should also be noted that although some shows use the exact same recording of the main title music from season to season, it is also common for the main title music to be updated and re-recorded from year to year.

THE END CREDITS

The end credits come, as their name suggests, when the film or show has ended, and all the people that worked on the film are being named. Sometimes, the music in this part of the film is a song, rather than instrumental music based on the underscore. The reason for this is usually commercial. Producers hope that because the song is the last thing heard, that it will stick in people's minds and remind them of the film. This is a logical business decision, but often one that has strange dramatic implications. It can feel like an intrusion when at the end of a two-hour movie with an orchestral underscore, a pop song with a completely different instrumentation suddenly begins.

However, there are many films that do use music by the film's composer to accompany the end credits. In this case, the composer usually develops themes presented during the film. Because of the length of the end credits—often five or six minutes—and the fact that the composer is free from dramatic considerations, this is a chance to write a piece that is more like a suite. Of course, unless kept in their seats in the hopes of a bonus scene, few people remain in the theater to hear this music.

PART IV

Genres and Special Topics

CHAPTER 17

Adapting World and Period Music

One of the important skills for the modern film composer is to be able to incorporate music from different cultures, countries, or time periods into their scores. If the location of the film is a country other than where it was made, the characters are from different parts of the world, or the story takes place in an earlier time, a director may want to reflect that culture or time period to varying degrees in the music. How much of that music a composer integrates into the score can range from it being fully authentic to the culture, or to just being a hint or a taste that is part of a larger, traditional film score ensemble.

In this chapter, we will give an overview of the important issues to consider when composing this kind of score, as well as the decisions that need to be made based on the director's desires and the target audience.

It should be noted that this discussion will be largely from the viewpoint of a composer of an American production. This is necessary for the purposes of discussion within the confines of one chapter of this book. However, the concepts presented can be applied to any cultural combination. For example, a Korean composer writing for a Hollywood western, a Danish composer writing for a Japanese film, or a Mexican composer writing for a film taking place in Greece. In all cases, the composer must understand their own frame of reference and what the musical frame of reference is both for the audience in the country in the film's story and for the audience of its home country.

In addition, the semantics of this topic are admittedly troublesome. For decades, when Hollywood composers referred to music from around the world, they would call it "ethnic music." This meant everything that was not in the Western traditions of classical, pop, folk, or jazz. Around the 1990s, the term "world music" replaced that of "ethnic," attempting to be more inclusive, despite the obvious fact that all music is world music. For the purposes of this book, and to generally be in line with contemporary usage, we have decided to continue to use this terminology.

OUR SHRINKING PLANET

Our shared planet earth has seemed to become smaller over time, as travel and communication technologies have developed, and the cross-cultural sharing of ideas that once took months or years has become something we take for granted. In music, we see this manifest in myriad ways, as artists from many different countries and of diverse genres collaborate with each other. What once was exotic now feels like part of the everyday fabric of musical life. For example, in the 1960s, the Beatles began using Indian instruments, like sitar and tanpura, in their recordings—sounds that were unusual and stimulating to their listeners' imaginations, creating an aural image of far-off locations. A few years earlier, Japanese artist Kyu Sakamoto broke through to pop music in America, with his hit song called "Sukiyaki," which used a pentatonic scale to represent his country's musical stylings. As far as the American audience of the 1960s was concerned, combined with a distinct Asian voice, this was different enough from the music they were used to hearing that it could create an association in their minds that said "Japan."

Today's world is different. Because of the internet, people around the world have a familiarity with other cultures that was not previously possible. This results in the fluid exchange of music. Many musicians and non-musicians alike know exactly what the instruments, scales, and overall presentation of music from cultures other than their own should sound like. Again, take the example of the Beatles using Indian music. In the 1960s, there were few people in the West who could define the difference between Indian classical music vs. devotional music vs. popular music. However, today many people in different countries can quickly distinguish Bollywood or Indian popular music from a traditional presentation of a classical raga. In addition, our listening standards as a world culture are higher, and our need for some degree of authenticity is higher. Thanks to high quality sample libraries, instant communication via the internet, and the ease of international travel, composers today can achieve a level of authenticity not previously possible.

REALISTIC OR NOT?

When creating a score that incorporates music of a culture different from one's own, or needing to reflect a certain time period, there are many possible questions to answer (see the very end of this chapter), but here are some basic questions to ask up front:

- How "real" or authentic does the music need to be when used in a film?
- Who is the target audience, and what are their musical expectations?

The decisions regarding the amount of music a composer incorporates from the desired culture—what kind of instruments, scales, rhythms, and overall production—is derived from the desires of the director. The balance between culturally derived music and generic Western-style film score music can be heavily weighted towards one or the other, and can even shift during the course of a film. A composer must listen carefully to the director in conversations and understand the intentions of a temp track before deciding how realistic to be.

In addition, it is important for a composer to know the primary target audience of a film. Even though today an audience can ultimately be worldwide, if it is an English-language movie made in the U.S., then the primary audience would be different from that of a Hindi film made in Mumbai, or a Korean film made in Seoul. Audiences in these different locations have a different frame of reference towards film music, and it is the composer's job to understand the milieu in which they are working.

Let's consider a few films that illustrate different approaches to creating a hybrid of Western and world music. In *Life of Pi*, composer Michael Danna uses a combination of Indian instruments such as bansuri flute, sarod, and Indian vocals, in combination with a string section playing a drone and/or a shifting chord progression. This is done to represent the main character's home in Pondicherry, India. *Life of Pi* is an English-language Hollywood produced film that has strong influences from India in story, character, and music. In fact, the opening music of the movie is a song that is Western in form and harmonic progression, and Indian in melodic and vocal presentation. It also has a hint of French music, using an accordion, because Pondicherry was at one time a French colony. It is therefore a hybrid in the use of instruments from three traditions: Indian, French, and Western orchestral. The melodic ideas in the film itself (after the main title song) are based on a raga, but don't sound like a classical Indian music performance. This kind of hybrid fits the dramatic story perfectly, enhances the audience's experience of the unfolding story, and appeals to Western and Indian audiences, as well as audiences around the world.

Another example is *Black Panther* (2018). For this project, composer Ludwig Göransson was not just referencing a location or a character's heritage; he had to create the sound of the mythical world of Wakanda. Before writing the score, Göransson traveled around Africa for several weeks to research and absorb the sounds of various traditions. In Senegal, he met Baaba Maal, a popular Senegalese singer and guitar player, and was able to accompany him on tour before going into a studio to record some local musicians. Göransson used a talking drum to represent the king and a Fula flute for one of the other characters. In this way, the African instruments became interwoven with the characters and the unfolding story.

Another film that references Black culture in a different context is *Get Out*. This is a psychological horror thriller about a Black photographer from New York who goes upstate to meet his girlfriend's parents—with all kinds of dark events unfolding. Composer Michael Abels wanted to find a language that referenced African-American culture while still staying dramatically on point. He used voices in the Swahili language as well as some blues motifs, admittedly not trying to be authentic to any one part of the African or African-American experience, but simply creating a sound that would enhance the story and place the audience in roughly the right cultural context.

Yet another example is that of Germaine Franco, composer for Encanto and songwriter, music producer, additional music composer, and orchestrator for *Coco*. Franco's family is originally from northern Mexico, and she spent many of her college years researching and traveling to and from that country. For *Coco*, she worked with underscore composer Michael Giacchino to create the sound of Mexico, and she went to Mexico City to oversee and produce the recording sessions in Spanish for both the source music and the songs in the film.

> *On* Coco, *there are multiple indigenous flutes played by the amazing Pedro Eustache. He has an incredible collection of bamboo, clay, and wood flutes from around the world. Sometimes, we used an alto or bass flute if the key was too awkward for a bamboo flute. Most of the bamboo flutes are diatonic. It can be difficult to play parts that use too much chromaticism. Sometimes, one cue would require starting and stopping multiple times to employ different flutes for new key changes. Also, we used "toyos," which are large South American pan pipes with a thunderous sound. We didn't say "we can only use Mexican flutes," but in fact we used instruments from around South America and even some Chinese flutes, because given the migration patterns of people from Asia, there are many similarities between Mexican and Chinese flutes.*

Franco said this about her work on *Encanto*, which takes place in Colombia:

> *On* Encanto, *I worked with the filmmakers Byron Howard, Jared Bush, and Charise Castro-Smith to create my impression of the sound of magical realism specific to Colombian music itself. This project was produced during the pandemic. Unfortunately, I was not able to travel to Colombia. My quest was to blend traditional*

Colombian instruments such as the marimba de chonta, gaitas, bandolas, arpa llanera, tiple, and tamboras, with traditional Western orchestral elements. I spent many hours playing and studying the traditional styles of music within Colombia such as joropo, vallenato, cumbia, pasillo, Afro-Colombian, as well as contemporary pop, hip-hop, and classical music. After I immersed myself in the sounds of the country, I explored how to weave the sounds and rhythms into the score while synching them to picture, in order to mesh them with the beautiful world created by the film-makers. I think it is essential to explore sounds, styles, and instruments before sitting down to write. It was a wonderful project. I strove to elevate the incredible music of Colombia, a very musically diverse and beautiful country.

In all of these examples, the composer took great care to find the right melodic, harmonic, and instrumental tools that would blend with a larger orchestral ensemble in order to create the sound they desired that would tell the story of the film and enhance the audience's experience of the location and/or characters.

RESEARCH

One of the primary concepts to understand in adapting the music of another culture is how each culture hears certain musical gestures. Different audiences may interpret a music phrase—a melodic idea, a harmonic shift, or a rhythmic groove—in different ways. For example, if an American audience hears a complex raga scale played by bansuri flute, they may think that is exotic. However, an audience in India will take that in stride and perhaps might even know the emotional intent of that raga as it corresponds to the story of a film.

Composers must be able to distill an enormous amount of information and musical concepts into what will likely be a few succinct musical ideas representing a particular culture. So, when embarking on a project that involves the music from another culture, there are several tasks a composer may take on in order to assimilate and write music that communicates well. It is important to understand that when operating under a deadline, the composer must be efficient in how they go about researching or absorbing new music. It cannot be done as a musicologist might, spending years on a dissertation. Few projects offer a composer the luxury of spending weeks or months actually visiting a certain location, as Ludwig Göransson did for *Black Panther*. Instead, for most projects the film composer must cut quickly to ascertain the main musical concepts of the music of that culture that can be utilized in the score. Here are a few main tasks to consider:

- **Listening.** Composers will listen deeply to the music of the culture they are adapting—often listening for hours and to many different artists. In this way, they will absorb the sounds of the music and can extract melodic, harmonic, instrumental, and rhythmic ideas for their score.
- **Scale sources.** This can provide an enormous amount of material that immediately communicates "that culture!" to an audience. For example, a scale like this: C D♭ E F G A♭ B C, having two augmented seconds, immediately tells the Western audience that we are in the Middle East, India, Pakistan, or perhaps North Africa.
- **Instruments that are commonly associated with a certain culture.** Sitar in India. Balalaika in Russia. Bouzouki in Greece. All of these, as well as many other instruments specific to one part of the world, would instantly place an audience in those countries.
- **Rhythms and grooves.** Different rhythms can instantly place us in a certain country or part of the world. For example, a samba instantly says "Brazil." A tango tells us, "Argentina," and a tarantella lets us know "Italy."
- **Tuning.** As equal temperament (exported from Western Europe) is the standard for the performance of tonal music in any part of the world, music that is not performed to that standard can sound weird, odd, or out of tune to those who grew up with equal temperament. This is a concept that a film composer must take into serious consideration if the music being adapted is not based on equal temperament and is being used in a score with both the equal tempered

instruments and the non-equally tempered ones. People who only know equal temperament will have that tuning system as part of their deep-rooted musical expectations, and anything outside of it sounds "off." On the other hand, those who were raised in countries where the music is not equal tempered have a much different frame of reference.

When examining the traditional music of cultures around the world, we find that many, if not most, do not follow equal temperament unless hybridized with Western influences. For example, the traditional music of Japan, China, India, many African cultures, Native Americans, and so many others are based on scale sources that are not equally tempered. In these traditions, it is important to note that they are often essentially monophonic in nature. In other words, they do not follow a harmonic system of changing chord structures. So, when adapting instruments or vocal lines from different cultures, a composer must be sensitive to the tuning and the ability of the instrumentalist or vocalist to fit with a Western arrangement of chords.

CULTURAL APPROPRIATION

When incorporating the music of other cultures—that is to say, cultures other than your own—into a film, there is the need to be sensitive and respectful. As part of the filmmaking team, a composer will be following the lead of the director and producers, in terms of how different cultures are represented. That representation is critical, both in telling the story of the movie, as well as how the movie is received by the world at large.

This idea of how a film is received brings us to one of the hot-button topics of the past few years, both in Hollywood and in our society at large: cultural appropriation. Simply put, *cultural appropriation* can be defined as one person's inappropriate borrowing from a culture they do not come from. It is when musical and other traditions of different cultures are used in the arts by people not of that culture in a way that could be seen as trivializing, disparaging, or misrepresenting important icons, symbols, social mores, or even clothing.

Many pop music stars—Katy Perry, Iggy Azalea, Pharrell—have created controversy in recent years for incorporating sets and costumes from places like Japan, Egypt, and India in their music videos, even if the song has nothing to do with that culture. Some people think that this is okay because it is entertaining and falls under "artistic license." Others think it is inappropriate and falls in the category of cultural appropriation, where the artist is harming or denigrating a particular culture, even if inadvertently. The issue is not cut and dry.

It is in this environment of what constitutes cultural appropriation and who gets to decide if the threshold of appropriateness has been crossed that composers of the mid twenty-first century find themselves. However daunting that might seem on the surface, the way to navigate this issue is not difficult. Spending as much time as possible learning about not just the music but also the social, spiritual, religious and even political traditions of a culture, gives one a broad understanding that hopefully will translate to a sensitive and respectful approach.

It must be mentioned that until about the 1980s, Hollywood as a filmmaking community did not try to be realistic or even respectful to either the traditions or the music of other cultures. Many different cultural groups including Native Americans, Mexicans, people from any Middle Eastern countries, and Asians were often depicted in a stereotypical and disparaging manner. Music scores unfortunately often followed suit in that they used melodic and instrumental clichés that may have a distant connection to a certain culture but were so homogenized that in hindsight we can say that they often fit the definition of being insensitive and even disparaging. This includes the famous parallel fourths in a low octave to represent Native Americans, a generic pentatonic scale for anyone from Asia, and the cliché major scale with an augmented second played by oboe to represent anyone from various countries in the Middle East or northern Africa. However, as we have seen with the previous examples, it can be said that there has been a huge improvement in the attitude and respect toward other cultures both in the music and in the overall filmmaking process.

ADAPTING PERIOD WESTERN MUSIC

In addition to adapting the music of different cultures, sometimes a film composer must adapt the music of different time periods of Western history (and possibly the musical history of any culture). This can be equally as tricky as adapting the music of different cultures when it comes back to the recurring question: How authentic do I have to be? For example, the 1994 film *The Madness of King George* takes place in England in the late 1700s, when the sonata-allegro classical style of Hayden and Mozart was in full bloom. However, the score uses the music of Handel, which was written in a Baroque style of some fifty to seventy-five years earlier. The question becomes: Does it matter? Would anyone but someone extremely knowledgeable about Western classical music even notice? Is the early 1700s music of Handel close enough to a story taking place in the 1790s? To take another hypothetical example, if a film takes place in Italy in the 1300s, but the music used is that of Palestrina from the 1500s, would anyone know, and does it sound ancient enough to work for most audiences?

In order to determine how much music should be used from a particular time period, the composer needs to listen carefully in the beginning stages of conversations with a director. Directors have made thousands of decisions regarding the sets, costumes, dialogue, lighting, pacing, etc., and these decisions can reflect a finely tuned attention to detail that will indicate their intention for historical authenticity and accuracy. So, the film composer must have a clear understanding of the wishes of the director in terms of how much the score incorporates the music of the time period when the film takes place.

Although there are many times when authenticity can be flexible, there are times when it is required. If a film takes place in Europe between about 500 CE and 1000 CE, there is a good chance that a director might desire some reference to the music of that time in the score. That music would be plainchant throughout that time period, or organum (early polyphony) in the last hundred years of that timeframe. As there are thousands of recordings of these styles, theoretically, all a film composer would have to do is a lot of listening. On the other hand, there are hundreds of books and thousands of articles written about chant and organum, and diving into that material is the life's work of a musicologist. So, the job of the film composer is to do some deep listening and commit to some research of the music of the time in order to gain a deeper understanding and distill any ideas that become dramatically appropriate for the project.

Once the composer has done the necessary research, usually the next task is to come up with a hybrid sound with a modern sense of orchestration, harmony, and melody. The reason for having a hybrid is that the musical styles of older times do not speak emotionally to the modern audience in the way they did at the time of their composition. As music has developed, so have the expectations and understanding of the audiences. Therefore, a modern hybrid film score will often include choices from this menu: a contemporary orchestra, modernized harmonization of an ancient melody, authentic instruments of the time period, voices utilized in a style that evokes the time period, rhythmic ideas, and electronic and synthesized instruments.

DELIBERATE ANACHRONISM

One approach that is being used is to inject references to popular music of the twenty-first century in a period movie. A great example is that of the Netflix series *Bridgerton*. This show takes place in the early 1800s in England, but uses covers and arrangements of contemporary songs from artists such as Beyoncé, Rihanna, Harry Styles, Adele, and others. For some, this can be a major disconnect—watching a scene taking place two hundred years ago with a string quartet playing an arrangement of a pop or R&B song. However, the intention of the show's creators is to place the audience in that time period without being historically accurate. Indeed, many of the characters represent different races, ethnic groups, and nationalities, when the aristocracy of England at that time would have been 100% white. The show is intended to be in a reimagined world, not one that is historically authentic or correct.

With that intention of the show's creators, a composer can take their direction in creating the covers, arrangements and quotes from twenty-first century artists. In addition to the covers of pop artists, the producers of *Bridgerton* used the classical music of *The Tales of Hoffmann* by Offenbach, composed in 1881, and Shostakovich's *Suite for Jazz Orchestra No. 2* from 1938—clearly historical inaccuracies, but somehow fitting the mood and overall presentation of the show.

This chapter has presented many musical considerations as well as social issues to be aware of when composing a score that adapts music of different cultures or of a particular time period. Earlier in this chapter, we proposed two guiding questions—how realistic must the music be, and what are the audience's expectations? In light of the material presented here, here is a more comprehensive set of questions for composers to ask themselves that sum up the concepts presented in this chapter:

1. What do I need to know about the people, cultural traditions, and religion/spirituality of this culture or these people, and how would that knowledge interact with the music?
2. What are the broader stylistic divisions and genres of this particular music?
3. Which of these styles is most relevant to the film?
4. What are the primary instruments used?
5. What kind of scale sources are used?
6. What tuning system is used?
7. Are there any musical gestures or clichés that immediately inform the non-musical audience of the location or origin of the people in this film? (instruments, scale sources, etc.)
8. How will people of this culture perceive my use of their music? How realistic or historically correct does the music need to be?

CHAPTER 18

Documentaries

Scoring documentaries (and other nonfiction genres) is in many ways the same as scoring fiction. The process of scoring goes through the same steps, and the roles in both the filmmaking and scoring teams are generally the same. However, documentary stands as a distinct form that has special considerations for composers. Unlike their scripted, fictional counterparts, these films at least purport to deal with truth, offering their audiences a window into real lives, events, and phenomena in a way different even from "inspired by true events" biopics and docudramas, which are still fictionalized. Documentaries, by their very nature, embody a commitment to authenticity, seeking to capture something essential without the embellishments of scripted narratives. The responsibility implied in this mission can also impact the approach to their scores, as the ethical implications play a bigger role in the composer's decisions. Documentary composer Miriam Cutler notes:

> *There's an important component of documentary filmmaking that has to do with journalistic ethics. In the documentary community, these are constant, public discussions of how they deal with these things.*

Composers working on documentaries must be aware of these discussions and what their responsibilities are as part of a documentary filmmaking team to adhere to these ethical standards musically. That might mean being more attuned than normal to how authentic the music should be to its subject, or how much the score should lead the audience towards a particular feeling or viewpoint about the topic of the film.

DOCUMENTARY FILM HISTORY

The history of documentary films goes back almost to the beginning of filmmaking, with the term "documentary" initially being used to refer to a film in 1926.[6] The first film generally accepted to be an example of this genre is Robert Flaherty's 1922 *Nanook of the North*, though since several scenes in the film were staged, and family relationships simulated, it isn't a pure documentary. In these early days of experimentation with cinema, filmmakers were still feeling out the boundaries and potentials of these forms, not to mention the ethics involved. In the opening title cards of the film, Flaherty acknowledges that he cast one man in the role of the "typical Eskimo," following the failure of his more purely ethnographic filming of Inuit life. The film's subtitle *A Story of Life and Love in the Actual Arctic* likewise nods to the combination of staged story and actual events.

Of course, *Nanook* and other documentaries of that early period were silent films, but the role of music in documentary films was clear since the beginning of the sound era. A hundred-plus years of film history later, documentaries make up an important, if lower-budget and scrappier, part of the film landscape, and a significant portion of broadcast television and streaming media is some form of nonfiction.

DOCUMENTARY SUBGENRES

Present-day documentaries can be subdivided into several subgenres or "modes," as analyzed by film critic Bill Nichols in his book *Introduction to Documentary*.[7] Each mode calls for a different scoring approach:

1. **Observational Documentaries.** Observational documentaries take a fly-on-the-wall approach, capturing real-life moments with as little interference as possible. Examples include *Salesman* (1969), which uses no underscore, and

Hoop Dreams (1994), which features both contemporary songs and a jazz-inflected underscore. There is often little to no music in these types of documentaries to go along with the *verité* style of filmmaking and keep it feeling raw and real.

2. **Expository Documentaries.** In expository documentaries, the primary goal is to convey information or present an argument. Examples include nature documentaries such as *March of the Penguins* (2005), which has a sweeping hybrid synth and acoustic score, or historical series like *Victory at Sea* (1952 to 1953) with its iconic melodic orchestral themes. This kind of documentary often employs narration or other voiceover to make explicit points, and music to serve as a guiding force, reinforcing key points and creating a cohesive narrative. In this style, as in many fiction films, clear motifs and structured compositions can help tell the story or, in this case, make the needed expository point. A well-crafted score can also enhance the viewer's understanding and engagement by allowing them to keep their focus through sometimes dense information.
3. **Participatory Documentaries.** Participatory documentaries involve the filmmaker as an active participant, though unlike performative documentaries (see #6, following), the filmmaker is not personally a subject of the film. Examples of this approach include films by Erroll Morris (*The Fog of War*, 2003) and Michael Moore (*Sicko*, 2007), both of whom are audibly and/or visibly present in their films. The music can echo this involvement by incorporating the filmmaker's perspective into the score, being more directly emotional or subjective than is favored in other genres.
4. **Reflexive Documentaries.** Reflexive documentaries prompt viewers to question the nature of documentary filmmaking itself, as in Orson Welles' fascinating *F for Fake* (1973), which is also a participatory documentary. In such cases, the music can play a pivotal role in reinforcing the self-awareness of the documentary by experimenting with

unconventional timbres and forms, and playing with levels of reality by employing source scoring approaches.

5. **Poetic Documentaries.** Poetic documentaries prioritize aesthetics and emotion over traditional narrative. Here, the music can be a powerful tool to evoke feelings and enhance the visual poetry of the documentary. Famous examples are *Koyaanisqatsi* (1982) and its sequels by Godfrey Reggio, in which the minimalist scores by Philip Glass, which use mostly triadic ostinato-type figures and percussion that mirrors the changes in tempo and intensity of the editing and film speed of the various scenes. These scores take an equal role with the visuals in creating the experience of the film for the audience. Just as the films in this subgenre are themselves experimental and abstract, composers can be equally unconventional in scoring these films, with nonlinear compositions and unique timbres.
6. **Performative Documentaries.** Performative documentaries weave the filmmakers' personal journey into the narrative, and range greatly in style, from 1926 Soviet silent film *Man with a Movie Camera* by and about Dziga Vertov (a film that also pioneered multiple film and editing techniques still employed today) to 2004's *Supersize Me.* The music in these types of films can be wide-ranging in style, and often overlaps in tone with one of the previously described subgenres.

HYBRID DOCUMENTARIES

The preceding analysis only covers pure documentaries—those that aim to show something real, or at least to express something true. Several prominent nonfiction-adjacent genres, notably reality television, purport to be a form of documentary (often observational), but behind the scenes, they are heavily scripted or fictionalized. As we saw in the very first documentary, *Nanook of the North,* seemingly unscripted moments can be set up or manipulated in editing to be more dramatic or follow a predetermined plot arc. Since the aim of reality television shows (such as *Survivor* and its many spin-offs and imitators) is to build and keep viewership, this is especially true in these forms.

There are also *mockumentaries.* These fully fictional comedy films are parodies of documentary forms, making use of the tropes of each subgenre to poke fun at documentaries themselves or at the subject of the mockumentary. Famous examples of this form include 1984's *This Is Spinal Tap* and several subsequent films by its co-writer and star Christopher Guest, and the mockumentary series *Documentary Now!,* which systematically spoofs each of the most famous documentary films. Even some sitcoms, such as *The Office,* adopt a fake documentary style and premise. Mockumentaries are not new, however—in fact, they are as old as documentary films themselves. The first, *A Tough Winter,* is a parody of *Nanook of the North,* and was released just one year after its target, in 1923.

COMPARISON TO FICTION FILM SCORING

The process of scoring a documentary is essentially the same as that of scoring a scripted, fiction film, as mentioned previously. However, the process of making a documentary film often takes many years. During that process, which subjects are most interesting emerges, as more information is gathered. For this reason, composers working on documentaries need to be aware that they may be on an extended timetable, and that even main characters for which they may have developed themes may be changed or eliminated in the course of post-production.

The actual music written for a documentary film may be more or less similar to music in a narrative fiction film, depending on the subgenre and the filmmaker's tastes, though in documentaries meant to educate an audience about an issue, it's more common for the filmmaker to take pains for the audience not to feel manipulated by the music. As audiences grow more familiar with filmmaking techniques, if a film feels like a propaganda piece, it may in fact be less convincing than one in which the audience feels free to make up their own minds. In these cases, filmmakers and composers often favor ambient sounds and minimalist compositions to enhance the immersive experience for the audience without prodding them towards any particular emotion. This is more difficult to do than it sounds, as "neutral music" is almost a contradiction in terms given the great power of music to affect our emotions. One technique called for a lot in documentaries to remain ethically neutral, while also making room for often extensive narration or voiceover, is to write what are called "beds"—essentially, underscore cues that stay in the background, avoiding things like big percussive events or strong melodies that might distract or lead the audience.

Miriam Cutler again:

> *There's not as many music-driven moments in independent documentaries, so there's a lot of beds, but I feel very strongly that those beds can have integrity as music. You can do wonderful variations of your theme: stretch them out, make them shorter, faster, a lot of things. You just always have to be really careful about not imposing the music on the film. You have to leave enough bandwidth for the dialogue.*

Since independent documentaries are also more likely to be labors of love for a filmmaker (especially if it's participatory or reflective), and the markets for these types of films vary greatly based on the entertainment potential involved, documentary films often have lower budgets and longer timelines. Like documentary filmmakers, composers who are called to work in this space are usually motivated not only by a desire to be a film composer, but also out of a desire to use their music to make a difference and effect positive change in the world. Cutler shares:

> *I became a documentary composer because the people that are making these films are my kind of people. They're my tribe. They're people who are deeply committed to what they're doing. They're artistic, they're independent. And it really is based on sharing values and sharing common interest and respect, and respecting them as artists and creators, and committed humans with high values, ethical values.*

One compensation for working within a lower budget, in addition to the personal satisfaction that's possible, is that composers can often successfully negotiate to keep the copyright in their music, as opposed to being forced to accept the terms of "work made for hire" contracts that are expected in bigger-budget studio and network productions. We'll explore this further in chapter 22.

CHAPTER 19

Animation

Though the word "animation," at least in the U.S., is likely to evoke a particular subgenre based on *Looney Tunes* and early Disney animations, there are as many types of animated films and shows as there are live-action. (Note that films with real actors are referred to as "live-action" films, in order to distinguish them from animation, where the characters are drawn.) Animated films or shorts encompass the full range of filmmaking expression; they can be overtly comedic, poignant, tense thrillers, mysteries, romances, and every other variation of the human story. Animation can be scored in an old-fashioned style, with lots of sync points, or it can be scored in the same manner as a live-action film. The process of scoring animation is similar to scoring live-action. However, there can be differences in both the aesthetic and technical approaches that are notable enough to be worth exploring.

THE EARLY DAYS OF ANIMATION

As discussed, film music styles were very different in the first decades of talkies from what they are today. In the 1930s, the music was likely to hit many pieces of action and comment on almost every emotion the actors showed. When the first cartoons came out, the musical approach was the same, though taken to an extreme. Almost every movement—whether the characters were falling in love, having a knock-down-drag-out fight, or simply pacing in a room—was reflected in the music. The term "mickey-mousing" refers to this style where the music mimics every little thing, as in the early Mickey Mouse cartoons.

Two of the most successful composers for cartoons in the early days of film were Scott Bradley, who did most of the *Tom and Jerry* cartoons, and Carl Stalling of Warner Bros.' *Looney Tunes.* These two composers set the standard for the industry. At first, cartoon music was a thrown-together jumble of snatches of different melodies taken from other sources—an extension, really, of the silent film fake book. Both Stalling and Bradley decided that something different could be done, and went about finding a way to accompany the cartoons that was interesting and had musical integrity. The dilemma facing them (and composers today) was the sheer number of sync points—as many as thirty or forty in a thirty-second cue—coupled with the fact that the action of the cartoons was irregular, in terms of musical beats. Somehow, a way had to be found to make the music seem regular. Mixed meters were a way to make musical accents fall on downbeats, yet cartoons had so many places where the music needed to hit the action that it was impossible to have every hit on a downbeat. One solution was the creation of a melody line that stretched over an entire sequence, and the hits in the music would be mostly in the accompaniment to the melodic line. This was more elegant than simply stringing together bits of folksongs, nursery tunes, and arias, which was the prior practice and tended to sound quite choppy.

In addition to mickey-mousing everything in the early cartoons, and despite the desire to achieve a more musical solution than simply linking familiar melodies, it became a convention to parody familiar pieces of music in a humorous way. This is probably a logical extension of the way well-known tunes were used during the silent film era. For example, sunrise became the "Morning Mood" from Grieg's *Peer Gynt,* and if a character was drunk, a song like "How Dry I Am" or "Little Brown Jug" would play. Many classical and popular pieces were quoted or parodied. To score these moments, composers still used the old silent-film fake books of Rapée or Becce, since these books provided dozens of excerpts of many different kinds of melodies.

The process for the composer in the early days of cartoons was different from today. Today, the composer generally receives a digital copy of the film, and the composer scores to that cut of the picture. In the early days of animation, the composer often would not even see the film before the music was recorded. After a spotting session with the director, the composer would receive a *detail sheet*, also called an "exposure sheet." (This nomenclature varied from studio to studio.) Prolific cartoon composer Richard Stone described the exposure sheet, as it was called at Warner Bros.:

> *These sheets laid out the action on paper and were a sort of mini storyboard. The director would decide, for instance, how fast a character was walking, and would have this very elaborate sheet saying, "Daffy is walking across the street taking a step every eight frames." This information would be copied onto the exposure sheet giving Stalling a description of all the action and the frame measurements of all the action. That is what he wrote to.*

Once the composer had the frame measurement, it was just a matter of math to figure out the rhythm and timings of these moments. The exposure sheet also had music staves below these verbal descriptions so the composer could fill in the sketched music. In order to hit all of the sync points, simply conducting freetimed with a clock or punches-and-streamers for reference proved inadequate, so these composers innovated. The first use of a click track on a scoring stage was for cartoon scores, and was accomplished by repurposing film reels to generate sound at regular intervals by punching holes in the film on certain frames. Today, the click track (now in digital format) is ubiquitous as a synchronization tool for scoring sessions, and it owes a great deal to its origins as a mechanism for effective mickey-mousing.

Occasionally, the composer would receive a pencil reel or a storyboard of the film. A *pencil reel* is a black and white rough-cut with line drawings as opposed to complete animation. A *storyboard* is a series of boxes on a page, like a comic book, that sums up the story and the action and includes timings for each box. Storyboards are still used today, but since animation is more often digital now rather than hand-drawn, pencil reels have given way to *animatics*—a rough animation that might be partly animated and partly storyboard with timings. Animatics are what today's composers are usually scoring to.

The composers of the early cartoons were remarkable and often unappreciated. They had fine music skills in composition, orchestration, and conducting, and they were often self-taught. They had an innate sense of drama and what was needed in a film. They were innovators and inventors. And, of course, they had a great sense of humor.

LOONEY TUNES'S NEXT GENERATION

Even as other genres of animation were on the rise in the 1990s, Warner Bros. continued to use the musical style originally developed by Carl Stalling in the 1930s. Cartoon series like *Tiny Toons, Animaniacs,* and *The Sylvester & Tweety Mysteries* all used devices that were popular in the early days of cartoon scoring: traditional orchestras, mickey-mousing action to the smallest detail, and quotes from well-known songs and classical pieces. Creating this kind of show was demanding because the music is constant and there are so many hits. Richard Stone was the supervising composer of many of these next generation Warner Bros. cartoons, and he describes the process:

> *It's like anything else. We still sit with the producer and have a spotting session. In our case, the music is wall to wall; the decisions are not where the music starts and stops, as in a feature film or a live-action television show. In our shows the music never stops. So the question at the spotting session is always about musical style, and what specific things we're going to hit—how loudly and with what instrumentation. We might talk about which public domain tunes we will use....*
>
> *What we do is an outgrowth of Carl Stalling's style, trying to stay in sync with as many things on screen as we can. Characters walking across the screen with pizzicato celli and a bassoon; if a boulder falls on somebody, it will have a piano glissando on it; the xylophone eye-blink, and*

all the rest of those clichés. We also try to do musical puns with folk songs—public domain tunes that we can use. We quote from the classical literature all the time.

A team of composers worked on these shows. Typically, they rotated and did one show every two weeks. William Ross describes being one of several composers working on episodes for *Tiny Toons*:

They were about as hard as anything you want to do. It's like working inside this little tiny box because of the number of hits. Music has seams, let's say, and so the number of seams you have to do in cartoons is a lot. As a composer, I find that most of my time is spent making the seams seamless. Once I get a texture I like, it's easy to continue it for five, six, seven minutes. But every time I have to transition that texture to another one, it takes a lot of thought.

Tiny Toons *takes that to a whole new level. In the course of a few seconds, you may have ten hits. I know that sounds ridiculous, but there are lots and lots of hits—things you need to address where the music has to do something in these few seconds. So I would have a thirty-second cue that had forty things I had to hit. I tried to limit the number.*

It was difficult for any of the composers to take on an entire episode and finish it by themselves. It was essentially nineteen minutes of music that had to be done in a week or two. It wasn't for the faint of heart. People would be on the floor trying to figure out how to get through this nineteen minutes of music. Those that had arranging experience and could manipulate melodies seemed to fair well. I got to where I could do two minutes a day.

This honest assessment of the difficulty of writing for an old-style cartoon makes one appreciate the work of Stalling and Bradley even more. That they could crank out enormous amounts of music that worked effectively with the picture, day-in and day-out, shows the high degree of skill they had.

ANIMATED DRAMAS AND ACTION SHOWS

Another type of animation that became popular in the 1990s and has remained so through today is the dramatic or action show. Such shows are often based on popular and established intellectual property such as a comic-book series or film franchise, and are scored like regular live-action shows. The music does not mickey-mouse every move on screen; rather, it simply tries to support and enhance the visual action.

The process of scoring is also largely the same as in live-action for these shows. The composer receives a video copy of the show, there is a spotting session, and the score is composed, recorded, and mixed using anything from fully in-the-box to fully live orchestra, with a lot of room in the middle for hybrid production. Whereas the Warner Bros. cartoons feature wall-to-wall music, in an animated drama, the music comes in and out as needed. The biggest difference between scoring this kind of animation and live action shows is that by the time the composer's work begins, the dialogue is already final, because it must be recorded first for the animators to lip sync the characters, but the visuals may still be in animatic form, or at least, not fully rendered. This means the composer must use their imagination more to get a sense of the final look of the film, but can rely on the timings when underscoring dialogue.

Batman: The Animated Series was one of the first such shows to gain wide popularity, beginning in 1992. Lead composer Shirley Walker described a writing process for that show, which will sound familiar from chapter 10:

> *It has been an interesting process on the* Batman *show. From the beginning, I was establishing the musical style of the series. I wrote the first several shows myself just to get the whole thing up and going. I also wrote the themes for the major characters. So for the first number of years of* Batman, *any main theme was mine.*
>
> *Ultimately, all of the composers that are in the rotation now worked their way up from orchestrating on the shows I was writing. Then they got to write a few cues,*

then maybe a half of the show, and then finally, I would give them a whole show of their own. So it's a great way to reward the people who really paid their dues. I like to go to the spotting, and I look at their show once they've got everything on its way. We go through every cue and make sure that there's not a misread somewhere, or something that I think could be handled in a different way. But the composers working for me now are excellent, and it is satisfying to see how they've all come along in their careers.

Watching some of these shows from the 1990s to 2000s, like *Batman*, *Superman*, and *Justice League*, one can see the aesthetic transition that had been made, from wall-to-wall music in a previous era to music used in the same way as a live action series, coming in and out as needed, with periods of no music at all: just dialogue and sound effects.

COMEDY BEYOND *LOONEY TUNES*

One of the most difficult things to decide in any comedy film, whether live action or animated, is when to be musically funny and when to be musically serious. In a *Looney Tunes* style show, the choice is obvious: the music must be as goofy as the drama. However, there are many comedies where it is much more effective to have the music be more serious or neutral, and let the comedy routines speak for themselves. *The Simpsons* is a great example of a show where the music essentially uses both techniques. At times, it hits some of the action, but for the most part, it paints with a broader brush. Alf Clausen was the composer for *The Simpsons* from 1990 to 2017, and he explains the concept:

Matt Groening [producer and creator of The Simpsons*] and company told me in our first meeting that, "It's not a cartoon, it's a drama where the characters are drawn." And when in doubt, he said, score it like a drama, not like a cartoon, not to mickey-mouse everything.*

I have an old friend that came up with the phrase, "You can't vaudeville Vaudeville." That has also served me really well on The Simpsons. *The producers keep saying, "We don't want the music to comment on the scene. We don't want the music itself to be funny." I'm always in agreement with that; we kind of joke in some of the spotting sessions about how the more serious I can play the music, according to the way the emotion is laid out, the more we pull the audience in and make them think that the situation is real. Then "boom," all of a sudden the gag comes, and it becomes twice as funny than it would have if I had tried to set up something leading up to the fact that there was going to be a gag.*

The Simpsons is an example of an animated show whose intended audience is adults. However, even shows aimed at a younger audience may employ this subtler approach to comedic scoring. Composer Ben Bromfield, who has scored several DreamWorks TV shows, such as *Boss Baby: Back in the Crib* (2022 to 2023), also draws from experience with live theater comedy in his scoring:

Scoring animation and accompanying improv comedy [for Second City] is kind of similar in that it's so heightened, and the music is a very big presence. The types of moves that I do in some animated shows are similar to moves I would do in improv. Obviously, the process is slower in scoring, so I can refine individual moments and make them more special. But there was definitely a musical idea I used to play a lot in improv scenes, that became a Boss Baby *cue that was used all the time in the show for similar purposes. For example, when characters were talking, and you wanted something in there that was kind of neutral and gave it a little bit of bounce.*

ANIMATED MUSICALS

Musicals, whether animated or live action, are extremely complex endeavors, from a production standpoint. The composer of the songs is involved during pre-production and writes the songs based on a script and conversations with the production team.

There is a lot of back and forth between the songwriter and the production team regarding the musical feel and the lyrical content of the songs. This can be an efficient process or it can be drawn out, because in pre-production, people feel less pressured and take their time getting the music just how they want it. Finally, after everyone—the producer, director, songwriter—has agreed and signed off on them, the songs are recorded. The animators take the final recording of the song and synchronize the singing and movements of the animated characters. Finally, months, or even years later, when there is a locked version of the film, the underscore is written by either the same composer as the songs or by someone different. David Newman did the underscore to *Anastasia* (1997), and talks about this experience from the composer's perspective:

> *I used all material from the songs because I thought that would be the right artistic choice for the movie. That's what my dad (Alfred Newman) would do with all those musicals, with all those Rodgers and Hammerstein musicals. I really liked that in shows like* Carousel *and* The King and I, *he interwove the score right with the song, and then right out from the song back into the score. I approached* Anastasia *like that, just like it was a traditional film. Steve Flaherty and Lynn Ahrens did the songs long before I began the underscore. Taking their themes and developing them in dramatic ways made the movie seem really unified.*

Alf Clausen wrote both underscore and songs for *The Simpsons*. His process for the songs was exactly the same as if it were a feature film musical and not a half-hour television series. The songs needed to be recorded before the animation was begun, months before the show aired. The process is complex whenever music is done like this during pre-production, and requires a lot of planning:

> *The procedure is that normally, I am given the script pages that have a lyric already written by one of the writers on staff. Then, I'll have a conference with the writer and the*

producers about what they feel the thrust of the mood of the piece should be, and what the intent should be.

Then, once I've composed the song, I write out the rhythm-section parts, we do a demo of the song, and record the rhythm-section track first. If the song is going to be recorded by cast voices, then I'll record scratch vocals, which are thrown away, eventually. They're just used for demo purposes for all the cast members to learn the material before they go into the voice-record session. The animators then animate to those tracks that are given to them with the rhythm section, the cast voices, and the click track. Nine months later, when the show is finished at the animation house, it comes back to us, and hopefully, they've left the songs alone, and I don't have to do any major surgery.

So, when I score the underscore cues for that particular episode, I'll also sweeten the song tracks that have come back, which means that I replace the rhythm section track with an orchestral track so it sounds as if the orchestra is accompanying the voices in the finished piece. So, there also needs to be new orchestrations written.

As the composer's task in a musical is to weave songs and underscore together, the relationship of musical keys and tonalities becomes very important as songs and underscore transition back and forth. There also must be a sonic unity in the textures between the songs and underscore. In addition, sometimes the animated story is about animals who need to be given human qualities, as in many of the Disney pictures. Mark Mancina produced many of the songs for *The Lion King* (1994), and wrote the underscore—in addition to producing the songs written by Phil Collins—for *Tarzan* (1999):

When you do an animated movie, it's hard, because you're not only scoring the same way you score a normal movie, but you're having to bring a certain sense of realness and humanness to characters that are animated.

Mancina also discusses the need for good collaboration with other musicians, as well as constant awareness of the flow between underscore and songs:

> *Key relationships between songs and underscore are tremendously important, especially in a movie where the music doesn't stop. Basically, in Tarzan, the music never stops. There needs to be continuity between the songs and the underscore. I don't like going to a movie, and when the song starts, I yawn, or I start going, "Oh God, here comes the song." I hate that. So does Phil (Collins). One of the ways we achieved a unity between the two elements was by me playing on his songs, and by him playing drums on some of my cues. That way the score and the songs can sound very similar. Not only the key relationships, but also the sonic relationships between cues.*

In addition to collaborating with other musicians, the process also involves collaboration with the production team. Because music is driving animated musicals, there is a whole team of people, from the director to the head of the studio, that gives input to the composer and songwriters. Mancina describes this:

> *There's not just one person that comes in and listens to what I do; there's a group. There's the director, the producer, the executive producer of music, the VP of theatrical, Michael Eisner, Joe Roth, the chairman of the board. All of 'em. They're all going to hear it! They're all going to have their own opinions on every note of the music, every frame of film—and they're all going to have something to say about it. Five of them might think it's the best cue they've ever heard me write, and three of them might say, "I don't like it, and it's gonna have to be changed.*

ANIME

Of course, not all animation happens in the U.S., and there is an especially notable animation industry in Japan that has a long history of producing amazing animated films and shows known as "anime," that has grown in worldwide popularity. Though anime's early form, through the 1960s, was heavily influenced by Disney and other Hollywood animation, it quickly became its own unique form, especially in that its audience went beyond just children far earlier than Hollywood was willing to consider it as a draw for adult viewers. In fact, anime encompasses practically every genre of film, from comedy to tragedy, and sci-fi and fantasy to realistic fiction.

In general, anime has less mickey mousing than a lot of U.S. animation. This is also related to the genre variety and target audiences of anime, which are more likely to include adults than much of U.S. animation.

In many anime films and shows, there will be a song written for the main title and closing credits, often by a different artist than the underscore composer. These songs often build a strong following on their own, outside of the movie they were written for. In fact, these songs are popular enough to be considered their own music genre: anison.

One of the anime studios with the widest international acclaim is Studio Ghibli, founded in 1985. Films by director Hayao Miyazaki, such as *My Neighbor Totoro* (1988), *Spirited Away* (2001), and *The Boy and the Heron (2023),* are especially beloved by audiences both inside and outside of Japan. Almost all of these films were scored by one composer, Joe Hisaichi, whose writing encompasses a broad range of the animation scoring styles mentioned above. At times, Hisaichi employs light mickey-mousing, but often, he prefers a dramatic scoring approach, using musical language that can include modern dissonance, traditional Japanese instruments, and lyrical melodies.

No matter what form it takes or where it is made, animation can be an interesting, and sometimes grueling scoring assignment. There is the opportunity to have fun with the music, as well as write serious underscore. Depending on the project, the composer can use traditional instruments, a full orchestra, or electronic sounds. The creative scope is wide, and though the process is difficult at times, animation can be among the most inspiring and fun genres of film scoring.

CHAPTER 20

Songs, Soundtracks, and Source Music

Many films use music other than the instrumental underscore. In addition to the kind of composed score that has been discussed so far, film scores frequently include songs. In musicals, as well as some dramatic films, the actors sing on-camera. Often, there is source music (as previously described, this is music that comes from a source on-screen that the characters can hear). A song can be used in place of instrumental underscore to heighten or comment on the dramatic action. For example, in the last scenes of *Michael Collins* (1996), when Sinéad O'Connor sings, "He Moved Through the Fair," the picture alternates between Michael Collins driving to what is ultimately his assassination and his fiancée trying on her wedding gown. This creates a poignant bridge between the two characters in their different locations.

There are several ways a song can end up in a film. If an established song is used in a new movie, the producer must obtain the rights to use it, either in its original form or by having a new version, or cover, recorded. Alternatively, the producer might commission a new song to be written for the film. Of course, if the movie is a musical, then several songs must be commissioned.

The composer's participation in a score that contains songs will vary from project to project. They may be involved in composing the songs, or they may only compose the underscore. For musicals, the songwriter might also write the underscore, as Alan Menken has done for many Disney films and Justin Hurwitz did in *La La Land* (2016). If used as background source music (as opposed to a character singing on camera), then the composer is usually not involved in the choosing of those songs.

Regardless of whether or not the same composer is used for the underscore and the songs, there are always dramatic considerations to keep in mind when choosing or writing songs for a motion picture. Hopefully, if a song is used in place of underscore, it will enhance the drama in some way. But the hard reality of the entertainment business is that there is always a pull-and-tug between creative considerations and those of commerce and profit, and this duality has a large influence on the use of songs in a film. This chapter discusses the many aspects of using songs in movies and the process that lands a song in the film, from the featured songs in musicals to the more subtle and less memorable—but still dramatically important—songs used as source music.

COMMISSIONED SONGS

Many times, a producer or director wants a song, or songs, to be written specifically for the film. One obvious case for this is a musical, where there are many songs that are essential to the plot. Another possibility is when a producer wants an individual song either for the main title or end credits, or for an important moment in the film. Let's take a look at how a commissioned song for a dramatic film (not a musical) might progress from inception to inclusion in the movie.

First, as with instrumental underscore, the director is usually the decision-maker of what songs appear in the film. The director (and sometimes the producer) will often take an active role in approving various stages of the song's creation, wanting to make sure it is appropriate both musically and lyrically.

Once it is determined that a commissioned song is required, a songwriter or songwriting team either reads a script or views a cut of the film to get a sense of the overall drama and emotional content. They then come up with a song that specifically reflects that. Then, the songwriters do a demo of the song, and it gets played for the decision makers. This could be just the director, but often involves producers and even studio executives. Once approved, the composer (if different from the songwriter) will hear the song, and with the director, will decide whether or not to incorporate thematic material into the underscore.

The song may be used only in the main title or end credits, or it could be featured as a dramatic statement in the body of the film. The thematic material in a song could come from a theme composed for the underscore, as in "My Heart Will Go On" from *Titanic* (1997), or the song could be created first, and thematic material from the song could then be used in the instrumental underscore.

"How Do You Keep the Music Playing," from *Best Friends* (1982), is organic to the score of the picture, and it also became a huge hit on the pop charts. For this song, composer Michel Legrand uses the thematic material in his underscore, as well as in the song itself. Lyricist Alan Bergman (who wrote as a team with his wife Marilyn) describes the evolution of "How Do You Keep the Music Playing?":

> *This film has two people involved in a relationship. The woman overcomes the man's resistance to marry, and they go back East to meet their respective families. The visits don't go well, and by the time the honeymoon is over, the marriage is almost over. There is a sequence in which they are on a people-mover in the airport, separated and not talking to each other. It was a marvelous sequence for us [as songwriters] because there are no sound effects or dialogue. Here was an opportunity to find a new way to say, "How do you keep romance alive?"*
>
> *After viewing the entire film several times, we watched this scene over and over again. Then we said to [composer] Michel Legrand, "What if the first line of the song is 'How do you keep the music playing?'" And he said, "I like that." He wrote the whole melody from that line. We then wrote the rest of the lyrics to that melody.*

When writing a new song and tailoring it for a certain movie, writers try to reflect either a single dramatic or emotional moment of the film, or to make a statement about the entire film. In *Life of Pi* (2012), composer Mychael Danna composed and produced a song called "Pi's Lullaby" for the opening credits, which uses lyrics in the Tamil language, a well-known Indian singer, several Indian instruments, and a Western-style harmonic scheme. All of this establishes both the original location of the characters (Pondicherry, India), as well as a kind of sweet and nostalgic mood. At least one of the main musical motifs in this opening song returns again and again throughout the underscore, creating a sense of unity in the music as well as a subconscious anchor for the audience.

MUSICALS

Musicals are the ultimate genre where songs are tailored to fit a film. They must be, because the characters are singing them. The words must further the story, and the genre of the songs must fit with the overall musical style of the film. The process of writing songs for a musical, whether animated or live action, can be different from that for dramatic-action films. In a dramatic film, the songwriters might not be involved until post-production. They may not see a script in advance; therefore, they must develop their ideas based on a working cut of the film. However, for a musical, the songwriters must be involved at an earlier stage. They read the script and discuss with the director where the songs shall go, what the feeling of a song should be, and what the lyric content will be. This is necessary because the songs must be completed before production begins. Then, they write the songs, make demos for the production team to hear, and make any requested changes. The process of approvals can be a lengthy one with musicals, and composers must adhere to the maxim, "there is always another solution," as director and producers weigh in and changes must be made.

After gaining approval, a recording is eventually made that is sometimes a finished version and sometimes a hybrid of finished tracks and guide tracks that will be replaced. The actor's vocal track needs to be a finished version because this recording is then played back on the set so that the actor(s) (or animators) can lip-sync accurately. So, the tempo and structure of the song will also be set in place at this juncture. (It is called a "prerecord" when the music is recorded prior to shooting or animating.)

If this recording is not the final arrangement of the accompaniment, the composer can still go into the studio and replace tracks, because a click track will keep the synchronization. For example, the playback may have been a MIDI orchestra, to be replaced later with live musicians. However, the vocal is usually not replaced, as that is what was used for lip-sync. Then, once the final music is recorded, it is ready to go to the mix and dub stages. Note that because the songs must be written, approved, and recorded before shooting or animating, the writing and recording of the songs will be completed well before the release of the movie. This entire process, from writing to release of the film, can take anywhere from one to three years.

Alan Bergman talks about the process of creating the music for *Yentl* (1983) with songwriting partners Marilyn Bergman and Michel Legrand, as well as Barbra Streisand—producer, director, and star of the film. What is clear is the connection to the arc of the story that the songwriters took great care to incorporate in the lyrics and music:

> *We agreed that this was a wonderful book for a musical. From the moment Yentl puts on the clothes of a boy and begins the masquerade, she cannot express to anyone her true feelings as a woman. This inner monologue was a perfect opportunity for music.*
>
> *So, first we spotted where the songs should be. Then we started writing. Michel is a dramatist; the best composers are dramatists. For one song, we said to him, "Yentl's father has just passed away. This is the first time she's been away from her village. It's a dark night in a forest and she is alone. In a way, she's pleading with her father." Michel wrote the melody that expressed in musical terms what our thoughts were for this song, and we wrote "Papa, Can You Hear Me."*
>
> *When he writes, or when anybody writes the music first, which we prefer, there are words on the tips of those notes, and we have to find them. It's a search.*

Exploring, being a dramatist and a storyteller, and finding just the right words to go with a character and a story are the jobs of the songwriter in a musical. These songs are often the reason the audience goes to see the film and remembers the film for years.

SOURCE MUSIC

Source music (see chapter 13) is diegetic music that appears to be coming from a source on screen. Said another way, it is any music the characters in the scene can hear. Car radios, home stereos, bands in a nightclub, street musicians, and actors humming in the shower are all examples of source music. Source music can be familiar songs by known artists, songs or instrumental tracks by new artists, or music written by the composer specifically for the film. Source music can be strictly in the background as part of the aural landscape along with various sound effects, or it can become a strong dramatic statement.

When songs are used as source music, they are sometimes written into the screenplay, and ultimately approved or chosen by the director, often with the assistance of the music supervisor. In the case of instrumental source music, it can be chosen from existing recordings, the underscore composer can write or arrange something, or another composer can be brought in to produce the source cues. Which of these methods are used depends on the kind of cue being written, and whether or not the composer has the musical background to write what is needed. Using existing recordings can be easy if the rights are available. If originally composed source music is asked for, and is in a style unfamiliar to the composer, it may be preferable to hire someone else to do those cues. In addition, if there are moments in which the source and underscore cues need to segue or otherwise interact, then the composer must at least be aware of the key, instrumentation, style and tempo of the source cues.

Whether or not the composer is involved in the source music also depends on dramatic considerations. Often, songs used as source music are taken from existing recordings and the composer is not part of the selection process. However, there are times when the composer is asked to write a source cue that is not a song, most likely an instrumental of some kind. The composer can utilize the players at the recording session for the underscore to record the source music. For example, if the requested music is a classic rock song, but the rights to that song are not available, then the composer could have a rhythm section create something close to that original song, but not be close enough for a copyright violation. This is an efficient way to create source music without getting clearances and having extra recording sessions.

People often wonder why they don't remember hearing many of the songs listed in the end credits or on the soundtrack from the movie. The answer is, they probably did hear those songs, but they were source cues played for only a few seconds at a low volume under dialogue. However, many record companies are content to have their artist's songs in the film as source cues, as that can still generate income for the publisher, writers, and artist.

MUSIC SUPERVISION

Helping to pick and negotiate clearances for the songs in a film is a large part of the music supervisor's job (see chapter 12). Although the process sometimes goes smoothly, many problems can arise in navigating the interpersonal relationships of producer, director, and others on the filmmaking team, as well as in the clearing of publishing and master recording rights. The music supervisor must be politically savvy in ascertaining the various power dynamics of a project, as there are often many different voices trying to influence the song selection process.

Producers and directors often request specific songs. Some are artistically appropriate and budget-friendly, some might seem kind of wacky depending on one's point of view, some are out of the budgetary range, and some will not be released by the artist, record company, or publisher. There is the screenwriter, who may have written the idea for a specific song into the script and advocates to keep that song no matter what. Then there is the movie studio, which might own a certain record company, and want to promote its artists. The film editor, who has worked with the film for several months, can have their own ideas as to what songs will work. The director will usually have a final say, but the music supervisor still must be able to sort out the various opinions. This situation is familiar to music supervisor and editor Daniel Carlin:

> *It's not just picking any song that will work. Anybody that listens to the radio can do that. We've got to have a budget. We've got to think about a soundtrack deal, we've got to think about the politics. For example, say I go in and I put this great Mariah Carey song into a scene. What if the budget is $300,000 for thirty songs and I have just spent $100,000 of the budget? Because the director falls in love with it and will not have it any other way, that does not do anybody any good. Now, everybody is fighting. The director is fighting with the studio, and somebody goes, "Who is the jerk that put this Mariah Carey song in there in the first place?" I don't want to be the guy who raises his hand.*

We've mentioned the role that budgets play in deciding what songs can be obtained for a film. There is no one rule, or guide, for how much a song will cost. If it is going to be the main title of the movie, obviously, the owner of the copyright will ask for more money. If it is a well-known song by a well-known artist, then that will cost more than an unknown song by an up-and-coming artist who wants the exposure. If a song is going to be used as source music in a bar that is heard at a low volume, that song will be cleared for a low dollar amount. The music supervisor will use their networking connections, knowledge of the industry, and familiarity with many different genres of music to choose the songs that fit the budget of a particular film. Daniel Carlin creates a hypothetical example of the kinds of negotiations that take place:

> *There is no law or rule about this stuff. You go to the publisher with hat in hand, and you say, "Here's our movie, here's our budget, and here's how much money we have to spend. Can you help us out?" And it depends. I mean, if it's a $100 million movie, they're not going to*

give you the song for $8,000. But if you make a $3 million movie, and you can them tell it's a labor of love for everybody, then they might say: "Here's what I'll do for you, I'll make a deal if you use five of our songs, and I'll give them to you for $6,500 each." And that way, they get paid not only what I pay them for the songs, but then, when it goes on television, they get those royalties. Then, it gets released overseas and gets more royalties. The volume helps them, and it helps me too. And it also means that I'm not going to put in a competing singer. I'm gonna have five of their songs, and it makes everybody's life easier.

Costs of movie making are constantly shifting as a result of many factors both within the industry (labor, creative costs, etc.) and in the economy. So, in addition to the specific costs of a song or package of songs, the music supervisor must be aware of the overall economic climate. Evyen Klean:

Since 2013, music costs have risen dramatically, probably along with everything else on the planet. I would say, song fees have risen over 50 percent from what they were—and in some cases, double what they were—a few years ago. So, it's more expensive to license music, and it's more expensive to create scores, and the challenge is that most production budgets haven't necessarily kept pace.

As you can see, the job of music supervisor has many dimensions and requires a broad skill set. There are countless ways that songs can end up in a film, and many different motives for using them. The balance between creative and financial considerations is a tricky one that everyone in the filmmaking business experiences, and because royalties and sales profits generated from songs can be substantial, there are many interested people other than the filmmakers who try to sway the choices. The director might want it one way, the producer another, the movie studio a third, and an interested record company a fourth. Therefore, there are often two conflicting goals in the choosing of songs: the creative choice, based on the director's vision for the film, and the commercial choice, which is based on what will make the most money. The music supervisor guides this process, and hopefully, can steer everyone involved towards serving the drama as well as serving the financial bottom line.

PART V

Business

CHAPTER 21

Making the Deal: Agents, Attorneys, and Contracts

Many musicians seem to want to avoid discussing the business aspect of film scoring. They would prefer to live in lofty heights above the humdrum, mundane world of money-changing hands. Some are simply scared at having to actually deal with making money doing music. But every artist, every working creative person, is also in business. Because of the freelance nature of our work, we are typically in business for ourselves and must learn to handle our financial affairs, deal with contracts, conduct ourselves in negotiations, and make the best deals possible. Many young composers have the impression that they will somehow get a gig writing music for films, be compensated handsomely for their music, and then someone else will handle the money. Unfortunately, this is far from the truth. Whether or not you have representation or business partners, ultimately, it comes down to having control over and being knowledgeable about your own business.

AGENTS, MANAGERS, AND ATTORNEYS

It is crucial for a composer to have competent and honest people to help with the deeper aspects of the business. These are the agents, managers, attorneys, and financial advisors who have expertise in specific areas.

Many film composers have agents who help them obtain jobs, negotiate deals, and provide career guidance. These professionals have thorough knowledge of projects in various stages of production, and can contact the producer or director to pitch one of their composers for that project. They constantly network with people in every facet of the entertainment business, always looking for opportunities for their clients. Then, once the composer is hired, the agent or manager negotiates deals and sees that the terms of a contract are honored.

Agent and manager David May:

> *What we depend on for our work is, number one, our relationships. This includes the music people out at the studios, the major production companies, and the major music supervisors. We are constantly calling them, and they are constantly calling us about what they have on their plate and what they are looking for and who we have that might fit the bill. It's our business to be providing them with constant information about our clients, and also to suggest appropriate candidates wherever we can.*
>
> *We want to find out when projects are occurring, when they are going to be looking for a composer, who the key people are that will be influencing that decision, whether we are going through a music producer or music supervisor or directly to the director—just who do we deal with? So, at the appropriate time, we can make the calls we need to make to that person, and get our people in there. And then, the next step—once we have some kind of entry, when we know what kind of person they are looking for and what kind of budget they have—we put together music or credits, whatever we can put together to hopefully make them interested in our client.*

Most agents and managers have a roster of many composers, so the trick for the composer seeking representation is to find the person or agency that works best for their style of music and stage of career. There is no way that an agent can give their full attention to one composer 100 percent of the time. For the agent, it is a constant juggling act that also involves an intuitive sense as to which client to pitch for a particular job. The composer must also be active in searching out work, and then let the agent handle negotiations once the job is offered. Agents welcome this kind of aggressive job seeking by a composer; it makes their job easier. But the good agent will always be looking out for your best interest and putting your work in front of multiple directors and producers. Also, the agent or manager must be someone you can trust and count on to be honest and up-front with you. David May:

> *It's a partnership between an agent and a composer. The theory is that if both of us are doing everything we can, and communicating as frequently as we can, then we're going to stand a much, much better chance in moving a composer's career forward.*
>
> *For new composers, it is difficult to get an agent. There is a catch-22: you must have done some work before they will take you on. And then, you are at the low end of the food chain, so to speak. It behooves the composer to pursue their own contacts and gigs as much as possible. When the gigs start coming in, this will get the agent's attention.*

Once a composer has signed with an agent or manager, they are said to be represented by that agency, and will sign a contract assigning a certain percentage of their fee from each job to that representative. This percentage can range from 7.5 percent to 15 percent, with some agents and managers offering a sliding scale based on the type of deal. For example, in a package deal where the composer is responsible for paying for the recording costs, they may charge a lower percentage than a deal in which the composer's creative fee is separate. (Additional details about different types of fee deals for composers' contacts are discussed later in this chapter.)

The difference between agents and managers for film composers can be subtle, and the two roles may even overlap. One difference is financial. In many states, including California and New York, agents must be licensed, and the fees they charge are regulated and capped. Managers, however, can take whatever percentage of an artist's income that the artist agrees to.

Other than the financial arrangement, the biggest difference is one of focus. An agent is completely focused on getting a composer specific projects, and planning for future jobs. A manager looks at a composer more holistically, helping them focus and develop their career. They may serve the same role an agent would in pitching a composer for jobs and negotiating the deals. Additionally, they may also serve a similar role to a publicist (someone hired to increase positive press about the composer), helping to promote the composer's image and brand as well as musical work, strategize with the composer about how to break into a new market, and even helping with things like managing the music budget. Manager Keith C. Anderson describes his role this way:

> *Managers wear many hats. We do a bit of tracking and pitching as an agent would—so then, we put on our agent hat. We also might put on our negotiation and contract hat. Budgeting for various film scores is something else we might help with. If the composer doesn't have a publicist, the publicist hat is another we might wear. We may also do something like artist development: really mapping out a one-, three-, or five-year plan. As a manager, I want to know not only what the artist's strengths are, but what their desires are—for their career, and even personally. That's where I find the biggest difference between management and agency lies: the long term strategy for an artist to succeed in a way that fits that individual person.*

Like May, Anderson also emphasizes the importance of trust in these relationships:

> *If you do find someone who is trustworthy and loyal, my advice is to build that rapport, build that relationship, and continue working with them. Of course, that's hard to identify when you're first starting out, because you might not be able to tell the difference until you get going. So, there's a lot to be said about learning from people that have that experience already, whether it be a seasoned composer or an experienced manager. Just talking to these people can provide valuable insight that you would not otherwise get except by learning it the hard way.*

It's also important to understand that an agent or manager is not a requirement for a film composer, and shouldn't be rushed into. The best time to get representation is usually once a composer has started to establish a name for themselves and is looking to take their career to the next level. In fact, bringing a relatively high-profile scoring job (like a film accepted to the Sundance Film Festival, or a streaming series) to an agent or manager and asking them to represent you in negotiations for that particular deal is often a good time to interest an appropriate representative.

ATTORNEYS

Perhaps the most important and most lampooned of all career advisors is the attorney. All shark jokes aside, a good attorney's advice (or an attorney's good advice) is invaluable. For a film score, after the agent negotiates the deal, the attorney reviews the contract's specific legal language. This can include different kinds of residuals, reuse, or new use of the music, worldwide copyright protections, and a number of other legal details. All of these items may be further negotiated through the agent, or the attorney may negotiate directly with the production company's legal representatives. In addition, the composer's attorney also may make deals with publishers and record companies.

Your attorney will know exactly how much money you are making as well as other sensitive details of your financial and legal situation, so (and you may sense a theme here) you need to find someone you can trust—someone whom you feel is looking out for your best interests. They should also have a specific expertise in the area of entertainment law, and film scoring in particular, since there's so much about this field that is not obvious without specialized training and experience. In other words, don't hire your cousin Vinny who usually works in estate planning, even if it means spending more money to hire an entertainment lawyer.

Unlike an agent or manager, who is paid a percentage of each scoring job's fee, attorneys are paid by the hour. They may be put on retainer if they need to be on call, but even this is based on an hourly rate, not a percentage fee. In those cases where an attorney is the only representative you have on your team, they can also sometimes step into more of the deal negotiation role that an agent would otherwise take on.

One final note about both agents and attorneys: any deal they strike with a producer, publisher, or other executive must be approved and signed by you. And that brings us full circle. In order to know that you are making the best decision for yourself, and sometimes for your family, you must be informed and have a good grasp of the issues and items in your contract. Let the attorney and agent give you advice, but don't let them run your life. Also, remember that they are working for you, so if you don't like the way they do business, you can walk away and find someone else.

CONTRACTS

Before any music is written, before any money is generated, the composer signs a contract with the producer that specifies the services the composer will provide and the compensation the producer will pay. The terms of this contract and the fee paid by the producer are ultimately coupled with the popularity of the film and its ability to generate royalty income, determining how much the composer will make inclusive of both up-front fees from the producer and back-end royalties from various sources.

After the composer is offered the gig, then usually, a *deal memo* or *short-form contract* is drawn up. These are simplified but legally binding agreements that summarize the terms the composer and production office have agreed upon, and can serve to allow the scoring process to get started while the finer details of the final contract are completed by the attorneys. (Note that any document needs to be signed by all parties in order to be legally binding.) Agent David May:

> *Once we have verbal terms for whatever creative deal we finally come up with, I will typically generate a deal memo. If it's a studio, sometimes they will generate it, and different studios have different policies. Sony does a*

short-form agreement first—they don't do deal memos—followed by a long-form contract. Others go straight to a long-form contract, but I want to make sure that there is something on paper as quickly after the verbal agreement has been transacted as possible.

Based on the deal memo, attorneys draw up the final long-form contract. Where the deal memo is a plain-language summary of the terms agreed upon, the final contract is a complex legal document. Even without the benefit of a law degree, every composer should understand the basic items that are covered. There are many clauses in the film composer's contract that must be addressed and approved. Some of the important ones are:

- Copyright ownership
- How much is the up-front fee?
- How will that fee be paid?
- Is it a package or all-in deal?
- The length of time for composing the score
- Screen credit
- Advertising credit
- Use of the music outside of this particular film
- Suspensions/terminations/defaults
- Royalty fees
- Exclusivity of the composer's time

Some of these items are fairly straightforward. "Screen credit" refers to how your name appears on-screen and where it is placed in the credits. Before the costume designer, after the cinematographer? On its own card in the main titles or just in the end credit scroll? Should it read:

Music by [Your Name]

Or do you want the full treatment:

Music composed, conducted, and orchestrated by

[Your Full Name]

Advertising credit is similar, referring to where and how your name is placed in newspaper, magazine, and billboard ads.

"Exclusivity of the composer's time" means that the composer will not work on other projects during the time indicated in the contract. This is a protection for the producer to ensure that they get your full attention. Composers are freelance and are always juggling schedules and projects, and the producer is investing a lot of money in your coming through. So, it makes sense from the producers standpoint that you are working exclusively for their project during the specified time, though it may not be something you are able or willing to commit to. Another variation of this clause is "non-exclusive, but first priority." This means that the composer may work on other projects at the same time, but must give the other party of the contract first priority.

It is worth reiterating what David May has said regarding the importance of putting everything in writing—even when dealing with friends or family. There is nothing like a written agreement in the form of a contract, or at least a deal memo, to prevent misunderstandings down the line. It is actually a protection for both parties in the event that one person has a different interpretation of what had been agreed upon several months before. Or in a worst-case scenario, if one party tries to deliberately misrepresent or distort the agreement, a written contract can settle the dispute. Handshake agreements are lovely, altruistic, and perhaps philosophically desirable; we all want to believe that our business partners are honorable. But in reality, verbal agreements sealed on a handshake can be a recipe for business disaster. If someone actually tries to avoid signing a written contract or a deal memo with you, walk out the door as fast as possible! This is a sure indication of a person who knows they may not or will not honor the terms of your verbal agreement, and this kind of person cannot be trusted.

The contract is a supremely important document. It is your security that certain terms have been agreed to by both sides. Make sure you understand the points of the contract, are comfortable with the agreement, and have had it reviewed by your attorney. This will be a strong protection going forward.

FEE STRUCTURES

One of most important issues in the film composer's contract is how they will get paid by the production company, which, as noted previously, may either be a fee paid directly to the composer just for their creative work, or a package deal where the composer is given an amount that is meant to include production costs from which they must then manage the budget. There are several dimensions to both these options, and they require in-depth discussion.

STRAIGHT FEES

When we refer to a "straight fee" or "composer's fee," it means that the producer is simply paying the composer for writing the music. If the composer accepts this kind of fee deal, then the film production studio will be responsible for any music production costs including studio time, orchestrators, musicians, etc. Composer fees for a feature film can cover a wide range, from about $50,000 for a low-budget film and a less well-known composer, to over two million dollars for an "A-list" composer on a big-budget feature. However, these days straight fee deals are a relative rarity, generally only found at the high end of studio feature-film scoring. Smaller budget films, television, streaming, and other forms of scoring are more likely to have a package deal model.

There are several ways the composer's fee can be paid. Often, the fee is paid in three parts: the first when the spotting is completed and the composer begins writing, the second at the beginning of recording the music, and the third at the completion of the dubbing session. Sometimes, a specific number of weeks are written in the contract, like "the composer shall commence services on the spotting date of the picture and will complete the score within twelve consecutive weeks from that date." Sometimes, the completion date is tied into the post-production schedule. Other contracts give a specific month, day, and year by which the composer shall deliver the finished score. If the composer is needed beyond the set time frame in the contract, there is another clause that provides additional compensation.

PACKAGE DEALS

The other form of fee structure for original music, which is by far the most common these days, is the *package deal.* Sometimes, also called an "all-in" deal, this is when the composer agrees to accept a certain amount of money in return for both writing and getting the music produced and recorded. As opposed to receiving a fee for composing the music with the producer paying for all production-related costs, in the package deal, the composer is responsible for almost all of these costs.

Since the biggest cost of producing a score is hiring musicians and a recording studio, when a composer accepts a package deal, they are either planning on producing most or all of the music in their home studios, or they must work out in advance a reasonable budget for these expected out-of-pocket costs. Of course, the danger to the composer in a package deal is that something unexpected could happen causing the recording session or other costs to escalate beyond the original budget. Then, the composer can be responsible for paying the extra costs, and maybe even losing money on the score, in order to deliver the final music. Luckily, there are often exclusions to what the composer is responsible for. These vary from deal to deal, but some of these common exclusions from a composer's package deal costs are:

- Music editing costs
- Licensing of songs or other music not written by the composer
- Reuse, new use, and other special payments to union musicians
- Rescoring for creative reasons not due to the fault or omission of the composer

The final item on this list is extremely important. It protects the composer from directors or producers that make arbitrary, capricious, and frequent changes in the film, or ask for changes in the music after a recording session. Often, a specific number of minutes of music will be agreed upon as a ceiling, and if this number is exceeded, the composer is entitled to extra fees. That said, this clause does not apply to versions of the mockup created by the composer on the way to approval of a given cue. Most composer contracts have no limit on revisions because the most important thing is the director being happy with the end result, though some composers do negotiate in a commercially reasonable number of revisions, especially on smaller budget projects.

An advantage to the composer of a package deal is that if they work quickly, and/or enjoy the production side of scoring, a healthy profit can be made. The composer can also choose whom to work with, since they are hiring all the roles from the orchestrator, to the music contractor, to the score mixer—or they can decide to do any or all of these themselves, rather than hiring others. The disadvantage is that the pressure of music production and the music budget is on the composer's shoulders. The reality of the film scoring business today is that in many instances, if a composer does not agree to the package deal, they will not get the job. The producer will simply find someone who will agree.

Composer Miriam Cutler discusses both the pros and cons of working on a package deal basis:

> *There's so much financial pressure of making it all work with package deals. You've got to do it on what you have. So do you put food on the table, or do you get that clarinet player or that string group? But on the plus side, I find when I'm part of a small crew, we can make decisions really quickly and have a clear vision of what the film is and what the music should be. And for me, it's just more fun to do that kind of work. It's not that it couldn't also be fun to have big budgets, but the price you pay for that is often very high.*

Mark Isham speaks about package deals:

> *A real important point for newcomers to understand is, because you're a newcomer, you're probably going to get package-dealed from the beginning, these days. It's*

very rare to just walk in and have someone say, "Here's a fee and we'll pay any costs you have." The important thing to remember is that everything [else] is negotiable. You can negotiate for gross points. You can negotiate for publishing. You can negotiate for how many musicians you guarantee to employ. Every aspect of a package deal is negotiable. And make sure you do your homework, because if you miscalculate, and you agree contractually to supply twenty strings for forty minutes of music, you better know what that's going to cost you.

And you'd better do things like go to the director and say, "I will accept this on the condition that you sign off on everything that I play for you in demo form." Sometimes, the director is sitting on the scoring stage and says, "What if this were faster?" Then, you're looking at writing more music, changing your tempo, and somehow getting new music on the stand while the musicians are waiting for you. That could eat up your profit right there. So, it's very crucial that you have a good line of communication with your director.

Even if you can't get it in writing that they'll sign off on the mockups, at least, get them to agree that this is a package deal, and you're going to try to help each other.

Package deals need to be approached with care and planning. Everything must be in writing, and communication with the director/production office must be clear. The best package-deal situation is when you are planning to produce most, if not all, of the music in your home studio. As soon as you venture into the world of studios, engineers, and live musicians, you are leaving yourself open to cost overruns for which you may or may not be protected contractually.

For this reason, when a composer is working on a package deal basis for a very large budget (for example, a million dollar package deal), they often will hire a specialist just to handle the score production. This role may be called "score coordinator," and involve handling the budget, booking studios, and generally keeping an eye on the bottom line. In fact, oftentimes, the best score coordinators are former studio music executives who have gone freelance. In general, the package deal is a way of life, so until you have the clout to negotiate a large enough package to afford a score coordinator, you'll need to know how to budget on your own so you can make a reasonable amount of money when you get the opportunity.

CHAPTER 22

Copyright and Publishing

Copyright and publishing are aspects of the film composing business that are fundamental to the composer's financial wellbeing. They are extremely important to understand because they address the actual ownership of music, which is the basis of your income stream in both the present and the future. Most of the time, for feature films and television in the U.S., film composers do not own their music due to a type of agreement called "a work made for hire" (or just "work for hire"). However, this is not always the case, and whoever holds the copyright to your music determines who can publish and monetize it, as well as some aspects of how much money in royalties you see down the road (see chapter 23). Let's talk about what makes a work copyrighted, what it means to have it published, and what is a work made for hire.

WHAT IS A COPYRIGHT?

"Copyright" refers to the ownership of an original creative work—in this case, music. (It could also be a book, a poem, a photograph, an artwork, etc.) It sounds somewhat circular, but copyright means "the right to copy," or the right to reproduce a certain work. The person who owns the copyright owns the rights to that work. Therefore, the person who owns the copyright controls how it will be published—that is, *offered for sale to the public.*

The history of U.S. copyright laws is a complex subject. Simply put, in the earliest days of the nation, laws were enacted that gave authors and publishers exclusive ownership of their creative works and protected them from theft of those works. In the last century, there were three significant copyright laws enacted: in 1909, 1976, and in 1998.

The first of these was the Copyright Act of 1909. This act set the length of the original copyright at twenty-eight years with a copyright renewal, making the potential life of the copyright protection fifty-six years. After that fifty-six-year period, the work would enter the *public domain* (become PD), and no royalties would need to be paid because the copyright would have expired. Public domain means that there is no ownership of a copyright, so anyone can reproduce or use the work in any way. Older songs, such as folk songs with no known author and classical music written before the earlier part of the twentieth century, are examples of works in the public domain. So, under the 1909 law with a fifty-six year expiration, if someone wrote a song in 1910 and filed the renewal form in 1938, in 1966 the copyright would have expired and that song would enter the public domain.

By the 1950s, this law had become outmoded, and Congress began to look at ways to change it. It took until 1976 to enact a new law: the 1976 Copyright Revision Act. This law made the duration of the original copyright to be the life of the author plus fifty years. So under this law, the copyright stayed in effect for fifty years after the composer or writer died.

Copyright law took its current form in 1998, when the U.S. Congress amended the Copyright Revision Act of 1976 to make the length of copyright protection the life of the author plus seventy years, often referred to as "life plus seventy." This means that if a composer created a work in the year 1990 and lived to the year 2020, the copyright will continue to be in effect for their heirs or estate until the year 2090, a total of one hundred years. If the same composer created a work in the year 2015, and passed away in 2020, the length of the copyright is only seventy-five years. This law is beneficial for composers (and all copyright holders), for it guarantees that as long as the creator is alive, their work is protected by the copyright law. Many composers outlived the previous fifty-six years protection of the 1909 law and saw their works enter the public domain while they were still alive. And some suffered the loss of copyright by forgetting to file the renewal forms, thus seeing the work enter the public domain after only twenty-eight years. This newest law insures the heirs or estate of the composer seventy years of copyright protection and potential income, whereas under the previous laws that protection was usually much shorter. In addition, the life-plus-seventy provision brought the U.S. in line with European and other countries around the world who had already adopted that timeframe.

Even more important is how copyright is established or registered since the 1976 act. Whereas before 1976 works needed to be registered with the copyright office in order to be protected by copyright, now copyright is established automatically as soon as an original work is created and "fixed in a tangible medium." A tangible medium in the case of a piece of music is notated sheet music or a recording of the piece. So if you compose some music and record it in your DAW or notate it either digitally or on paper, technically, it is now "fixed" and protected by copyright. However, if sometime down the line, you believe that this music has been stolen and used by someone else, you would have to prove exactly when you created it and precisely how that person could have had access to your creation. As you can probably imagine, this could become a thorny legal issue. Therefore, the best protection of your music is to register it with the U.S. Copyright Office.

Registering a copyright is easy, and most copyright registration is now done online. Go to copyright.gov and follow the link to the Electronic Copyright Office. You will fill out the form and upload a recording of the music to be registered along with the current fee. After a period of about three weeks to three months, you will receive a copy of your completed form with a stamped seal of the U.S. Copyright Office indicating completed registration and full copyright protection. However, your protection begins on the day your form is received by the Copyright Office, as long as it is filled out correctly. Note that for a film score, you may not be the one responsible for doing this step (for reasons to be discussed later).

So far, we've been discussing United States copyright laws, which do have some unique aspects. However, in general, copyright functions in largely the same way in all 180 countries that are signatories of the Berne Convention, which establishes a portable, international concept of copyright. In other words, whether you write a piece of music in the United States, France, Japan, or Nigeria, you can rely on these same basic concepts of what is copyrighted, what the author of the work has the right to do, and the length of the copyright term.

PUBLISHING

A copyrighted work is considered to be published if it is offered for sale to the public. If a composer writes an incredible heart-stopping symphonic suite but leaves it on a shelf for years, that work is copyrighted but not published. However, if copies of the same work are printed and consequently offered for sale in a classical music store, that work is then considered published. If a band records an album and just gives a few copies away to friends and family, that work is not published because those copies were not sold. If the same album is offered for sale at gigs or released on streaming services, that music is then considered to be published. When a film is released in theaters, streamed, or shown on TV, the music in that film is also considered to be published. (A reminder that in all the above examples, the works are protected by copyright whether or not they are published.)

When a work is considered published, by natural implication, that work has a publisher. A publisher can be an individual, such as a film composer or songwriter, who is self-publishing their own catalog of works; it can be the movie production company or studio; or it can be a company whose sole business is publishing music with hundreds or even thousands of titles to oversee. The duties of the publisher are to register the copyright, oversee the financial administration of a work, collect royalties, negotiate new uses, and make sure that there is no infringement of the copyright.

THE RIGHTS OF THE COPYRIGHT OWNER

What exactly does it mean to own a copyright? To sum it up, the owner of the copyright has the right to reproduce the copyrighted work, to distribute it through "phonorecords," to create "derivative works" from the original work, and to perform the work publicly. ("Phonorecords" used to apply to just that—records that go on a turntable; now it legally means anything that reproduces sound. Digital files, CDs, and any future invention of reproducing sound is covered by this term.) If you own the copyright to a piece of music, you have the exclusive right to decide how to initially reproduce copies of it, where and when the initial performance takes place, and who initially performs it.

Notice how that word "initially" snuck into those last few phrases. This is important since, after the work is initially offered to the public, i.e., published, your ability to control the use of your copyrighted material changes. Remember that a copyrighted work is not necessarily a published work. A work can be under copyright but not yet be published. So, if someone wants to use your music on their album or perform it in public, and your music is copyrighted but not yet published, they absolutely need to get your permission. You have the right to decide about the initial performance or re-production of copies. However, if the work is already published (for example, you have already recorded and released it on an album, or if it has been released in any medium as a film score), then your permission is not necessary for them to record or perform their own version, as long as they pay you a royalty (to be discussed in the next chapter). Note that this right to record or perform a cover of a published work does not extend to the use of that work in a film or otherwise synchronized to picture. This requires permission from the copyright holder in all cases.

COPYRIGHT INFRINGEMENT

Another question that often comes up is "What constitutes copyright infringement?" There are two types of copyright infringement: the unauthorized use of a copyrighted work, and the copying of substantial portions of a work.

The unauthorized use of a copyrighted work is the more clear-cut type of infringement. This is when someone records or performs copyrighted material without paying royalties to the owner of the copyright. This can happen if a performer records a copyrighted song, sells thousands of units, and doesn't pay the appropriate royalty. Even though the copyright owner does not have to give permission for use of a published song, they must still be notified that the song will be used, and must be paid at least the minimum statutory rate. In a film score, if a producer uses music from another film or recording but does not obtain a *sync license* (written permission to use the music and synchronize it to picture), that producer is guilty of copyright infringement; they have violated the copyright owner's exclusive rights.

"The copying of substantial portions of a copyrighted work" is a more difficult issue to determine. Many composers and songwriters are under the impression that you can copy up to four bars, or five seconds, or some other amount of actual music before you are in danger of violating the copyright laws. This is a misconception. The copyright law says that you must have music that contains a *substantial similarity* to the copyrighted work before you are guilty of copyright infringement. This is a vague term that allows for great leeway in interpretation on a case-by-case basis. Whether or not a work is infringing on the copyright of another work would be decided in a civil court by either a jury or a judge. Musical experts would be presented by both sides, and the judge or jury would make a determination if they believe the two works are substantially similar.

In addition, the law says that for there to be infringement, the owner of the copyright must show *proof of access*. In other words, if you are being accused of copying a substantial portion of a copyrighted work, the owner of the copyright must prove that somehow you had access to hearing the work in question. For example, if the earlier work had substantial streaming, radio, or TV airplay, then it is assumed that you had access to it. You cannot claim that because you do not own a TV or don't subscribe to Netflix, you therefore never heard that sitcom theme song. The same applies for a film score. You cannot claim that you never saw the movie and therefore are not guilty of copyright infringement. If the music is widely disseminated to the public, either in theaters or on the radio, TV, or streaming, then it is assumed that you had access to it.

On the other hand, say you have written a song that has only been performed at your weekly gig in your city of Burlington, Vermont. Suppose that a composer based in Los Angeles comes out with a hit movie theme or song that sounds just like your song. In this case, you would be hard-pressed to prove that a composer from Los Angeles had access to your song that was only played in a nightclub in Vermont once a week. However, if you can prove that the composer in question had recently spent time in Burlington, or even was present at your gig, then you would have a case.

In songs, infringement could be based on musical or lyrical similarities. In film scores, there is only music. Actually, you often will hear similarities in two or more different scores of the same composer's work. For example, John Williams uses the interval of a fifth as the opening motive for the main themes of *Star Wars* (1977), *Superman* (1979), and *E.T.* (1982). Is this copyright infringement on the part of the latter two scores? The answer is no, because the rest of the music after the opening interval in each of these scores continues on in different melodic, harmonic, and rhythmic directions. One could find similar examples in the work of many of the top Hollywood composers.

You will hear similarities in themes, harmonies, and instrumentation that run through almost every composer's work. One could dissect Mozart or Beethoven in this way and find that they often repeated themselves, though mostly in small musical ways, such as cadences or melodic connection devices and ornaments. Some self-repetition is bound to happen, since every composer has their own style. When it becomes copyright infringement (stealing from themselves) once again depends on whether the corresponding parts of the music are considered to have substantial similarity, and whether or not someone has the desire to file a lawsuit.

Copyright infringement is an area in which you should hope never to be involved. Always check (better yet, have someone else check) if you are subconsciously borrowing someone else's music. Try to always be original. These kinds of lawsuits can be messy, lengthy, and expensive, and they have happened to major artists in high profile cases relating to both songs and film scores.

In the case of film scores, often, the pieces for which the copyright holder alleged infringement were used as temp score, thus removing the need to prove proof of access. For example, Zack Snyder's film *300* (2006) used cues from Elliot Goldenthal's score for Julie Taymor's film *Titus* (1999) as temp score. Goldenthal sued Warner Bros. Pictures for copyright infringement, and the settlement of that suit included Warner Bros. issuing this public statement:

> *Warner Bros. Pictures acknowledges and regrets that a number of the music cues for the score of 300 were, without our knowledge or participation, derived from music composed by Academy Award-winning composer Elliot Goldenthal for the motion picture* Titus. *Warner Bros. Pictures has great respect for Elliot, our longtime collaborator, and is pleased to have amicably resolved this matter.*

In another case, Huey Lewis and the News's song "I Want a New Drug" was used as temp score for the main titles of *Ghostbusters* (1984). Ray Parker Jr. was directed to use it as a model for the now instantly recognizable *Ghostbusters* theme song, resulting in a lawsuit which was also settled out of court.

SYNCHRONIZATION AND MASTER USE RIGHTS

When it comes to film music, there are actually two different copyrights that come into play. One is the copyright of the music itself—what the composer composes, which could at least plausibly be written down in some kind of notation (whether or not that step is actually taken). When a piece of music is used in a film, the right that needs to be obtained by the filmmaker for the music itself is called a "synchronization right." This gives a filmmaker the right to use the musical composition—the melodies, harmonies, etc. The other copyright relates to the particular performance and recording of that piece of music. In a film this right is called the "master use right." If a composer writes and records a piece themselves in their home studio, they own the copyright to both the music and the recording. However, in many cases, the two copyrights may be held by different people or companies. It's common, for example, for a songwriter to have a publishing company that administers the copyright of the music, and a separate record company might own the master rights to a particular recording of that song.

If an already-published work is going to be used in any form of visual media, the person or company desiring to use the copyrighted material must obtain a sync license from the publisher. If they wish to use a particular recording of that work, they need to obtain a master use license from the record company. These licenses allow the filmmaker to synchronize the music to their visuals. Therefore, if you own the copyright to a song or film score and PepsiCo wants to use a portion of it for their next ad campaign, they must obtain a sync license from you allowing them to use the music for a specified amount of time, and for a specified amount of money. That amount doubles if they are also licensing your recording of that piece.

Note that in the somewhat rare instance that you have negotiated to keep your copyright when you agree to write original music for a film, the contract will state that you are allowing the producer to use both the music itself and the recording of that music for that particular film and for purposes related to the marketing of the film. Though this type of contract encompasses both synchronization and master use rights, it is commonly known as a "sync license." This is to differentiate it from the more-common "work made for hire" contract, which we will look at next.

WORK MADE FOR HIRE

Work made for hire is yet another dimension for film composers in the complex, yet important area of copyrights and publishing. Many of the preceding hypothetical examples assume that the composer actually owns the copyright of the work. However, the usual conditions under which a film composer signs a contract and delivers the score for U.S. films is as a work made for hire, or simply, work for hire. This legal term, established in the Copyright Act of 1976, requires that a work, in this case a film score, is created as a commission. The composer is hired to write the work by the producer, and while writing, despite being an independent contractor, that work is treated as though the composer were an employee of the production. During the writing of this music, all of their work, including every draft of every cue, demos, and even the software files upon which the music was created, belong to the producer, as though the producer were in fact its legal author. (Many composers will relate how at the end of a project, they had to turn over every external hard drive used in the project.) The producer then owns the copyright and can decide how the music is to be used (subject to any other conditions negotiated in the contract), both in the project it was composed for and possibly for other projects in the future.

In both the case of the project contracted for, as well as future uses of the music, the composer still receives the *writer's share* of royalties (we'll come back to this in the next chapter), but cannot control the use of the music. For example, a cue might be composed as 2M08, but the producer or director decides they like it better at the end of the movie, and it becomes 6M42. The composer has no control, in this kind of situation. It is important to know that this is standard procedure, with some exceptions, in the U.S. film-scoring business.

Unlike other copyright concepts, which as noted, are fairly standard around the world due to the Berne Convention, work for hire in this sense is unique to U.S. copyright law. That said, in many countries (Canada, for example), it is still most common for the film production company to own the copyright of the original music commissioned for the film. It just must be accomplished by the composer signing over (or "assigning") their copyright in the music to the production company after it is composed, rather than it legally never having belonged to the composer in the first place as a work for hire.

"Work for hire" can apply to both instrumental underscore and songs. If a composer is commissioned to write a song for a film under a work-for-hire contract, then that song is written as a work for hire. This is different from the song or piece of instrumental music that is already published, for which the producer must obtain a sync license from the publisher and master use license from the record company. When a song or piece is written as a work for hire, the producer becomes the publisher and also holds the master use rights to the recording.

Many composers have commented on the unfairness of this situation—that a person should spend weeks using their creative talents and training to produce a unique product, but have someone else legally be its author. This is also not the case in the classical or concert music scene, where a composer usually retains their copyright ownership even when writing on commission. In the film business, the future uses of the music are often controlled by a producer who has no artistic interest in the music, only a financial one. However, except in low-budget projects where a composer may have some leverage, this kind of rights deal is generally non-negotiable in any studio or network project. The reality of the scoring market is that production companies have the leverage to insist on this arrangement and composers who aren't willing to agree to a work for hire deal with them simply will not find work on those kinds of projects.

Especially problematic in this kind of deal is the possibility that the music will be used in a way that is creatively or personally reprehensible to the composer. To use a hypothetical example, a composer who has been a life-long vegetarian and animal-rights activist might not want their music to be used in a McDonalds commercial, regardless of any possible financial reward. Yet, if the music has been written on a work-for-hire basis, and a movie production company has the opportunity to sell the rights for a

McDonalds ad campaign, this composer would have no say in the matter, though they would receive royalties for the reuse of the music. There are some remedies for this; even a work-for-hire contract can include a clause limiting certain possible future uses of the music.

One instance where a composer might want to try to negotiate out of the work-for-hire clause and retain the rights to the music is on certain low-budget or independent projects. Occasionally, on such projects, the composer is offered a low amount of money to do a package deal. If this is the case, you can attempt to negotiate retaining ownership of the music—or at least sharing the ownership—in exchange for the lower fee. In this way, you can make some extra money down the road by licensing the music to other projects and collecting both writers' and publishers' royalties (see next chapter). However, even low-budget productions may be resistant to giving up their ownership of the music.

Also, it is a good idea to insist on retaining ownership of the music if you are scoring a student film, or any other project for no pay. The copyright is worth something, so if they're not able to pay even a small fee for your services, you might as well try to keep the copyright and be able to use the music somewhere down the road. The chances of a student film having a long theatrical life are low to none, so it is a shame to write some good music that gets lost forever under a work-for-hire contract clause.

As composers ourselves, we obviously have a bias about this issue. However, it is one of those unpleasant things, like taxes or getting cut off while driving, that is difficult to change and is a part of life. Therefore, composers who are at the beginning of their careers need to understand that this is a reality of the industry.

CHAPTER 23

Royalties

In chapter 21, we looked at the up-front fees a composer might receive from a production company (either as a straight fee or package deal). However, the most substantial income for the composer often comes after the fact, and from a different source: in the form of royalties. Money can be made for months or years after a film is completed from streaming, television, soundtrack albums, use of the music for commercials, showings of the film (in countries other than the U.S.), etc. Writing the score for a network TV series in particular can generate large amounts of royalties because of the number of viewers, episodes, and reruns. There is a difference in the amount and the way money is generated between underscore or song score, and the money generated in royalties from source music (known as "visual usage"). But first, let's define what kinds of royalties there are, where they come from, and who collects and distributes them.

PERFORMANCE ROYALTIES

There are two primary kinds of royalties to be collected for published music: performance royalties and mechanical royalties. *Performance royalties* are those that you receive after a work has been publicly performed. This covers some live performances, use in stores and restaurants, radio, television, movie theaters (though only those outside the U.S., which we will discuss), and streaming.

Performance royalties are divided into two portions. Half goes to the publisher, who is at least by default, the owner of the copyright, and half goes to the writer (composer), regardless of who holds the copyright. In some cases, the publisher and the writer are the same person or entity. In other cases, as in work-for-hire contracts, they are different. In addition, both the publishers' and the writers' portions can be divided into percentage splits, if there are co-writers or co-publishers.

In the U.S., performances are monitored by three main performing rights organizations (PROs): ASCAP, BMI, and SESAC. Every country around the world has its own PRO and the U.S. is the only country with multiple PROs. Worldwide, PROs are affiliated with their counterparts in foreign countries, so that if your music is performed in a different country than your own, the foreign society will report your earnings to your home country PRO, which will distribute them to you.

PROs issue licenses to anyone who uses music in their catalogs. This includes TV and radio stations, restaurants and nightclubs, streaming services, and so forth. An annual amount is paid by these venues and media outlets to the PRO for a blanket license to use any of the music in its catalog. The PRO then determines the amount of royalties owed to the various writers and publishers that are its members and distributes the money in quarterly statements.

Note that a writer in the U.S. can only belong to one of the three American PROs, and their publisher must belong to the same one. Many publishers have several different companies under the same umbrella, each with a different PRO, so that they can work with writers of any performing rights affiliation.

SMALL RIGHTS AND GRAND RIGHTS

There are two types of performance royalties: small rights and grand rights. *Small rights,* also called "non-dramatic rights," are the ones previously mentioned—performances on radio, television, nightclubs, etc. *Grand rights,* or "dramatic performance rights," are for live performances in a dramatic setting: Broadway musicals, ballet, or opera. The PROs do not issue licenses for grand rights and do not monitor this type of performance. So, if you write the music to a Broadway show or ballet, then either you or your publisher must negotiate the license for each live performance of that music directly with the producer.

Most of the time, film scores fall under small rights (non-dramatic rights). If a movie is shown on television or streaming (or is a show produced for one of those media to begin with), or if the music is played on the radio, it is covered by a small rights license, and your performance royalties will be collected and distributed by your PRO. However, if the same music from a film is adapted for a ballet, then the publisher must arrange for a grand rights license.

ROYALTIES FROM THEATRICAL PERFORMANCES OF FILMS

The other thing to be aware of regarding performance royalties, especially in film scoring, is that in the U.S., no royalties are paid for the showing of a movie in theaters. This is a situation that came about in the late 1940s. At that time, ASCAP was the predominant performing rights organization; BMI and SESAC were only just getting started. In 1947, almost every U.S. film composer belonged to ASCAP and was receiving healthy royalties for scores that were shown in theaters around the country. Every theater paid a yearly amount to ASCAP for the right to use their members' copyrighted music, and ASCAP made quarterly distributions to the composers. However, in 1947, ASCAP tried to raise the fee substantially and the theater owners filed suit. On March 14, 1950, the judge handed down a decision in favor of the theater owners and against ASCAP, declaring that the raising of the fee was illegal. He also took this decision a step further, declaring that it was a violation of antitrust laws for ASCAP to demand any kind of license for the theatrical use of motion picture music. This meant that the theaters could show any movie with any music and not have to pay performance royalties at all.

This ruling was a blow to composers and greatly affected their royalty income. Unfortunately, it is still in effect today and is the reason why film composers do not collect royalties from the showing of films in the United States. However, most other countries do allow the issuing of licenses for theatrical performances, and if an American composer scores the music for a film that is released in theaters overseas, that composer will collect royalties through the foreign affiliate of their performance rights society.

The distribution of royalties from the performing rights societies is determined by complex formulas. For film composers, royalties from television and video streaming performances are the most relevant. For broadcast and cable channels, this is determined by a census survey, meaning that everything that is performed in a given area, whether it be ABC, CBS, NBC, WB, HBO, TNT, etc., is counted and prorated, and then a royalty is paid. The size of the station, the time of day of the broadcast, and the kind of performance will determine how much the royalty actually will be. Performances on large, urban stations are weighed the heaviest. Prime time slots (7:00 P.M. to 1:00 A.M.) are the best time of day to have performances. The major networks (ABC, CBS, and NBC) still pay the most, with the other broadcast and cable networks trailing behind.

These days, of course, a lot of media is produced by and for streaming, and even content made for broadcast is likely to be viewed on a streaming service rather than over the airwaves or on cable. In this case, the royalties are calculated based on the number of streams. The rate per stream is still low compared to the equivalent royalty rate per viewer on legacy media formats, so overall, the income available to composers from royalties has diminished in recent years. Composer Ben Bromfield, who writes for some of the most viewed streaming shows, compares the royalties for those shows to be what he'd expect to see for similar cable shows, but not as much as broadcast royalties. For example, on one recent streaming show, his royalties were about fifty percent of his up-front fee in the first year. That said, he is still adamant that royalties are essential to a composer's long-term financial success, and that composers need to hold the line and not accept deals in which they sign away their writer's shares.

> *Performing rights organizations are the closest thing we have to a union for composers. They are able to collectively bargain for us with other large entities. And even though we can't get everything that a union can bargain for, like health care and weekends off, the fact that we've gone all-in as an industry on keeping our royalties is something a lot of other sectors of the entertainment industry are jealous of. If it weren't for the royalties, this wouldn't be that good of a job, frankly. The fact that you are creating intellectual property that gets distributed around the world is a major advantage to what we're doing. One way to describe what we're doing is writing music. But another way to describe it is that we're creating long-term assets for ourselves. And the fact that we own a tiny sliver of the success of a film or a show is amazing, and we have to hold on to that.*

CUE SHEETS

The way that each broadcast of a film or show gets translated into the right amount of payments to each writer and publisher is that the producer or studio submits a *cue sheet* listing the cues in a particular show or film to RapidCue, a service that all of the PROs have agreed to use. As previously noted, the music editor is responsible for creating this cue sheet, if there is one attached to the project, though in situations where there is no music editor, the composer may be called on to draft it. This cue sheet notes the usage type for each cue, its duration, and its writer(s) and publisher(s). The PRO then cross-references that cue sheet with the data from the broadcaster about when the show aired, and calculates the appropriate monetary distribution.

Performance usages fall into the following categories, and each category gets paid a royalty at a different rate: visual vocal or instrumental, background vocal or instrumental, and main or end titles. So-called "feature performances" including "visual cues" (what we would call source cues) and "main and end titles" get paid the most. Background cues (underscore or song score) get paid the least. Some PROs further distinguish between instrumental and vocal cues, with vocals being paid a higher rate; others have abandoned this distinction.

PERFORMANCE ROYALTIES FROM RADIO AND STREAMING AUDIO

Performance royalties cover all public broadcasts, which includes terrestrial and satellite radio and streaming audio. Since film music rarely gets radio airplay, the main way these types of royalties might enter a film composer's income stream is through streaming audio of a soundtrack album. Currently, streaming audio pays only a tiny fraction of a penny for each stream, so even big name music artists can't rely on streaming audio royalties as a primary source of income.

In some cases, there will be a breakout hit that has significant streaming or even radio airplay, especially when it comes to songs from a popular show. This was the case with two of the songs co-composed by Sonya Belousova and Giona Ostinelli, first from the Netflix shows *The Witcher* (2019) and then *One Piece* (2023). In 2023, for example, the duo had 47 million streams on Spotify, so even given the low $0.003 to $0.005 per stream, that adds up a six-figure annual amount. And that's only for the Spotify performance royalties, not any up-front fees paid for the score, performance royalties from the video streaming, or sales of the music through downloadable files (to be discussed).

MECHANICAL ROYALTIES

Mechanical royalties are those received from the sales of recorded music, as digital downloads or physical albums, as opposed to public performances, broadcasts, and streams. Although mechanical royalties are much more important to songwriters than film composers, they can create a significant royalty income for film composers when there is a soundtrack release from a popular film or show.

Mechanical royalties came about when, at the turn of the twentieth century—before radio, before stereo recordings, before vinyl records—the home music entertainment machines of choice were cylinder records, pianos, and player pianos. At that time, the 1909 Copyright Act was passed, guaranteeing the writers and publishers of music a royalty for every record, piano roll, and piece of sheet music sold. Because those records and songs were reproduced on machines, they were called mechanical royalties. Sheet music and piano rolls became the biggest income generators for composers and songwriters, with records running a distant second. As the technology changed over the years, records (of the various kinds), cassette tapes, CDs, and finally digital files have replaced printed music as the primary source of mechanical royalty income.

There are actually two types of mechanical royalties. In the previous chapter, we discussed how someone can perform and record your copyrighted material without receiving your permission, as long as your work has been published (distributed or offered for sale to the public). When they do this, they are acting under a *compulsory mechanical license*. This license allows a person or company to use your published material without having to receive your permission, as long as they abide by certain rules, including:

- They agree to notify you within thirty days of making or distributing the work that they are using your copyrighted material,
- They will send you a monthly statement and payment of royalties earned, and
- They will pay the statutory mechanical rate based on the number of units manufactured.

The other kind of mechanical license is a *negotiated mechanical license*, which is similar to a compulsory mechanical license, only it is more flexible. This license is simply referred to as a mechanical license—the license that is issued to someone who wants to use your music, and would like more lenient terms from you than those in the compulsory mechanical license. Its terms usually involve the receipt of a quarterly statement instead of a monthly one, an agreed-upon lower rate than the statutory minimum, and the payment of royalties on units sold, as opposed to units actually manufactured. For film composers, the negotiated mechanical license is usually the one in effect.

Mechanical royalties are administered by the record company (or other publisher), which keeps track of how many units are sold, and they pay accordingly. For film composers, this can be a significant (but not huge) amount of money. Soundtrack albums traditionally sell small amounts compared to hit pop albums. However, as the soundtrack craze waxes and wanes, there are sometimes conditions under which a significant amount of royalties add up for the composer of the score.

Usually, the film composer's contract specifies a dollar amount per album sold as their mechanical royalty. This is because film cues are not like songs; they can be much longer in duration, especially after the music editor is finished editing. This editing can involve cutting as many as fifteen short cues together to make eight or ten long selections for soundtrack release. Remember, mechanical royalties for songs are based on the statutory minimum, 12.4 cents per song, or even lower if you negotiate a different rate. Therefore, if the film composer goes by that rate, for ten selections on an album that is actually a compilation of fifteen or twenty cues, they will receive only $1.24 for every album sold.

REAL DOLLARS

Here is the nitty-gritty of royalties, and after reading this section you might be wetting your lips anticipating your pot of gold at the end of the royalty rainbow. Note that performance royalties are the main source of royalty income for film composers, so they take up the bulk of this discussion.

Let's look at some of the possible numbers in performance royalties. The rates that the different performance royalty organizations pay are generally comparable, although they all have slightly different formulas for computing the rate. As of this writing, the highest rates for a main title playing on 200 stations for a major network broadcaster are between $600 and $700. In the same primetime broadcast scenario, underscore (a.k.a.

background instrumental cues) would pay about $200 per minute. That means if you write twenty minutes of underscore for a show that is broadcast nationally on ABC, CBS, NBC, or Fox between 7 P.M. and 1 A.M., you will receive about $4,000 for the writer's share of performance royalties. If you score a full season (twenty-two shows in a year), you'd expect $88,000 a year in royalties. If you also wrote the main title theme, that amount would climb to as much as $4,800 per episode, or over $100,000 in a year. (Keep in mind that this is the writer's share; the producer is receiving an identical check for the publisher's share, assuming you have signed a contract making the score as a work for hire.) These royalties are in addition to the up-front fee or package deal you were already paid by the production company for composing the music.

In addition, after the initial airings, many television shows will be rerun on other channels, and each time that happens, you will receive performance royalties scaled relative to that broadcaster and timeslot.

Note that songs played as background music are considered the same as instrumental background by ASCAP and BMI. (SESAC pays a higher rate for vocal cues regardless of whether they are background or visual uses.) However, if someone is singing a song or playing an instrument on-camera, that is considered a visual vocal, or featured performance, and the royalty rate is considerably higher.

When we drop down from big broadcast networks (which pay the most) to cable or streaming services, these rates fall considerably. Cable rates vary tremendously, depending on how big the cable station is. Royalties for featured cues can range from over $100 to just pennies per minute, and background cues trail far behind these featured use rates. Streaming continues to pay the lowest, with their rates being calculated per stream. It is difficult to pin down numbers on streaming service royalties, as their data is confidential. However, overall, it's clear that composers with multiple hit shows on streaming can still earn six figure performance royalties annually, whereas composers of shows and movies with fewer views can't rely on their royalty income as much, and may need to negotiate more money up-front or find other ways to make the bulk of their money.

Let's take a look at some hypothetical examples for feature films and television that take into account performance royalties from several possible sources, mechanical royalties from sales of CDs and downloads, as well as the composer's fee (or profit from a package deal). Note that these examples leave out possible future revenue from commercials and other reuses. And please also note that the following scenarios are hypothetical, and that rates will vary tremendously based on multiple factors.

POSSIBLE SCENARIO 1: FEATURE FILM

Let's take a look at some of the possible numbers for music in a feature film that has sixty minutes of music, was a moderate success, and is an example of a mid-budget studio production. It is shown on cable two months after the theatrical release, and network TV one year later.

Income Stream	Calculation	Amount
Composer's fee		$500,000
U.S. cable television (HBO), multiple broadcasts	(60 minutes x $7 per minute x 50 showings)	$21,000
Network broadcast, prime time	(60 minutes x $200 per minute)	$12,000
Foreign theatrical and other foreign performances (1st year)		$150,000
Local television performances and streaming	(5 years)	$50,000
	Total Income:	**$733,000**

Again, keep in mind that this scenario excludes many possible future royalties, such as more television performances, possible use in commercials, or even use in other films. In addition, a film can continue to earn performance royalties for the composer over many years of airings. (And remember that in the U.S., there are no performance royalties when the film is shown in a theater, but there are for overseas theatrical performances)

POSSIBLE SCENARIO 2: PRIMETIME NETWORK TV SERIES

Here is how the money—fees and royalties—can add up for music in a network, prime-time TV series. Let's assume there are twenty minutes of music in each of twenty-two episodes, with each episode broadcast twice (the initial airing and reruns) on a prime-time network over the course of one year.

Income Stream	Calculation	Amount
Composer's profit from package deal, twenty-two episodes	$5,000 x 22	$110,000
First year, U.S. network prime time, initial airing, and summer reruns	44 shows x 20 minutes x $200 per minute	$176,000
Main title theme royalties	44 shows x $800	$35,200
First year, foreign television performances	(1 year)	$30,000
First year syndication		$50,000
Strip syndication (1 year)		$40,000
	Total Income:	**$441,200**

You might have noticed that if the up-front fee is taken out of these examples, the TV series composer is making more money in royalties than the film composer in the example we presented. However, for a blockbuster movie that gets significant foreign box office and multiple reruns on network television, the royalties can really add up. There are, however, several big differences between TV scoring and film scoring when it comes to total income. First of all, the TV composer is working steadily, maybe even six days a week for twenty-two weeks, whereas the film composer will probably spend four to twelve weeks on a feature film, and can score three or four films a year if they're on a roll.

You can probably also see that when it comes to network television scoring, royalties will far outstrip up-front fees, even with the somewhat generous assumptions in this scenario about how much profit a composer will clear from a package deal. It's common for television to pay $5,000 to $10,000 per episode up front as a package, but the composer is often paying most or even all of that on players, engineers, and even additional music writers to be able to write all the music within the deadline. Therefore, a TV composer may rely on royalties for the entirety of their take-home pay.

POSSIBLE SCENARIO 3: CABLE TV MOVIE

With a cable TV movie, having left the area of feature films and episodic television, you can see the numbers drop significantly. When you have a film on cable or local television, the royalties are paltry in comparison to the national broadcast networks. This is not to say such movies are not worth scoring. They can still be a good source of income, as well as a step towards bigger and better things. Note that for a movie on a streaming network, these numbers likely look similar.

Income Stream	Calculation	Amount
Composer's profit from package deal		$15,000
Primetime airing of film	(45 minutes x $22)	$990
Re-airing on smaller sister network	(45 minutes x $7)	$315
	Total Income:	**$16,305**

POSSIBLE SCENARIO 4: (RELATIVELY POPULAR) STREAMING SHOW

For a streaming show, you can see that compared to a TV movie, a series is going to generate more revenue for a composer, though just as in the broadcast vs. feature film examples, you have to remember that the time it takes to score a series is more than for a film. Here, the ratio of up-front to royalty payments for streaming is a very different proposition, at least currently, than it is for national network broadcast television. In fact, the royalty rates are closer to that for cable than network television. This may still change, of course, as PROs and other organizations representing composers lobby for updates to rate calculations.

Income Stream	Calculation	Amount
Composer's profit from package deal, twelve episodes	$5,000 x 12	$60,000
First year streaming royalties		$15,000
	Total Income:	**$75,000**

In any of these scenarios, you can see that performance royalties are a film composer's friend. They can provide steady income during slow times and can add up to substantial amounts from all the different possible sources. In addition, the composer does almost no administrative work. The performing rights society takes care of it all. The only thing a composer must do is make sure that the cue sheets are filed properly with the performing rights society. Even that task is administered by the production office of the film; all the composer has to do is review the summary of cues.

The more work you do, the more you build up a catalog, the more money will flow to you in the form of performance royalties. Shows or movies that you scored ten years ago can still generate both domestic and foreign or syndicated performances, so the more of these you have, the more money you make. Even if it's not the bulk of your income, it can be like an annuity for retirement.

CHAPTER 24

Finding Work

There comes a point when a dream can become a reality. The musician who has dreamed about working as a film composer is ready to live that dream once they've achieved the appropriate composition and orchestration skills, has mastered storytelling and drama, has built their home studio and knows how to use music technology effectively, and above all, is ready to start making money writing music for movies. The questions are: How to get started? Where is the work? What materials are needed? Whom should I call? Am I good enough? On and on these questions go, with many variations on these themes.

There is no one answer; there is no one best route to scoring success and a sustainable career, let alone stardom. Every working composer has a different story to tell. They all involve some combination of hard work, persistence, preparation, and sheer luck. Maybe the 347th door you knock on will be the one. You never know when a director will hear your self-released album and decide that your music is perfect for their film. You could knock on every door in Hollywood, New York, London, or Mumbai for years, only to get into a fender-bender with a director who is looking for a composer. So, the best thing a composer can do is be persistent, keep writing, study, and be prepared so that when that opportunity comes around, you're ready to run with it.

In the early days of film scoring, there were few avenues for a composer to make a living. There were feature films, documentaries, and a small amount of *corporate films*—often in-house training movies. Then, television came in and expanded the opportunities. Now, in today's world, with the explosion of streaming services in addition to network television, cable, podcasts, music libraries, and video games, there are countless more content creators who need original music.

With all of this new content needing music, there are also thousands of aspiring film composers around the world right now, hoping to catch that big break. How can you hope to compete? One of the biggest distinctions between the wannabes and the real composers is perseverance.

Mark Snow puts this angle well:

> *You knock on every door and you're merciless, you keep persevering like crazy and pray, and one out of ten composers who come to town make it. I don't know, maybe one out of a hundred. Maybe one out of four.*

There are many ways to get started in the film-composing business. You can move to Los Angeles and try to join the world's biggest scoring market. Or you can go to a smaller media center, get some smaller projects, and gain experience and credibility. Either way, there are two things that must happen while you are getting started. First, you need to be actively involved in making or writing music on a regular basis. Second, you need to have your act together in terms of presenting yourself and your music. Take the time to organize your materials in a professional way. Remember that this is a business based on person-to-person relationships, and your demos, your website, your Spotify tracks or YouTube videos, and even your business card could be the first step of this relationship. Create a logo and a company, make a compelling and professional-looking website, invest in business cards, set up a business bank account. When you go to meetings, be appropriately dressed, arrive on time, and be confident. In short, create an aura about yourself that says to a producer or director, "This person has their act together and would be good to work with."

WEB PRESENCE

The old cliché in commerce and marketing is that the key to success is "location, location, location." In the old days, if your business was on busy Main Street, that was a whole lot better than off on one of the lesser-used side streets. Today, a similar maxim applies, only it could be reworded to apply to digital as well as physical spaces. Obviously, the internet is where a large portion of commerce and networking takes place these days. This hasn't diminished the centrality of personal relationships in the entertainment business, but there are now composers who have been hired without ever meeting the director or producer because they had great stuff posted on their websites or socials.

WEBSITES

Today's website is a combination of yesterday's business card, résumé, and demo reel. It is the composer's public face, and is often the first impression a director or producer will have of you. Or it may be the second impression, after you get the opportunity to meet someone at a networking event, and rather than calling you and chatting, that director checks out your webpage to decide whether or not you might be a good fit for their film. Though some composers may opt to skip the website and focus instead solely on social media, it is generally advisable to at least have a landing page to link all your other accounts in one central location. You have more control over how this site will show up in search engines, and social media companies are constantly in flux, so it's more reliable long-term to have a website. Here are some things to take into consideration when designing your site:

- **Presentation.** Make your site professional and pleasant to look at. The graphics should be clear and have some flair. Not too dry, not too flamboyant. A sense of humor is great, but remember that all different kinds of people might be checking it out, so go for the middle ground. Keep the language clean, and for those of you who are the exuberant type, keep a lid on the tendency to be goofy.
- **Organization and layout.** The site should be easy to navigate and well organized. Make clear divisions in the options for pages that represent different facets of your career and who you are. For example, you might have different places

to navigate to such as biography, credits, photos, film music samples, rock performances, songwriting, concert music, director recommendations, contact information, etc. It is fine to have one site for everything you do as a musician, but another option is to create one site dedicated to music for film, and have another one for everything else, such as your work as a jazz pianist, for example. Both ways have potential pros and cons.

- **Demos.** First and foremost, if you are presenting more styles than just film scores, make sure you have made clear distinctions and options for the visitor. The last thing you want is for a director to go to your heavy metal rock band's examples thinking that is all you do. This is where the clarity of your design is paramount. Make it easy to find the different pages that showcase your skills as a film composer as opposed to a concert composer, performer, or songwriter.

  Be ready to include as many different styles of writing as you can, but not to the extent that it becomes like the proverbial box of chocolates. Your unique compositional voice should be discernable in all of your music, while offering up different kinds of cues: love themes, comedy, action cues, suspense cues, etc. If there are genres you especially want to work on that call for a particular kind of writing, be sure to include those.

- **Streaming video.** Many composers stream at least some video examples of scenes with their music to show their ability to score to picture or because this can double as a way to show off your scoring credits. Just remember, you should absolutely not include any rescores here (clips from an already released movie where you replaced the original music with your own). Not only do you not have permission from the copyright holder to share video clips from a released film that you didn't score, but this also risks making it seem like you're not yet a professional with real credits to show.

SOCIAL MEDIA

There are as many ways to participate in social media as there are ways to interact in the real world. You have a choice of many different platforms and how to show up there. Though the specific companies change so fast that it wouldn't be productive to explore these in a book, the principles behind choosing where and how to leverage these platforms changes far more slowly.

- **Quality over quantity.** It's far better to focus on one or two social media platforms and really build a presence and engagement there, rather than to try to be on all of them but only post once in a long time on each. Social media algorithms vary, but all of them reward engagement, making your posts more visible to your audience the more effort you put in. It's also important to learn at least a few basics of social media marketing for each platform. Is there an etiquette to likes or shares? Do you get more views when you include an image rather than just text? Are hashtags in wide use? And so forth. Until you can hire a specialist (social media manager or publicist) to handle your social media presence for you, as with other scoring-adjacent skills like budgeting, mixing, and orchestration, you may need to get up to speed yourself—at least as an advanced beginner in managing social media.
- **Professional vs. personal.** Social media blurs the boundaries between private and public in ways that can be difficult to navigate. The first thing is to decide if you'll have a separate social media presence for your scoring persona or company, or if you'll use your personal accounts for your professional work as well. There are pros and cons to each decision, and various factors are unique in each person's case, such as how established you are already on a platform, what kind of work you do, and what kind of professional facade you want to project. Even if you have separate accounts for your business, you will need to keep your personal social media posts consistent with your professional image. Don't be lulled into thinking that your

personal account is private just because your posts are set to "private" or "friends only." Assume anything you put up can and will be findable publicly.

- **Be helpful.** You may think you need to constantly be promoting your projects—and you're not wrong!—but actually, the most effective way to interact on social media can be finding ways to be helpful. Join online groups, and answer questions for which you have expertise. Create a YouTube channel dedicated to a niche area for which you can create tutorials. Spending time seeking to be helpful to the scoring community or, even better, the communities frequented by your potential clients is a great way to build a strong reputation and can lead to job offers.

DEMO REELS

The music that you present on your website, socials, and demo reel submissions are an expression of your musical personality. People listening will be getting a sense of your creative ability, what kind of person you are, your sense of taste, and ability to interact professionally. So, this music must sound great to the non-musical listener. It must be well-produced, and the visuals that accompany it must be professional looking, as it represents your "brand."

The majority of film scoring demos are most effectively presented in audio form, rather than video. This is in part, perhaps counterintuitively, because of filmmakers' strong sense of visual language. Let them imagine your music in their film. In addition, using video can work against you if the film scenes you have the rights to show from past work are from student films or other projects of less than ideal quality. Even in cases where you have excellent film clips to include, most filmmakers watching them for the first time will be distracted by things like the acting, editing, and camera work, and may not be able to focus fully on your music. Sticking to audio also removes issues around copyright for the film clips, which may be much harder to get permission to post publicly.

There are two basic types of presentation to filmmakers. One is a selection of publicly available tracks on your website, YouTube, SoundCloud, or other such service. For this kind of showcase of your work, be sure to demonstrate as many sides of your composing as possible (orchestral, electronic, ambient, etc.), but make sure to keep it sounding like film music. The other presentation of your work is a custom-made demo reel for a particular project. In this case, you want to show off your skills in the genre of music that the director describes, or that you think they want.

In the case of demo reels for specific projects, the next question is how to make and send this reel. These days, really the only way to send a demo reel is electronically, but do you just share the files via email, create a custom web page for each reel, or use a site specifically designed for demo reel creation and sending? The last of these is generally the best option, as it allows you to create custom demos for each job quickly, craft the look and text that accompanies the reel, and in some cases, track how the reel has been opened and viewed. For these reasons, most composers will subscribe to a service dedicated to this task, such as ReelCrafter. However, when just getting started, either of the other two options can be cheaper and can work in a pinch. Just be sure to customize the reel you send for each job, if you're applying for a particular film. Don't simply share your generic demo reel on your website that includes a range of genres if you know the filmmaker is looking for dissonant, textural horror music, or is making a bouncy cartoon comedy. Showing that you understand their vision by sending only relevant tracks will go a long way to advancing you in the pool of composers under consideration.

There are also some principles common to both general and specific demo reels.

- **Recording quality.** Make sure all the musical examples on your demos are well recorded and mixed. Do not include projects played by students or amateurs if they have questionable intonation, or projects with poor mixes and less than terrific sound quality. A director may not know that the reason your wonderful composition sounds bad is because the clarinet is a quarter-tone flat or the shaker is too up-front in the mix, and the worst thing you can do in an early meeting with a potential client is apologize for some aspect of your demos. Use high-quality sample libraries, sweetened with live performances where appropriate, and have someone with experience check your mixes.

Composers have gone to various lengths to make great demos. Some have hired small orchestras, to the tune of several thousand dollars, in order to make the best presentation. There are demo orchestras that you can book at reasonable rates in Los Angeles and in Europe. Sometimes, they offer group sessions where you can go in with several other composers so you only have to pay for fifteen or thirty minutes. Whether you go to this extent or stick to orchestral mockups for your demos, the key is to make it sound as good as possible.

- **Give it a hook.** Try to include as much material as possible that is either thematic in nature or has a unique timbre or musical concept. Cues with catchy melodic material or a sound that catches the audience's ear are generally more interesting than cues that were originally conceived as underscore for a scene with dialogue. As we've seen, most film music is background music, and as such, is not meant to be listened to without also seeing the film. If there are sections in a cue that are really static, see if you can make an edit and just include the more interesting parts.
- **Film cues, not concert works.** Choose pieces that are from films or are film-like in nature. Cues from projects you have actually worked on are best, but cues for an imaginary scene can work fine. Excerpts from classical concert pieces or jazz band arrangements are not recommended, because they do not usually sound like film music. The majority of films don't use these kinds of ensembles.
- **A rose by any other name...** Go ahead and label your demo cues either with their original title (if they came from a real film for which you earned a scoring credit) or with a descriptive title to entice the listener. For example,

a cue that was originally titled "Sally Meets Bill" in a film could be retitled "Love at First Sight." Or an action cue that was originally called "The Garbage Man" could become "Madison Avenue at 70 MPH." In this way, the visitor gets a sense in advance of what they are about to hear. Whatever you do, don't use a title from a project you didn't actually have credited work for.

NETWORKING

Once you have all your materials together, you are ready to go out and get some gigs. That means meeting people anywhere you can. Be prepared for a lot of rejection that has nothing to do with your skills as a composer. Most of all, be prepared to talk to and be interested in other people.

There are many avenues for the beginning composer, but the most important thing to do is to expand your circle of contacts. Whether you live in Los Angeles, New York, or anywhere else, find the places where film and music people gather. This could be trade organizations like ASCAP, BMI, or the Society of Composers and Lyricists. It could also be a more local organization like the Massachusetts Production Coalition, which offers regular networking meetings that include producers, directors, actors, composers, and many others associated with the entertainment business in the state. Film festivals and screenings are also great places to meet people and to hang out with emerging filmmakers or people attending filmmaking seminars. Go to these events, take your business cards, and don't expect to get offered a gig. Just meet some people, and then stay in touch with them. You'd be surprised how much fun you can have and at how effective this can be in your career path.

You could also get a job as an intern in a trade organization, at a recording studio, or at a production house. The Television Academy offers an internship every year, as does the Society of Composers and Lyricists. Opportunities like these are often posted at colleges or universities and on the web, but you will need to be resourceful to win a seat in one. Make a list of potential internship sites, and then email—or, preferably, call—and find out if a recording studio, composer, or post-production house ever needs interns or entry-level assistants. Keep a log of the responses, including the names of all the people you talk to, even the receptionists. If they say, "No, but maybe in the future," wait a couple of months and call again. If they say, "No, we never hire unknowns," then cross them off the list.

Want ads were never a good way to find the rare film scoring related jobs, and that remains the case even in the age of internet hiring sites. That said, occasionally, people advertise internships, jobs as composer's assistants, and even put out a call for composers to submit music for a film on social media groups and even traditional job sites. If you want to include these in your career strategy, be prepared to check them all frequently, even several times a day, as the competition for these jobs can be fierce. One former student of ours responded to an internet listing where an independent film company was looking for a composer to do sixty minutes of music—for free. He responded within the first hour of the posting, and eventually made it to the final three. He was told that they had received over three hundred inquiries by the end of the first day! That means that there were three hundred people who were at least willing to investigate a project where they could be spending dozens of hours working for nothing. This is one of the many reasons that building your network person-by-person, though painstaking, is generally time better spent.

Fish where the fish are! If you are looking for films to score, you can network all day with other musicians, but you'll never get hired. Instead, you need to find filmmakers—specifically, filmmakers at the same approximate level in their career as you are in yours. Early on in your career, that probably means film students. Though perhaps only one in a hundred film students will make it big, if you establish a strong bond early on with a talented young director, you can sometimes ride their coattails to your own success. A famous recent example of this was the composer-director pair of Ludwig Göransson and Ryan Coogler. The two met as students at USC, where Göransson scored Coogler's thesis film. They then went on to work together on all of Coogler's films, from *Fruitvale Station* (2013) through *Creed* (2015), and eventually *Black Panther* (2018), for which Göransson won the Oscar Best Original Score.

Another approach is to send your materials to producers of low budget films and documentaries, but keep in mind that most unsolicited demos never get played. The question becomes, how to get your demo reel into the "solicited" category. The best way is to somehow make personal contact with a producer or director. This can happen in any number of ways. You might meet someone at a party, at a seminar, or in line at a coffee shop. Ideally, you won't ask everyone you meet this way for a job, but do keep in touch with them. Then, when they are looking for a composer, they are likely to think of you and invite you to apply.

Once you have sent your materials, follow-up is extremely important. Wait about a week, and then call to make sure that your submission was received. This is not the only reason you will be calling. The other reason is to keep your name on their radar. Be careful here, though. There is a fine line between persistence and annoyance. People get busy. While it is sometimes important to remind them of your existence, it is also possible to become a pest and create a negative association with your name. Oftentimes, the response will be that the producer has not listened to your demos, or that they are not interested. This is difficult for some composers to hear because most of us want to believe that the world is waiting to hear our musical creations. However, finding work is often a form of self-promotion. The trick is to become thick-skinned, and not to take rejection as a reflection of your musical ability, personality, or worth as a human being. Take it as simply a result of where a particular person is at that particular day. Perhaps they already have another composer. Perhaps they really didn't like your music, and that's okay! Music is subjective, and you need to have the confidence that someone else will like it.

COMPOSER'S ASSISTANTS

These days, most composers have at least one and often several assistants who work for them either part-time or full-time, in-house or remotely (see chapter 11). Starting one's career as a composer's assistant has become the de facto standard entry-level job, and it brings multiple benefits of learning on the job: not only the skills involved in scoring and music technology, but also the much harder to acquire skills of client management, communication, and collaboration that are best learned by watching someone already skilled in these elusive arts. Ideally, an assistantship also has an aspect of mentorship, where the composer employer considers the needs of the assistant to learn and grow their own career.

When an established composer is looking for an assistant, it is usually to help relieve the pressure of short deadlines. That translates to someone who has excellent technology skills, knowledge of both MIDI and traditional orchestration, and perhaps could help with additional writing. Of these, it is usually the technology skills that come first, though which of these skills will be needed will vary from composer to composer, and the actual duties performed by the assistant will differ depending on each composer's modus operandi. There are hundreds of aspiring composers angling for jobs as the assistant to an established composer. What we hear over and over again is that in addition to the skills listed above, the most important quality a composer is looking for in an assistant is someone who has a great and helpful personality, who is a problem solver and self-starter, and is willing to go many extra miles to "make it happen."

The daily life of the composer's assistant can be rich and varied, or it can be dry and dull. Most assistants report that it is interesting, intense, creative, and demanding. One day, the assistant could be answering phones and filing paperwork. The next day, they could be orchestrating or composing a cue for a feature film or network TV show. This makes these great, terrific jobs for an aspiring composer, and although they are generally entry level, these opportunities immerse the budding composer in every aspect of the film-scoring process: making demos, spotting, taking a meeting, meeting deadlines, recording sessions, mixes, and dubs. The assistant is usually getting a hands-on education in how the scoring process and business works. Pay is not usually high, but when you consider that you are getting paid while gaining what is essentially the equivalent of a graduate degree skillset, it is often well worth considering.

That said, it's important to note the possible downsides of composers' assistant jobs, especially for some established composers who take advantage of the young, ambitious, just-starting-out composer by requiring over-long working hours and offering unreasonably low pay. An ethical employer will set up reasonable working hours and conditions, with adequate pay, and provide credit for original work written by an assistant (for example, sharing writer's credit on the cue sheet, and requesting an additional music credit in the film for them). Unethical employers may not do one or more of these, and in the worst cases, can be verbally abusive. Assistants in such problematic jobs may not feel they have options, because the work is so hard to find and the opportunities so valuable. There's also no human resources department in most composers' studios, and since there is no union or guild for composers either, an assistant who's being exploited may not know where to turn. The advice often given is, "If the working environment is emotionally or physically toxic, get out!" though that advice may be harder to follow than it is to give. It is important to remember that there are many ethical and fair employers out there, and that it is worth holding out for one of those, rather than putting up with unacceptable conditions in the hopes of finding your big break.

Many young people working as composer's assistants stay in touch and network with each other. There is a kind of informal assistants network that starts humming as both long-term and short-term jobs open up. This is helpful in finding work since, as with films, composers' assistant jobs are not to be found in traditional job listings. Communicating with others working as assistants also helps in calibrating expectations and getting support in standing up for your rights as an employee, and in solving job-related problems that may be unique to the job of composer's assistants.

Finally, it's important to understand that if your goal is eventually to score your own films, you should continue to score student and independent films on the side, even while assisting another composer. Since your credits for your assistant work, if any, will likely be "additional music," at best, you will also need to build up some credits and a filmmaker network of your own. This is difficult to do around the long hours generally expected of assistants, but it's also good preparation for the type of work ethic required to sustain a composing career.

MUSIC LIBRARIES AND TRAILERS

Another avenue to explore for the emerging composer is to look into work composing for music libraries and trailers. There are some similarities in how the business operates for both of these.

Music libraries can also be an opportunity for added income, or even a full-time career. It's important to note though that there isn't really a path from music library scoring to getting custom film scoring work, and the two skillsets are related, but different. There are many library companies that license cues to TV and film producers who either don't have the budget for a custom score, or prefer the relative control and simplicity of working with pre-existing tracks. Each music library has lists of genres and moods that can be browsed, and they get paid according to the usage: how big the project is, where it will be shown, etc. The arrangement with the composer, however, will depend on the company. Some libraries pay an up-front fee for the music, and the composer retains the writer's share of the royalties. Some libraries offer a buy-out, where the composer is forfeiting the writer's share and just receives a one-time, up-front payment. This is not the norm, but at least one library company offers no money at all unless the cue is picked up by a producer, and then there is a small payment for the use of the cue as well as the composer keeping the writer's share of the royalties.

Music library work is, in part, a numbers game. If you write one or two tracks, you may get lucky and get a big placement, but if you write a hundred tracks or more each year, eventually, you're bound to get some placement. The 80/20 rule truly applies here: about 20 percent of music library tracks make at least 80 percent of the money. The library itself also makes a huge difference. The music library is acting as a publisher. If they have great connections in a particular market—for example, if CBS selects most of their music from that particular library—then writing for that library will be much more lucrative than writing for one that isn't on most producers' go-to list, even if the terms of the deal for the composer are much better in the smaller library.

There are also several specialized music houses that write music just for trailers, and these can be well-paying jobs. It's rare, in fact, for the music in a trailer to be pulled from the original score for the film, both because the film's music is usually not ready by the time the trailer is released, and because trailer music is in a way its own unique genre—very different from the conventions and functions of film scores. Usually, these companies will offer custom scoring for trailers, but most of their music will come from the distribution of trailer-specific music libraries, which trailer companies will pull from to music-edit the trailer score. If you are interested in this career avenue, you'll need to immerse yourself in trailer music specifically, and also get adept at sequencing, synthesis, and instrumental sound design so you can find the next must-have trailer sound.

SURVIVAL OF THE MOST PERSISTENT

Regardless of which path you decide to try in establishing your career, in order to survive in the entertainment business, you must develop a strong sense of who you are and what your music is about. Then, all the rejections in the world will not phase you, and you can keep on plugging away. Artists in every aspect of the music industry face this same problem. Billy Joel was rejected from over twenty record labels before he got a shot from Columbia Records. Brian Epstein shopped the Beatles' demo to every label in London before he went back to EMI a second time and got George Martin to give them a try. In interviews for this book, over and over again, composers spoke about times when they could barely find work even after having had some degree of success and recognition.

There are many projects involving music happening all over the country, yet the number is finite. Like every other segment of the entertainment industry, there are many more people trying to get work than there are jobs. Who gets what jobs often has less to do with who writes the best music or who is more experienced, and more to do with who has the personality and presentation of a team player, and who has created the most solid relationships, as they navigate the industry. The important thing is to enjoy writing music and even find a way to enjoy the constant search for work. Composer Lolita Ritmanis speaks about this issue:

> *It's hard to know why one person works and another doesn't. You have to stop wondering why because there's no point to it. There are great composers working on projects that have very little visibility. Their music might be brilliant. So why are they not scoring big studio films? It's often not fair, and worrying about it not being fair doesn't change a thing. I've seen quite a bit of disaster as well as success in this business. If you're only waiting for the big break, it can be a long wait, and you can really get sick over it. You have to try and enjoy your life, and live a life too.*

One thing that beginning composers should be aware of is that it takes some time to get established. There are no overnight success stories; these are all a figment of publicists' imaginations. Every composer has paid their dues somewhere, whether it's as an orchestrator, as a composer's assistant, as a rock musician, or as a waiter. If you are just starting out and you don't have the playing skills, or if your cutting-edge band hasn't provided enough income, then you must figure out a way to create an incoming cash flow. Although this might mean getting a job in an office or as an Uber driver, it is important to create a cushion for yourself so that you can afford to make those demos and keep writing.

In addition to the economic realities, it is important to remember that the film business is based on personal relationships. Many composers at the top of the field tell stories about producers or directors that they met when they were just starting out. So, nurture the relationships that you make all along the way. Enjoy people as human beings first, as business contacts second. The composer that is looking at every new person as a possible connection or source of income is causing themselves a lot of stress, as well as creating shallow relationships. If you treat people well, if you treat yourself well, then others will pick up on this and want to be around you. The entertainment business can be difficult, so reaching out to others as people and having a strong personal center and confidence will carry you through the most difficult situations.

Finding work is not easy at any level of the entertainment business. Film scoring can be wonderful, rewarding work. If you love it, if there's nothing else in the world you would rather do, if you are willing to possibly endure several years of struggle and countless rejections, then go for it! There is no single road to the top. It can happen a million different ways. But you will never find out if you can get there until you try.

NOTES

1. Lauzen, Martha M. "The Celluloid Ceiling: Employment of Behind-the-Scenes Women on Top Grossing U.S. Films in 2022." SDSU Center for the Study of Women in Television and Film, 2023. https://womenintvfilm.sdsu.edu/wp-content/uploads/2023/01/2022-celluloid-ceiling-report.pdf
2. McCarthy, Justin. "In U.S., Library Visits Outpaced Trips to Movies in 2019." Gallup.com, November 20, 2021. https://news.gallup.com/poll/284009/library-visits-outpaced-trips-movies-2019.aspx
3. George, Alison. 2019. "The Earliest Storytellers." *New Scientist*, December 14.
4. McKee, Robert. *Story: Style, Structure, Substance, and the Principles of Screenwriting*. New York: Harper Collins, 2010. Page 45.
5. Parks, Suzan Lori. "From *The Elements of Style*." *The America Play and Other Works*. New York: Theatre Communications Group, 1995. Page 9.
6. Oxford English Dictionary, s.v. "documentary, n.," September 2023. https://doi.org/10.1093/OED/9071432593
7. Nichols, Bill. *Introduction to Documentary*, Second Edition. Indiana University Press, 2010.

INDEX

ABOUT THE AUTHORS

Photo by Scott Snyder

Richard Davis is an educator, composer, orchestrator, record producer, performing musician, and author. His film credits include orchestrations and transcriptions for *Robin Hood, Prince of Thieves*, *The Last Boy Scout*, and *The Fall Guy*; original music for *Monsters*, *Walking at the Edge*, and others. His musical experience spans multiple genres, including jazz, classical, pop, folk, and Indian ragas.

Richard studied guitar with Barry Galbraith, jazz composition and arranging with Dick Grove, and classical composition with Daniel Kessner and Aurelio de la Vega. He recently retired after twenty-seven years as a professor of film scoring at Berklee College of Music. Dozens of his students have gone on to success as composers for feature films, television, and streaming, and as music editors, orchestrators, and conductors.

Photo by Suzie Katayama

Alison Plante is previous chair and current professor of Screen Scoring at Berklee College of Music, and program director for the Berklee Online Master of Music in Film Scoring. She plays keyboard and wind instruments and sings, performed in an Indonesian-style Gamelan for three years, and has conducted both orchestra and choir. Her composition honors include the Janet Gates Peckham International Award for Excellence in the Arts and the Olga and Paul Menn Foundation Prize for an original literary or musical work.

Her scoring credits include documentary films, educational television series, History Channel and PBS specials, national TV spots, trailers, corporate identity music, live action and animated shorts, theater (with a specialty in puppetry), and multimedia museum installations for the Smithsonian Institution and the Harvard Museum of Natural History.

More Fine Publications

GUITAR

BERKLEE ESSENTIAL GUITAR SONGBOOK
Sheryl Bailey and Kim Perlak
00350814 Book....... $22.99

BERKLEE GUITAR CHORD DICTIONARY
Rick Peckham
50449546 Jazz – Book....... $16.99
50449596 Rock – Book....... $12.99

BERKLEE GUITAR STYLE STUDIES
Jim Kelly
00200377 Book/Online Media....... $24.99

BERKLEE GUITAR THEORY
Kim Perlak
00276326 Book....... $26.99

BLUES GUITAR TECHNIQUE
Michael Williams
50449623 Book/Online Audio....... $29.99

CLASSICAL TECHNIQUE FOR THE MODERN GUITARIST
Kim Perlak
00148781 Book/Online Audio....... $19.99

COUNTRY GUITAR STYLES
Mike Ihde
00254157 Book/Online Audio....... $24.99

CREATIVE CHORDAL HARMONY FOR GUITAR
Mick Goodrick and Tim Miller
50449613 Book/Online Audio....... $24.99

FUNK/R&B GUITAR
Thaddeus Hogarth
50449569 Book/Online Audio....... $25.99

GUITAR SWEEP PICKING
Joe Stump
00151223 Book/Online Audio....... $24.99

JAZZ GUITAR FRETBOARD NAVIGATION
Mark White
00154107 Book/Online Audio....... $24.99

JAZZ GUITAR IMPROVISATION STRATEGIES
Steven Kirby
00274977 Book/Online Audio....... $27.99

MODAL VOICINGS FOR GUITAR
Rick Peckham
00151227 Book/Online Media....... $24.99

A MODERN METHOD FOR GUITAR*
William Leavitt
Volume 1: Beginner
00137387 Book/Online Video....... $27.99
*Other volumes, media options, and supporting songbooks available.

A MODERN METHOD FOR GUITAR SCALES
Larry Baione
00199318 Book....... $15.99

TRIADS FOR THE IMPROVISING GUITARIST
Jane Miller
00284857 Book/Online Audio....... $22.99

BASS

BASS LINES
Metal
David Marvuglio
00122465 Book/Online Audio....... $19.99

BERKLEE JAZZ BASS
Rich Appleman, Whit Browne, and Bruce Gertz
50449636 Book/Online Audio....... $25.99

FUNK BASS FILLS
Anthony Vitti
50449608 Book/Online Audio....... $24.99

INSTANT BASS
Danny Morris
50449502 Book/CD....... $9.99

READING CONTEMPORARY ELECTRIC BASS
Rich Appleman
50449770 Book....... $24.99

VOICE

BELTING
Jeannie Gagné
00124984 Book/Online Media....... $24.99

THE CONTEMPORARY SINGER
Anne Peckham
50449595 Book/Online Audio....... $29.99

JAZZ VOCAL IMPROVISATION
Mili Bermejo
00159290 Book/Online Audio....... $19.99

TIPS FOR SINGERS
Carolyn Wilkins
50449557 Book/CD....... $19.95

VOCAL WORKOUTS FOR THE CONTEMPORARY SINGER
Anne Peckham
50448044 Book/Online Audio....... $27.99

YOUR SINGING VOICE
Jeannie Gagné
50449619 Book/Online Audio....... $34.99

WOODWINDS/BRASS

TRUMPET SOUND EFFECTS
Craig Pederson and Ueli Dörig
00121626 Book/Online Audio....... $14.99

TECHNIQUE OF THE SAXOPHONE
Joseph Viola
50449820 Volume 1....... $24.99
50449830 Volume 2....... $27.99
50449840 Volume 3....... $26.99

PIANO/KEYBOARD

BERKLEE JAZZ KEYBOARD HARMONY
Suzanna Sifter
00138874 Book/Online Audio....... $29.99

BERKLEE JAZZ PIANO
Ray Santisi
50448047 Book/Online Audio....... $24.99

BERKLEE JAZZ STANDARDS FOR SOLO PIANO
Robert Christopherson, Hey Rim Jeon, Ross Ramsay, Tim Ray
00160482 Book/Online Audio....... $24.99

CHORD-SCALE IMPROVISATION FOR KEYBOARD
Ross Ramsay
50449597 Book/CD....... $19.99

CONTEMPORARY PIANO TECHNIQUE
Stephany Tiernan
50449545 Book/Online Video....... $39.99

HAMMOND ORGAN COMPLETE
Dave Limina
00237801 Book/Online Audio....... $27.99

JAZZ PIANO COMPING
Suzanne Davis
50449614 Book/Online Audio....... $26.99

LATIN JAZZ PIANO IMPROVISATION
Rebecca Cline
50449649 Book/Online Audio....... $29.99

SOLO JAZZ PIANO
Neil Olmstead
50449641 Book/Online Audio....... $42.99

DRUMS/PERCUSSION

BEGINNING DJEMBE
Michael Markus and Joe Galeota
00148210 Book/Online Video....... $16.99

BERKLEE JAZZ DRUMS
Casey Scheuerell
50449612 Book/Online Audio....... $27.99

DRUM SET WARM-UPS
Rod Morgenstein
50449465 Book....... $19.99

DRUM STUDIES
Dave Vose
50449617 Book....... $12.99

A MANUAL FOR THE MODERN DRUMMER
Alan Dawson and Don DeMichael
50449560 Book....... $14.99

MASTERING THE ART OF BRUSHES
Jon Hazilla
50449459 Book/Online Audio....... $19.99

PHRASING: ADVANCED RUDIMENTS FOR CREATIVE DRUMMING
Russ Gold
00120209 Book/Online Media....... $19.99

WORLD JAZZ DRUMMING
Mark Walker
50449568 Book/CD....... $27.99

Berklee Press publications feature material developed at the Berklee College of Music.
To browse the complete Berklee Press Catalog, go to **www.berkleepress.com**

SONGBOOKS

NEW STANDARDS: 101 LEAD SHEETS BY WOMEN COMPOSERS MUSICIANS
Terri Lyne Carrington
00369515 Book $29.99

STRINGS/ROOTS MUSIC

BERKLEE HARP
Chords, Styles, and Improvisation for Pedal and Lever Harp
Felice Pomeranz
00144263 Book/Online Audio $26.99

BEYOND BLUEGRASS
Beyond Bluegrass Banjo
Dave Hollander and Matt Glaser
50449610 Book/CD $19.99
Beyond Bluegrass Mandolin
John McGann and Matt Glaser
50449609 Book/CD $19.99
Bluegrass Fiddle and Beyond
Matt Glaser
50449602 Book/CD $19.99

CONTEMPORARY CELLO ETUDES
Mike Block
00159292 Book/Online Audio $24.99

EXPLORING CLASSICAL MANDOLIN
August Watters
00125040 Book/Online Media $24.99

FIDDLE TUNES ON JAZZ CHANGES
Matt Glaser
00120210 Book/Online Audio $16.99

THE IRISH CELLO BOOK
Liz Davis Maxfield
50449652 Book/Online Audio $29.99

JAZZ UKULELE
Abe Lagrimas, Jr.
00121624 Book/Online Audio $26.99

BERKLEE PRACTICE METHOD

GET YOUR BAND TOGETHER
With additional volumes for other instruments, plus a teacher's guide.
Drum Set
Ron Savage, Casey Scheuerell, and the Berklee Faculty
50449429 Book/CD $19.99
Guitar
Larry Baione and the Berklee Faculty
50449426 Book/CD $29.99
Keyboard
Russell Hoffmann, Paul Schmeling, and the Berklee Faculty
50449428 Book/Online Audio $22.99

MUSIC BUSINESS

CROWDFUNDING FOR MUSICIANS
Laser Malena-Webber
00285092 Book $17.99

HOW TO GET A JOB IN THE MUSIC INDUSTRY
Keith Hatschek with Breanne Beseda
00130699 Book $39.99

MAKING MUSIC MAKE MONEY
Eric Beall
00355740 Book $29.99

MUSIC LAW IN THE DIGITAL AGE
Allen Bargfrede
00366048 Book $29.99

PROJECT MANAGEMENT FOR MUSICIANS
Jonathan Feist
50449659 Book $39.99

MUSIC THEORY/EAR TRAINING

BEGINNING EAR TRAINING
Gilson Schachnik
50449548 Book/Online Audio $22.99

THE BERKLEE BOOK OF JAZZ HARMONY
Joe Mulholland and Tom Hojnacki
00113755 Book/Online Audio $34.99

BERKLEE CORRESPONDENCE COURSE
00244533 Book/Online Media $29.99

BERKLEE EAR TRAINING DUETS AND TRIOS
Gaye Tolan Hatfield
00284897 Book/Online Audio $19.99

BERKLEE MUSIC THEORY
Paul Schmeling
50449615 **Rhythm, Scales Intervals** $29.99
50449616 **Harmony** $26.99

CONDUCTING MUSIC TODAY
Bruce Hangen
00237719 Book/Online Video $24.99

JAZZ DUETS
Richard Lowell
00302151 C Instruments $14.99

MUSIC NOTATION
Mark McGrain
50449399 Theory and Technique $29.99

REHARMONIZATION TECHNIQUES
Randy Felts
50449496 Book $29.99

MUSIC PRODUCTION & ENGINEERING

AUDIO MASTERING
Jonathan Wyner
50449581 Book/CD $34.99

AUDIO POST PRODUCTION
Mark Cross
50449627 Book $32.99

CREATING COMMERCIAL MUSIC
Peter Bell
00278535 Book/Online Media $19.99

HIP-HOP PRODUCTION
Prince Charles Alexander
50449582 Book/Online Audio $24.99

THE SINGER-SONGWRITER'S GUIDE TO RECORDING IN THE HOME STUDIO
Shane Adams
00148211 Book/Online Audio $24.99

UNDERSTANDING AUDIO
Daniel M. Thompson
00148197 Book $49.99

WELLNESS/AUTOBIOGRAPHY

LEARNING TO LISTEN: THE JAZZ JOURNEY OF GARY BURTON
00117798 Book $34.99

MANAGE YOUR STRESS AND PAIN THROUGH MUSIC
Dr. Suzanne B. Hanser and Dr. Susan E. Mandel
00117798 Book $34.99

MUSICIAN'S YOGA
Mia Olson
50449587 Book $26.99

THE NEW MUSIC THERAPIST'S HANDBOOK
Suzanne B. Hanser
00279325 Book $34.99

SONGWRITING/COMPOSING

ARRANGING FOR HORNS
Jerry Gates
00121625 Book/Online Audio $24.99

ARRANGING FOR STRINGS
Mimi Rabson
00190207 Book/Online Audio $22.99

BEGINNING SONGWRITING
Andrea Stolpe with Jan Stolpe
00138503 Book/Online Audio $22.99

BERKLEE CONTEMPORARY MUSIC NOTATION
Jonathan Feist
00202547 Book $27.99

COMPLETE GUIDE TO FILM SCORING
Richard Davis
50449607 .... $39.99

CONTEMPORARY COUNTERPOINT
Beth Denisch
00147050 Book/Online Audio $24.99

COUNTERPOINT IN JAZZ ARRANGING
Bob Pilkington
00294301 Book/Online Audio $29.99

THE CRAFT OF SONGWRITING
Scarlet Keys
00159283 Book/Online Audio $24.99

CREATIVE STRATEGIES IN FILM SCORING
Ben Newhouse
00242911 Book/Online Media $27.99

ESSENTIAL SONGWRITING
Jonathan Feist and Jimmy Kachulis
50448051 .... $14.99

JAZZ COMPOSITION
Ted Pease
50448000 Book/Online Audio $49.99

MELODY IN SONGWRITING
Jack Perricone
50449419 Book $26.99

MODERN JAZZ VOICINGS
Ted Pease and Ken Pullig
50449485 Book/Online Audio $29.99

MUSIC COMPOSITION FOR FILM AND TELEVISION
Lalo Schifrin
50449604 Book $39.99

MUSIC NOTATION
50449540 **Preparing Scores & Parts** $25.99
50449399 **Theory and Technique** $29.99

POPULAR LYRIC WRITING
Andrea Stolpe
50449553 Book $17.99

SONGWRITING: ESSENTIAL GUIDE
Pat Pattison
50481582 **Lyric and Form Structure** $19.99
00124366 **Rhyming** $24.99

SONGWRITING IN PRACTICE
Mark Simos
00244545 Book $16.99

SONGWRITING STRATEGIES
Mark Simos
50449621 Book $27.99

THE SONGWRITER'S WORKSHOP
Jimmy Kachulis
50449519 **Harmony** $34.99
50449518 **Melody** $27.99

Prices subject to change without notice. Visit your local music dealer or bookstore, or go to **halleonard.com** to order